Lecture Notes in Computer Science 2897

Edited by G. Goos, J. Hartmanis, and J. van Leeuwen

Springer

Berlin
Heidelberg
New York
Hong Kong
London
Milan
Paris
Tokyo

Olivier Balet Gérard Subsol
Patrice Torguet (Eds.)

Virtual Storytelling

Using Virtual Reality Technologies for Storytelling

Second International Conference, ICVS 2003
Toulouse, France, November 20-21, 2003
Proceedings

 Springer

Series Editors

Gerhard Goos, Karlsruhe University, Germany
Juris Hartmanis, Cornell University, NY, USA
Jan van Leeuwen, Utrecht University, The Netherlands

Volume Editors

Olivier Balet
CS-SI, Virtual Reality Department, ZAC de la Grande Plaine
rue Brindejonc des Moulinais, 31500 Toulouse, France
E-mail: Olivier.Balet@c-s.fr

Gérard Subsol
Université de Perpignan, LTS
52, avenue de Villeneuve, 66860 Perpignan Cedex, France
E-mail: Gerard.Subsol@wanadoo.fr

Patrice Torguet
Université Paul Sabatier, IRIT
118 route de Narbonne, 31062 Toulouse Cedex 4, France
E-mail: torguet@irit.fr

Cataloging-in-Publication Data applied for

A catalog record for this book is available from the Library of Congress.

Bibliographic information published by Die Deutsche Bibliothek
Die Deutsche Bibliothek lists this publication in the Deutsche Nationalbibliografie;
detailed bibliographic data is available in the Internet at <http://dnb.ddb.de>.

CR Subject Classification (1998): I.3, I.2, C.3, H.4, H.5, I.4, I.7.2

ISSN 0302-9743
ISBN 3-540-20535-7 Springer-Verlag Berlin Heidelberg New York

This work is subject to copyright. All rights are reserved, whether the whole or part of the material is
concerned, specifically the rights of translation, reprinting, re-use of illustrations, recitation, broadcasting,
reproduction on microfilms or in any other way, and storage in data banks. Duplication of this publication
or parts thereof is permitted only under the provisions of the German Copyright Law of September 9, 1965,
in its current version, and permission for use must always be obtained from Springer-Verlag. Violations are
liable for prosecution under the German Copyright Law.

Springer-Verlag is a part of Springer Science+Business Media

springeronline.com

© Springer-Verlag Berlin Heidelberg 2003

Typesetting: Camera-ready by author, data conversion by Olgun Computergrafik
Printed on acid-free paper   SPIN: 10969625   06/3142   5 4 3 2 1 0

Preface

In September 2001, we organized the 1st International Conference on Virtual Storytelling in Avignon, France. This was the first international scientific event entirely devoted to the new discipline that links the ancient human art of storytelling to the latest high technologies of the Virtual Reality era.

Since this date, technology has not slowed its course. We all know that personal computers are even more powerful, but there have been huge advances in graphics boards. These are now programmable and can render in real time huge quantities of data as well as special effects that until recently required a dedicated graphics superworkstation. Applications that were in the research lab have now come to market. 3D Virtual Humans, the heroes of today's video games, are taking their first steps on e-business Web sites. These will be the stars of tomorrow. New topics are being intensively researched, especially, mixed and enhanced realities – the art of combining synthesized with real worlds.

This evolution raises many technical, applicational, artistic and even ethical questions. The occasion of the 2nd International Conference on Virtual Storytelling provided an excellent opportunity to once again gather researchers from the scientific, artistic and industrial communities to demonstrate new methods and techniques. This was the venue to show the latest results, and exchange concepts and ideas about the use of Virtual Reality technologies for creating, populating, rendering and interacting with stories, whatever their form, be it theatre, movie, cartoon, advertisement, puppet show, multimedia work, video games, etc.

We believe that participants in Virtual Storytelling 2003 found exciting guidelines for future scientific and artistic research as well as ideas for new applications and developments. Because Virtual Storytelling is a rapidly expanding discipline, new conferences are expected to be organized very soon to update the state of the art!

Toulouse, November 2003

Olivier Balet
Jean-Pierre Jessel
Gérard Subsol
Patrice Torguet

Acknowledgement

Organizing a conference on Virtual Storytelling was a joint initiative of the Virtual Reality Department of the Communications et Systèmes Group and the French Working Group on Virtual Reality (GT-RV).

However, Virtual Storytelling 2003 only came about thanks to the financial support of the IST Programme of the European Commission, of Grand Toulouse, the Paul Sabatier University of Toulouse, and the University of Glasgow. We really want to thank them all for offering the opportunity to organize a conference on so innovative a topic.

We would also like to thank the Eurographics Organization for supporting the conference as well as the members of the Scientific and Application Board who helped the organizers to define the conference topics, and proposed names of experts for the Program Committee. The members of the Program Committee deserve special acknowledgments for their amazing reviews of the large number of papers that were submitted (three times what we had initially expected!).

Last, but not least, we had the pleasure to welcome two companies, Immersion SA and NVIDIA Corporation, that offered prizes for Best Paper and Best Demonstration.

Finally, our thanks to the organization people from Sophie et Associés for their help during the conference preparation.

Organization

Chair

Olivier Balet	Communications & Systèmes Group, France
Jean-Pierre Jessel	IRIT, Paul Sabatier University, Toulouse, France
Gérard Subsol	LTS, University of Perpignan, France
Patrice Torguet	IRIT, Paul Sabatier University, Toulouse, France

Scientific and Application Board

Norman I. Badler	University of Pennsylvania, USA
Ronen Barzel	Pixar, USA
Maurice Benayoun	Z-A Production, Paris, France
Kevin Björke	NVIDIA Corporation, Santa Clara, USA
Bruce Blumberg	MIT MediaLab, USA
Ronan Boulic	EPFL, Lausanne, Switzerland
Marc Cavazza	University of Teesside, UK
Yves Duthen	IRIT, University of Toulouse 1, France
Franz Fischnaller	University of Illinois at Chicago, USA
	F.A.B.R.I.CATORS, Milan, Italy
Catherine Garbay	IMAG, Grenoble, France
Andrew Glassner	Consultant, Seattle, USA
Stefan Göbel	ZGDV, Darmstadt, Germany
Jonathan Gratch	University of South California, USA
Alain Grumbach	ENST, Paris, France
Barbara Hayes-Roth	Extempo Systems, Inc., USA
Paul Kafno	HD Thames, UK
Wim Lamotte	Limburgs Universitair Centrum, Belgium
Didier Libert	ENSAM, Paris, France
Sina Mostafawy	[rmh], Germany
Ryohei Nakatsu	Kwansei Gakuin University, Sanda, Japan
	Nirvana Technology, Inc., Japan
Jean-Christophe Nebel	University of Glasgow, UK
Sally Jane Norman	École Supérieure de l'Image, France
Catherine Pélachaud	University of Paris 8, France
Ken Perlin	New York University Media Research Lab, USA
Simon Richir	ISTIA Innovation, Angers, France
Leonie Schaefer	Fraunhofer FIT, Sankt Augustin, Germany
Barry Silverman	University of Pennsylvania, USA
Ulrike Spierling	University of Applied Sciences, Erfurt, Germany
Marie-Luce Viaud	INA, Bry-sur-Marne, France
John Wilson	University of Nottingham, UK
R. Michael Young	North Carolina State University, Raleigh, USA

Program Committee

Jan Allbeck	University of Pennsylvania, USA
Victor Bayon	University of Nottingham, UK
Stéphane Donikian	IRISA, Rennes, France
Patrick Doyle	Stanford University, USA
Knut Hartmann	University of Magdeburg, Germany
Junichi Hoshino	Tsukuba University/PRESTO JST, Japan
Ido Iurgel	ZGDV, Darmstadt, Germany
Michael Johns	University of Pennsylvania, USA
Pieter Jorissen	Limburgs Universitair Centrum, Belgium
Alexander Lechner	Vertigo Systems, Germany
Manuel Viñas Limonchi	University of Granada, Spain
Heidy Maldonado	Stanford University, USA
Maic Masuch	University of Magdeburg, Germany
Michael Mateas	Georgia Institute of Technology, USA
Chris Raymaekers	Limburgs Universitair Centrum, Belgium
Jean-Hugues Réty	University of Paris 8, France
Nadine Richard	ENST, Paris, France
Paul Richard	ISTIA Innovation, Angers, France
Oliver Schneider	ZGDV, Darmstadt, Germany
Magy Seif El-Nasr	Pennsylvania State University, USA
Alexander Sibiryakov	University of Glasgow, UK
Danaë Stanton	University of Nottingham, UK
Andrew Stern	InteractiveStory.net, grandtextauto.org, USA
Nicolas Szilas	IDtension, France
Bill Tomlinson	University of California, Irvine, USA
Daria Tsoupikova	University of Illinois at Chicago, USA

Table of Contents

Virtual Characters

Mixed Reality

Applications

Real-Time Technologies

Seizing Power: Shaders and Storytellers

Kevin Björke

NVIDIA Corporation
2701 San Tomas Expressway
Santa Clara, California
kbjorke@nvidia.com
http://developer.nvidia.com

Abstract. Graphics hardware has quickly moved past the challenges of previous years, such as realtime projection, simple lighting, heavy tessellations, and surface texturing. New hardware provides a richer context not only for final imagery in games and similar immersive environments, but also has begun to revolutionize the tools used to create entertainments both in realtime and in static formats like TV and motion pictures.

1 Introduction

Rapid change is typical in the electronics industry, but graphics has proven to be among the most rapid of all fields – the parallelism inherent in modern realtime graphics hardware is better-able to exploit the advantages in manufacturing that drive the famous Moore's Law. Not only are graphics processing units (GPUs) faster at creating graphics than the base CPUs in modern computers, the margin of difference is broadening.

In the year 2000 – when this year's undergraduate classes were entering college – the best GPUs were able to drawn shaded, OpenGL-lit triangles. Today those GPUs' ancestors are already performing tasks an order of magnitude more difficult – rendering more polygons, and shading them programmably using high-precision per-pixel shader programs. Manufacturers have heralded the newest generation of GPU's as "cinematic."

2 Cinematic Imaging

The "cinematic" label is generally applied as a catch-all for visual richness. Yet true cinematic imaging, in a cinema, isn't driven merely by a desire for baroque complexity. Instead, a key element of the cinematic experience comes from the fact that each part of the images we view in a theatre is sculpted and designed specifically to reinforce the demands and intents of film narrative.

These issues are evident in each part of the overall creation of a film, starting with the placement of the camera, the blocking of the actors, the materials chosen for their costumes and sets, the direction and mood and heightened dimensionality of the film's lighting. In live action filmmaking, and other narrative experiences such as theatre (whether proscenium, thrust-stage or "funhouse"), the experiences of the audience are deliberately shaped by the visuals as the story unfolds.

O. Balet et al. (Eds.): ICVS 2003, LNCS 2897, pp. 3–11, 2003.
© Springer-Verlag Berlin Heidelberg 2003

The new possibilities in hardware present us with both power and problems. We now have the ability to create more-advanced and complex scenarios, characters, sets – but unless there is also a means toward the creation and management of this power, it's useless.

Movie and TV audiences are passive – they can't control the camera, move, or "become" the characters on the screen. The screen is separated from the viewer, so the theatre experience is deliberately designed to make the experience "Bigger Than Life." We watch films in a dark room, free from distractions, and the staging, lighting, and art direction are all dedicated to drawing us in, to directing our attention, and getting us to the state called "suspension of disbelief," where we can become directly and emotionally involved with what's on the screen.

In realtime games and similar contexts, the controlled environment available to filmmakers may not be practical. The viewer may be moving the camera around freely, there may be other viewers influencing the staging, etc. This means that camerawork, lighting and stage design, etc, may need to be crucially different in such media, if it's our desire to still employ the mood and storytelling tools inherited from film and theatre.

3 Simulation, Stylization, Customization

In general, computer graphics scientists of the past years have focused on understanding and simulation of natural appearances. Photo-realism has become an advanced field – audiences in theatres today are no longer startled by walking skeletons or heroes who leap from building to building. It's accepted as a matter of course that it's somehow all done in a computer somewhere.

Yet the live-action footage to which this material is compared is in fact only slightly more "real." Films are always heavily stylized, altered by convention, fashion, and most importantly story points. The photorealism we see in films is only "realistic" – not "real."

Realism is only one genre in filmmaking, a useful dramatist's trick. Generally, creating a scene that is realistic, that the audience can readily accept, allows viewers to more readily suspend disbelief so that we the filmmakers can get on with the true "main business" of our narrative. But realism is only a style – Mickey Mouse cartoons are equally effective at narrative, but with a very low amount of realism. And even realism itself is subject to layers of "realisticness" – thus we see in modern films like *Full Frontal* or *Affliction* sections filmed in Super-8 or mini-DV, as if the film projection of the video image is inherently more immediate and "real."

Managing and manipulating these complexities of meaning and illusion require considerable skill on the part of the filmmakers. They need a large variety of tools at their disposal. No less so for creators of new realtime entertainments.

In older generations of graphics hardware, one single shading model was supplied – vertex-shaded plastic. This has evolved into textured shaded plastic, and is only recently advanced to generally-programmable surfaces. Most of the kinds of surface shading that had been explored in software rendering over the previous decades are now possible to implement directly in graphics hardware.

Variety in surface characteristics is crucial for giving images a look that approaches the richness we see around us every day. As painters have long known, there are an apparently-infinite number of tiny visual cues which we use to gauge the properties of the objects in the world around us. Without needing to touch or smell, we can surmise that an object is heavy or light, wet or dry, organic or metallic, living or dead, natural or man-made. Painters such as John Singer Sargent or Rubens became particular adept at recreating these sensations with a minimal means – Sargent was particularly known less for his meticulous apparent detail than for the way he could conjure-up worlds of apparently photo-like detail through a few well-placed, seemingly loose brushstrokes.

Strict adherence to a limited set of shading rules, even a large set, is antithetical to the creativity and expression we demand of modern entertainments. Compare to the rigid state of illustration during the medieval times, when artists were taught to copy the "correct" mannerisms, no matter how artificial they might be. It was only by throwing out the copybooks that art of later periods was able to reach the heights seen in narrative masters like Dürer or Caravaggio.

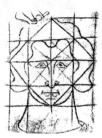

Fig. 1. Reduction of imagery to exact, formal rules suppresses personal expression, as in this 13th-century copybook credited to Villard Honnecourt, which instructs artisans to copy a narrow range of geometries valiantly, rather than to seek forms from nature

For some purposes, of course, such as CAD applications, close simulation of real-world materials is desirable. For such users, the world of scientifically-measured BRDFs and empirical simulation of nature is now available in real-time.

For the more complex visuals we expect from entertainment, we need the ability to go beyond simple simulation and handle our images with style. This doesn't always mean that the shading algorithms themselves are more complex – indeed, often we will find that simple algorithms are more appropriate and more flexible as artistic tools. The difference is in purpose.

For CAD and related applications, the goal is the actual creation of a physical object – an automobile, stereo, a new building. Narrative entertainments are created instead in the imagination, through the engaged participation of the audience. They are therefore amenable to abstraction and "purification" of their visual characteristics. As Thomas Aquinas wrote: "Corporeal creatures exist in the soul in a higher manner than they exist in themselves."

Just as in live-action photography, shading can subtly alter the appearance of objects that appear almost natural, but with differences appropriate to the medium. For example, photography and cinema often liberally employ large rim-lights and *contre-jour* effects, specifically to heighten the sense of contours and lines in the final frame. These lights are usually un-motivated (they don't appear to come from any specifically-identifiable source in the scene) but give the audience a heightened sense of dimensionality when projected onto the flat screen. Such lights permit cinematographers the same sorts of minute expressive control over the character of these contours and lines as those of a draughtsman.

Modern hardware is also capable of expanding our abilities to animate characters, particularly through the use of vertex shaders, which can alter static geometry that resides in the memory of the graphics card. The technique of matrix palette skinning, where a static model is deformed by the transform matrices of a set of "bone" objects, is one that was quickly adopted by game designers from similar algorithms that existed in software rendering.

Fig. 2. Realtime character rendered using a variety of different Cg shaders: *vertexLight, Dürer, putrid, terminator,* and the animated *flame* shaders

As a current example, consider the popular "Dawn" demo character created by NVIDIA. "Dawn" contains close to 300,000 polygons, which must animate and deform smoothly at high frame rates. Even if the available CPU were infinitely fast, those 300,000 polygons would still need to be transmitted over the AGP bus to the graphics pipeline, 30 or more times each second. This simply isn't possible for any existing AGP hardware.

Fig. 3. "Dawn" makes complex use of GPU shading, not only for the surface characteristics of skin, hair, wings, and costume, but also to drive the complex character deformations that make her performance expressive

Instead, Dawn's figure can be transmitted exactly *once* – in a static position – and all subsequent deformations can be calculated directly on the GPU while Dawn is displayed. The CPU needs only to provide the GPU with a handful of transformation matrices, a few hundred bytes per frame. This is easily attainable and provides a convincing result.

4   Power over the Means of Production

The power available from modern graphics hardware is great, but so far only available to a chosen few. Modern GPUs are complex – they usually have more circuits even than modern CPUs. And each different model has unique features and abilities. The knowledge associated with this hardware is highly specialized and changes rapidly. How can artists and storytellers hope to harness this power?

4.1   High-Level Languages

High-level languages are the first tool provided to handle the array of complex and changeable GPU power. A number of languages have been proposed and developed. NVIDIA distributes the open-sources Cg language, which can function in both of the common realtime APIs, either OpenGL or Microsoft DirectX. Each API also has their own localized language support, OGLSL (aka GLSLang) in OpenGL and HLSL for DirectX. In all of these languages, the ideas of shading and control are abstracted into a human-readable format. The shading-language compiler can read shader programs written in Cg or a related language, and execute code specific to the capabilities and features of the GPU hardware specific to any particular device.

This level of abstraction provides some transportability between people, since algorithms and shading methods can be easily communicated in a human-readable form without undue attention to ID#s of registers or register combiners, etc. It also provides transportability between graphics cards, so that shaders developed on one GPU may in the future run handily – or even faster – on future hardware.

High-level languages alone, however, still require an environment in which they can execute. To use Cg or HLSL directly, one must write the appropriate C++ program to load the shaders, to assign textures to hardware registers, set the API graphics state, etc. Programmers who have already been writing OpenGL and DirectX programs are completely comfortable with this notion, and high-level languages function perfectly within the scope of those programmers' usual work. Each language package also provides an API layer for easy integration into existing programs.

In environments where applications are being developed directly by programmers, this is an excellent solution. It does, however, require programming knowledge and expertise that may not be available to all who desire to use this power – particularly artists and animators.

Artists and animators are used to managing art assets like models and textures – it's desirable that they should also be able to apply and manage complex shading.

4.2   High-Level Metafiles

Cg and HLSL provide an additional level of abstraction, through a format known to both as "fx" (to distinguish clearly, fx files that use Cg are designated as "CgFX" files). Both forms are nearly identical.

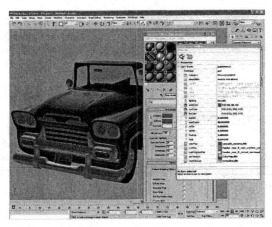

Fig. 4. CgFX plugin running in 3ds Max version 5.1. CgFX appearances are simply integrated into the existing Max Material editor, under the control of a Max Viewport Manager. All shaded views will display fx-driven hardware shaders, rather than the Max built-in view

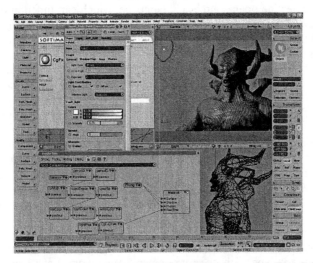

Fig. 5. CgFX Add-on shown operating in SoftImage XSI version 3.5. The CgFX appearance and its attributes are integrated seamlessly into the existing SoftImage RenderTree editor, and FX shaders are used in any XSI "realtime shaded" view. CgFX-enabled material descriptions can be dragged and dropped, or stored as presets, just like any other XSI surface description

CgFX files are simply text files that encapsulate shaders, their API definitions, and their user attributes into a simple, transportable package. CgFX files can handle complex combinations of shaders – not only joining-together pixel and vertex shaders, but also allowing the definition of complex appearances that may require the surface to be built-up across multiple composited passes. The handling of graphics state and related low-level issues is then left to the application, while artists and animators can simply swap appearances around between models in a manner not unlike assigning textures.

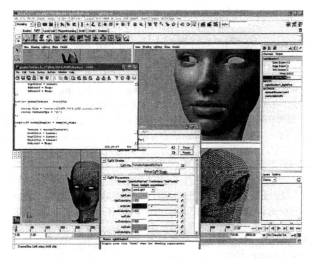

Fig. 6. CgFX plugin operating in Maya 5.0. CgFX shaders are incorporated as Maya shading nodes, with the same functionality as other Maya shading nodes. All objects in Maya shaded views can be drawn using Cg-driven hardware shaders. Mel control and on-the-fly shader editing provide a powerful, rapid look-development environment

Crucially, the CgFX format allows fx definitions to be freely shared between applications, using just the lightweight text file. This allows artists to define and share shading definitions even if they have no desire or aptitude at writing code – but still with a format that's open enough to permit flexible changes and re-editing for artists who are comfortable with that technology.

CgFX plugins have already been provided for many of the most-common 3D art applications, including 3ds Max, Alias Maya, SoftImage XSI, and Cinema 4D. While NVIDIA has created some of the code for some of these first plugins, the individual vendors have also been quick to adapt the technology themselves, providing their own fx parsers and integration.

4.3 Multiple Techniques

Shaders shared via the CgFX mechanism are easily moved not only between art applications, but also to other applications that are hardware-shader aware – these applications can either link to the CgFX runtime API, to provide CgFX support themselves, or the individual shaders can be compiled to GPU assembly language and incorporated into applications. They can be freely mixed with older code, such as assembly-language shaders from older APIs, or even the "hardware T&L" shading built-into DirectX and OpenGL.

CgFX files also permit the definition of multiple *techniques* within a single fx file. Each technique provided in a CgFX file provides potentially a different way to create an appearance. For example, there may be a technique which executed quickly on GeForce FX™ class hardware, and another that operates on older hardware such as the GeForce 3™. There may be a technique which supports bump-mapping, and another that does not. Balances can be freely chosen by artists and animators between performance, quality, and hardware choices, without requiring complex programming support.

Techniques can be used to emulate hardware that has no complex programmable shading – one U.S. game developer, when introduced to CgFX, provided their artists with fx shaders that always showed an accurate representation of their models as shaded by both highend and low-end hardware, including game consoles like the Playstation 2 and the Xbox. These emulations allowed artists and animators to work in a computer DCC application like 3ds Max and see their characters and sets *exactly* as they would appear on the final game hardware, without having to second-guess the conversion process or wait for a lengthy software build to see the results of their handiwork.

Techniques can also provide partial previews of specific portions of an appearance – for example artists working on a final film-rendered frame may use shaders that provide accurate highlight placement for a particular raytraced lightsource, without having to emulate all parts of the more-complex shading equation. This allows them to place lights quickly – normally infamous as one of the most time-consuming processes in computer animation.

5 Special Considerations for Multiplayer Environments

When providing entertainments to multiple viewers at once, programmable shading offers a number of special advantages over previous techniques.

5.1 Bandwidth and Compression Issues

- Shader files tend to be much smaller than texture maps, and can be broadcast easily with limited resources. This allows more customization and variety between characters and groups of characters. Shader parameters tend to be even more minimal, numbering in the bytes or hundreds of bytes. Compare to texture maps, which may potentially range in the hundreds of kilobytes or megabytes. Even a long shader file is rarely more than 20-30K, and its techniques may provide shading instructions for use on a variety of different target hardware – so users of high-end PCs might share the virtual space with low-end users or even game-console users.
- GPU-side skinning provides great data compression -- different LOD versions of the same character can be skinned by the same data stream, and the LOD levels flipped as the character approaches or recedes in importance to the viewer (or depending on their hardware profile)
- The low bandwidth demands of procedural shading encourage players and designers to create and trade their own shading "mods."

5.2 Complexity/Storytelling Issues

- In MMORPGs etc, players may experience different shading and different lighting according to their own roles and locations. For example, if a user is playing on a team, he may see the other members of his team rendered more realistically or sympathetically than members of other teams (such as the teams in *America's Army,* where all sides see themselves in American uniforms). In other scenarios, players may have different levels of detail and shading based upon their importance to the player, thus providing them with visual hints (not unlike the common cinema practice of lighting movie stars just slightly brighter than the other actors on screen).

- At a simpler level, large virtual spaces can mean that the perceptual space of the player may be significantly less than the global space of the environment. We can use shading to help each player see the elements that are most-important to that particular player, while ignoring those that are unimportant. Lighting can be redesigned for each player according to the pace of the game and their place in it. Crucial cues about space, location, goals and hazards can be provided by savvy shading, without depending on the user's CPU or the virtual-world server for this information.
- Better shading creates greater demands on models, artworks, and display AIs for camera and lighting. An important datum to recall is that render times in offline rendering have remained fairly constant for the past decade – even as computers become orders of magnitude faster, our appetite for increasingly-complex imagery increases at a parallel pace. The art we create today for entertainment is almost certain to look dated and crude within the span of a few short years – or months.

Acknowledgements

"Dawn" and the other animations from NVIDIA come from the demo team, headed by Mark Daly and Curtiss Beeson. The demon character was modeled by Steve Burke of NVIDIA. The DCC plugins and shaders shown in this lecture are available on the web through http://www.nvidia.com/developer/

References

1. Akenine-Möller, Tomas; Haines, Eric. *Real Time Shading*. 2002.
2. De Tolnay, Charles. *History and Techniques of Old Master Drawing*, 1943.
3. Egan, Walter G.; Hilgeman, Theodore W. *Optical Properties of Inhomogeneous Materials; Applications to Geology, Astronomy, and Engineering*. 1979.
4. Gritz, Larry; Apodaca, Anthony A. *Advanced RenderMan: Creating CGI for Motion Pictures*, 2000.
5. Hunter, Fil; Fuqua, Paul. *Light Science and Magic*. 1997
6. Klee, Paul. *Pädagogisches Skizzenbuch*. 1923.
7. Sargent, John Singer; Swinglehurst, Edmund. *John Singer Sargent*. 2001.

Real-Time Lighting Design for Interactive Narrative

Magy Seif El-Nasr and Ian Horswill

Northwestern University
Computer Science Department
1890 Maple Avenue
magy@northwestern.edu, ian@cs.northwestern.edu

Abstract. Lighting design is an important element of scene composition. Designers use light to influence viewers' perception by evoking moods, directing
their gaze to important areas, and conveying dramatic tension. Lighting is a
very time consuming task; designers typically spend hours manipulating lights'
colors, positions, and angles to create a lighting design that accommodates
dramatic action and tension. Such manual design is inappropriate for interactive
narrative, because the scene's spatial and dramatic characteristics, including
dramatic tension and character actions, change unpredictably, necessitating
continual redesign as the scene progresses. In this paper, we present a lighting
design system, called ELE (Expressive Lighting Engine), that automatically, in
real-time, adjusts angles, positions, and colors of lights to accommodate variations in the scene's dramatic and spatial characteristics accommodating cinematic and theatrical lighting design theory. ELE uses constraint-based non-
linear optimization algorithms to configure lights.

1 Introduction

Lighting designers rely on lighting to visually compose a scene. Lighting is essential
not only for visibility, but also for emphasizing visual tension, establishing depth,
directing viewers' gaze to important objects/characters/areas, and providing mood [1-
3]. Film Noir, for example, is distinguished for employing high contrast lighting to
project mystery and visual tension. These qualities are significant for interactive narrative, because they influence the participant's action, engagement, and mood [4].

Creating a lighting design that satisfies these goals for an interactive scene is a difficult problem. In a typical interactive narrative, player's choices and movements
affect the camera angle and position as well as the characters' orientations, positions,
and relationship values, and thus, influence dramatic intensity and action. Interactive
entertainment productions currently use statically designed lighting, which is context
insensitive and often result in partially lit or unlit characters (e.g. *The Thing*) leading
to player's frustration.

Lighting design is a complex problem. Lighting designers have identified several
lighting design goals and constraints, and developed many rules to satisfy them [2, 5-
8]. In many cases, however, these goals conflict, therefore, lighting design as any

O. Balet et al. (Eds.): ICVS 2003, LNCS 2897, pp. 12–20, 2003.
© Springer-Verlag Berlin Heidelberg 2003

design process involves many tradeoffs. For instance, establishing visibility for all objects in a scene often conflict with providing a clear visual focus or achieving intense and dark moods, because creating such moods require high contrast and less visibility [9]. Additionally, continually adjusting light angles and positions for visibility may cause distracting changes, and thus conflict with visual continuity.

This paper presents a lighting system, called ELE (Expressive Lighting Engine), which introduces a new approach to lighting design for interactive entertainment. As an alternative to static lighting, ELE automatically adjusts lighting angles, positions, and colors, to satisfy the lighting design goals and accommodate camera's and characters' positions and orientations, while maintaining visual continuity. Recognizing lighting design as an optimization problem that involves balancing many goals, ELE uses non-linear constraint optimization algorithms. In addition, it adapts theories discussed by Calahan [1] and the traditional lighting design theory addressed by filmmakers and theatre designers [2, 5, 7]. ELE has been implemented and tested within several scenes from *Mirage* – an interactive story that we developed based on the Greek Tragedy *Electra*.

In this paper, we will first review some of the current techniques used in interactive entertainment productions, and outline some of the related research in the field. We will then discuss ELE in detail outlining its components. We will then conclude by discussing summary of contribution and future research.

2 Related Research

Interactive entertainment productions use static manually designed lighting, e.g. set-based or ambient[1] lighting. Ambient lighting, used in many games, including *the Sims* and *Sim city*, is simple and does not require adjustments as the characters move or the shot changes. However, it has no cinematic quality and serves no dramatic or aesthetic functions [11]. To establish mood and visual focus, first person and adventure game (e.g. *Max Payne* and *Devil May Cry*) designers use set-based lighting, where they manually set positions, orientations, and colors for each light in the scene depending on the set design [4, 12]. While this scheme provides a workable solution for most games, it is inflexible due to the following reasons. First, it cannot be used to provide character modeling – a technique where more lights are added around a character to show depth and texture. Second, in some situations the character may not be sufficiently lit; a problem that surfaces in games such as the *Thing*. Third, it does not adequately accommodate the dynamic dramatic tension and visual focus.

Few research projects proposed an alternative approach to scripting or manually designed visuals (such as lighting or camera movement). M. He et al. used film-based cinematography techniques to guide an authored interactive narrative [13]. They, however, did not address lighting. Tomlinson proposed a system that manipulates

---

[1] The term ambient lighting is used here to define a light design where every object in the scene is lit equally using a constant intensity, and where the light has no direction. [10] T. Moller, and Haines, E., *Real-time Rendering*. MA: A K Peters, Ltd, 1999.

light colors and camera movements to present the user with an interpretation of the world based on the characters' internal states [14]. For example, it uses a low camera angle to show that a character is powerful or harsh red light to make a character look demonic. In his work, the function of the camera and lighting was restricted to portraying the emotional states of characters in a scene, and thus visual design goals and their link to the narrative as addressed by filmmakers and theatre designers were not addressed [15].

3   ELE (Expressive Lighting Engine)

ELE is designed to automatically set the number of lights used, their positions, colors, and angles based on rules formulated using theatre and film lighting design theory. ELE sits on top of a real-time rendering engine and is used to provide a level of abstraction from the low-level details of manipulating and placing lights individually through graphic engines.

I assume that there exists a system that passes several parameters to ELE, including a set of parameters describing style, local light sources, stage configuration and dimensions, characters' dimensions, dramatic focus (the area/characters towards which attention should be directed) and the dramatic intensity of the situation. Using these parameters ELE computes the number of lights used. For each of these lights, it computes the type of instrument (e.g. spot light or point light), color in RGB color space, attenuation, position as a 3D point, orientation including the facing and up vectors, range, masking parameters, and, depending on the light instrument used, Penumbra and Umbra angles. These parameters are given to a rendering engine to render the frame.

ELE is composed of three subsystems: a system that determines the number of lights used and the areas they affect, a system that selects a color for each light in the scene, and a system that selects an azimuth and elevation angles for each light in the scene. In addition, ELE interacts with the camera system to synchronize lighting changes with camera movement and to ensure that distracting changes are hidden between camera cuts, since Neuroscience and psychology literature have found that human vision does not perceive changes made between camera cuts [18]. I will describe these systems next.

3.1   Allocating Lights

Lights are expensive. Rendering time is proportional to the number of lights used. Most often rendering engines limit the number of lights used to achieve real-time rendering speed (30 frames/second). For instance, Wildtangent (a publicly available rendering engine) restricts the number of lights to eight lights. However, artists use many lights to model characters (i.e. show depth and texture of characters) and establish depth. Lighting designers at Pixar, for example, often use as many as thirty two lights to light one scene. ELE finds a compromise using optimization.

Following film and theatre lighting design theory, ELE finds a configuration of cylindrical areas, a_i, such that the visible area, V, is covered satisfying several constraints, including the maximum number of lights (which is limited considering the speed needed), desired visibility of objects, the desired visual focus (dramatic focus), desired modeling for each character, and desired depth, all of which are determined depending on the given style and situation.

To establish depth, ELE differentiates between areas in the foreground, middle ground, and background. It creates character areas, such that all characters are assigned an area, as follows:

- For each character c create a new area a and assign c to it
- For each area a, if $\exists a'$ s.t. $|a - a'| < \varepsilon$, and both are focus (or non-focus) areas

then merge a, a'

It then finds an allocation p, where $p: L \rightarrow A$ is an assignment of lights to areas, maximizing an objective function composed of the lighting design goals described above:

$$P_{opt} = \arg \max_p (\lambda_v V(p) + \lambda_d D(p) + \lambda_m M(p) + \lambda_c C(p)), \qquad (1.1)$$

where $V(p)$ is the percentage of visible areas that are assigned lights, $M(p)$ is the average number of lights assigned to character areas (to ensure desired modeling), $D(p)$ is depth measured by the difference between the number of lights assigned to the background and foreground areas, and $C(p)$ is visual continuity measured by the difference of the configuration p from the one used in the previous frame. The weights are set by default rules developed based on traditional lighting design theory.

3.2 Configuring Angles

ELE selects azimuth and elevation angles for each light in the scene, including key, fill, and backlights. According to Film and theatre lighting design, designers select angles for each light in the scene to conform to several requirements: ensuring visual continuity, maintaining the illusion of a light source established direction, provoking mood, establishing the desired modeling, and providing visibility.

These goals/requirements conflict; for example, an angle that provides best visibility may hinder modeling or mood. ELE balances these goals using a nonlinear optimization algorithm based on hill climbing. It selects a key light azimuth angle by optimizing a multi-objective cost function, where the objective functions correspond to the lighting design goals, as follows:

$$\text{cost}(k, k^-, m) = \\ \lambda_v(1 - V(k)) + \lambda_-|k - k^-| + \lambda_{m_a}|k - m_a| + \lambda_q \min_i |k - l_i| \qquad (1.2)$$

Where k is the key light angle, k is the key light angle from the previous frame, and m_a is the mood angle azimuth suggested by the artist or calculated by ELE (using a set of default rules as addressed in [9]), λ_v is the cost of deviation from an orientation that establishes best visibility and modeling, λ_- is the cost of changing the key light angle over time (to enforce visual continuity), λ_l is the cost of deviation from an established light source (e.g. torch, window) angle/direction. In addition, l_i is the angle of light from the light source i on the subject or area in question, and λ_{m_a} is the cost of deviation from an angle that shows a specific mood.

Thus, the cost function in (1.2) calculates the best angle given the value of the angle k relative to the objectives desired and their importance projected by the weights. The term $\left| k - k^- \right|$ calculates visual continuity by calculating the difference between the angle selected and the one selected in the previous frame. The third term, $\left| k - m_a \right|$ calculates the difference between the angle selected and the angle suggested by ELE or the artist for achieving the mood desired. Thus, the third term ensures that the right mood is provided in the given shot. The last term, $\min_i \left| k - l_i \right|$, calculates the difference between the angle of light selected and the angle of light emitted by the nearest practical source. $V(k)$ measures the quality of the key light azimuth angle relative to visibility and modeling following Millerson's guidelines [5], which we mathematically represented as follows:

$$V(k, s) = \sin(k)\cos(s), \tag{1.3}$$

where k is the angle between the key light and the camera, and s is the angle between the nose light and the key light.

Similarly, ELE uses the following multi-objective cost function to find the best key light elevation angle:

$$\cos t(e, m_e) = \lambda_{m_e} \left| e - m_e \right| + \lambda_l \min_i \left| e - l_i \right|, \tag{1.4}$$

where e is the elevation angle, m_e is the mood elevation angle suggested by the artists or computed by ELE (using rules documented in [9]), l_i is the elevation of the practical source i, λ_{m_e} is the cost of mood elevation angle, and λ_l is the cost of ensuring that the elevation angle conforms to the elevation of the practical source angle. ELE uses gradient descent to find the best e that minimizes the cost function above.

Fill and backlight azimuth angles are calculated depending on the value of the key light angle and the angle between the camera and the subject. According to the guidelines described by Millerson [5], fill light azimuth and elevation angles are calculated to be the mirror image of the key light angle. Backlight azimuth angle is calculated as follows:

$$b = \left(k - c + \pi \right) \bmod 2\pi, \tag{1.5}$$

where k and c, again, are the are the respective angles of the key light and camera. Backlight elevation angle is set to 45° as recommended in [5].

3.3 Color Optimization System

Colors of lights in a scene compose the contrast and feeling of the entire image. A change of one light's color may affect the entire image. Therefore, ELE manipulates the colors of light evaluating each color change and its effect on the whole image. ELE evaluates color using several parameters, including desired contrast, importance of visual continuity, color palette constraints, as well as ideal values for the hue, saturation, lightness, warmth/coolness for each light, and costs describing the importance of adhering to these values. Using default rules formulated based on film and theatre lighting theory, ELE determines default values for these parameters given the style, dramatic intensity, dramatic focus, and the dramatic situation.

Using the ideal values and their associated costs, ELE uses nonlinear optimization that searches through a nine-dimension space of RGB values differentiating between colors of focus, non-focus, and background areas to select a color for each individual light in the scene evaluating this color using a multi-objective cost function defined as follows:

$$cost(c^t, c^{t-1}) = \lambda_d \left(D(c^t) - d\right)^2 + \lambda_c \left(\text{contrast}_\phi(c^t) - \delta\right)^2 + v(x) + \sum_{i \in \{f,n,b\}} P(c_i^t, c_i^{t-1}),$$

(1.6)

where

$$p(c_i^t, c_i^{t-1}) = \begin{matrix} \lambda_{s_i} \left(S(c_i^t) - s_i\right)^2 + \lambda_{h_i} \left(H(c_i^t) - h_i\right)^2 + \\ \lambda_{l_i} \left(L(c_i^t) - l_i\right)^2 + \lambda_{w_i} \left(W(c_i^t) - w_i\right)^2 + \lambda_{ch} E(c_i^t, c_i^{t-1}), \end{matrix}$$

(1.7)

and where c is a vector of light colors for focus, f, non-focus, n, and background, b, areas at frame t. Color c_i^t is represented in RGB color space, $S(c)$ denotes the saturation of color c, $H(c)$ denotes the hue of color c, $L(c)$ denotes lightness of color c (in RGB color space). ELE uses CIEDE2000 – a well known formula for measuring color difference [16, 17]. The depth, $D(c)$, of a color vector, c, is defined as the color difference between colors of lights lighting the background areas and those lighting other areas.

Following traditional lighting design theory, contrast is used to establish visual tension that parallels the dramatic tension in the scene [2]. Using the guidelines documented by filmmakers and designers, contrast is defined relative to the dramatic focus of the scene [2] as the difference between colors of lights lighting the focus area and a weighted sum of the colors lighting the other areas as follows:

$$\text{contrast}_\phi(c) = \sum_{i \neq focus} w_i \left|\phi(c_{focus}) - \phi(c_i)\right|,$$

(1.8)

where ϕ is the color component (lightness, warmth, or saturation) over which we're computing contrast, c is a vector of the light colors, c_i is a color for an area type i, where $i \in \{focus, non-focus, background\}$ and $focus$ is the index of the dramatic focus area.

The optimization problem discussed above is a constraint-based optimization problem, where the color, c, is constrained to specific values. ELE uses a boundary method to bind the feasible solutions using a barrier function that approaches ∞ as the values approach the boundary defined by the feasibility region. Although gradient descent has major drawbacks, including occurrence of oscillations and being easily stuck in a local minimum, ELE uses gradient descent because a local minimum in our case is preferable since it provides a solution closer to the previous one, thus establishing visual continuity.

4 Results

ELE was implemented and tested within several scenes from an interactive story, called *Mirage* – an interactive drama based on the Greek Tragedy *Electra*. ELE was used to make real-time lighting design decisions that adapt to the story and the situations presented. ELE adapts the lighting to the scene's dramatic action and tension maintaining the established style and visual continuity.

To evaluate the performance of ELE in accommodating movements, figure 1 compares set-based lighting and dynamic lighting used by ELE in a shot where some unanticipated movements occur. As shown, set-based lighting results in partially lit characters due to character movement and changes in the camera view. On the other hand, ELE ensures visibility by dynamically adapting to the movements, as shown.

Figure 2 presents a sequence of screenshots showing how ELE adapts the lighting in a scene to accommodate movement and rise in tension. For example, in the moment after the choice point, ELE accommodated the steep rise in dramatic tension by first requesting a cut from the camera system, and then changing the color contrast within the cut, thus maintaining visual continuity. Comparing the contrast before the choice point to the contrast after the choice point, one can see the dramatic difference. However, viewers were not distracted by this steep change, since it was done within a camera cut.

Fig. 1. Shows two screenshots using ELE *(right)*, camera fill *(left)*

To evaluate the performance of ELE as a lighting designer, a web-based evaluation was conducted. We put the website up for 7 days and asked many visual artists to visit the site and conduct the evaluation test. The reviewers were first asked to view three movies of the same scene lit by (1) ELE, (2) ambient lighting, and (3) statically designed lights. The viewers were allowed to switch between movies, stop, pause, rewind, or forward any of the movies at any time. When ready to begin answering the questionnaire, reviewers pressed on the questionnaire button. (They were allowed to go back to the movies at any time). Reviewers where then asked ten questions comparing the scenes in terms of the lighting design goals (such as providing depth, visual focus, and dramatic tension). Since the test used the same models and scene content, the variables evaluated were constrained to only lighting. ELE rated higher than the other approaches for providing depth, dramatic focus, and dramatic tension.

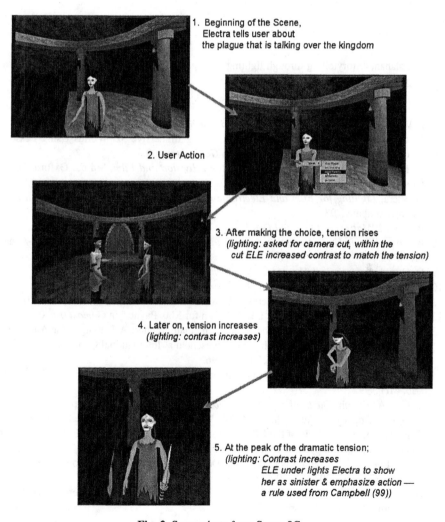

Fig. 2. Screenshots from Scene 8C

5 Conclusion and Future Work

Lighting is an important element of scene composition. Film and theatre lighting designers have long realized the importance of lighting and its implication in enhancing and enriching an experience. In this paper, we presented ELE – an Expressive Lighting Engine that follows traditional film, theatre, and animation techniques to provide a new lighting design technique suited for interactive scenes, where dramatic and spatial content unpredictably change. Due to the complexity of the lighting process and limitations of real-time rendering engines, we left several topics for future research, including shadows, interrelflections, and refractions.

References

1. S. Calahan, "Storytelling through lighting: a computer graphics perspective," presented at Siggraph Course Notes, '96.
2. B. Block, *The Visual Story: Seeing the Structure of Film, TV, and New Media*. New York: Focal Press, '01.
3. P. Ward, *Picture Composition for Film and Television*. Oxford: Focal Press, '96.
4. D. Carson, "Environmental Storytelling: Creating Immersive 3D Worlds Using Lessons Learned from the Theme Park Industry," in *Gamasutra*, '00.
5. G. Millerson, *The Technique of Lighting for Telivision and Film*, 3rd ed. Oxford: Focus Press, '91.
6. D. Viera, *Lighting for Film and Electronic Cinematography*. Belmont: Wadsworth Publishing Company, '93.
7. R. Lowell, *Matters of Light and Depth*. New York: Lowel-light Manufacturing, Inc., '92.
8. B. Foss, *Filmmaking: Narrative & Structural Techniques*. Los Angeles: Silman-James Press, '92.
9. D. Campbell, *Technical Theatre for Non-technical People*: Allworth Press, '99.
10. T. Moller, and Haines, E., *Real-time Rendering*. MA: A K Peters, Ltd, '99.
11. J. Birn, "Digital Lighting & Rendering," G. Maestri, Ed. Indianapolis: New Riders, '00.
12. A. Maattaa, "GDC 2002:Realistic Level Design for Max Payne," in *Gamasutra*, '02.
13. M. C. L. He, and D. Salesin, "The Virtual Cinematographer: A Paradigm for Automatic Real-time Camera Control and Directing," presented at International Conference on Computer Graphics and Interactive Techniques, '96.
14. W. M. Tomlinson, "Interactivity and Emotion through Cinematography." MIT Media Lab: MIT, '99.
15. D. C. a. A. Knoph, *The Book of Movie Photography*. London: Alfred Knopf, '79.
16. B. H. Hill, Roger, T. , and Vorhagen, F. W., "Comparative Analysis of the Quantization of Color Spaces on the Basis of the CIELAB Color-Difference Formula," *ACM Transactions on Graphics*, vol. 16, pp. 109-154, '97.
17. M. R. Luo, Cul, G., and Rigg, B., "The Development of CIE 2000 Colour Difference Formula: CIEDE2000," vol. 2000: CIELAB, '00.
18. H. a. Hollingworth, "Global transsaccadic change blindness during scene perception," *Psychological Science*, in press.

Interactive Out-of-Core Visualisation of Very Large Landscapes on Commodity Graphics Platform

Paolo Cignoni[2], Fabio Ganovelli[2], Enrico Gobbetti[1], Fabio Marton[1], Federico Ponchio[2], and Roberto Scopigno[2]

[1] CRS4
POLARIS Edificio 1, C.P. 25, I-09010 Pula (CA), Italy
http://www.crs4.it/vic/
[2] ISTI-CNR
Area della Ricerca, via G. Moruzzi 1, 56124 PISA, Italy
http://vcg.iei.pi.cnr.it/

Abstract. We recently introduced an efficient technique for out-of-core rendering and management of large textured landscapes. The technique, called Batched Dynamic Adaptive Meshes (*BDAM*), is based on a paired tree structure: a tiled quadtree for texture data and a pair of bintrees of small triangular patches for the geometry. These small patches are TINs that are constructed and optimized off-line with high quality simplification and tristripping algorithms. Hierarchical view frustum culling and view-dependendent texture/geometry refinement is performed at each frame with a stateless traversal algorithm that renders a continuous adaptive terrain surface by assembling out of core data. Thanks to the batched CPU/GPU communication model, the proposed technique is not processor intensive and fully harnesses the power of current graphics hardware. This paper summarizes the method and discusses the results obtained in a virtual fly-through over a textured digital landscape derived from aerial imaging.

1 Introduction

Virtual environment technology has been developing over a long period, and offering presence simulation to users as an interface metaphor to a synthesized world has become the research agenda for a growing community of researchers and industries. The motivation for such a research direction is twofold. From an evolutionary perspective, virtual reality is seen as a way to overcome limitations of standard human-computer interfaces; from a revolutionary perspective, virtual reality technology opens the door to new types of applications that exploit the additional possibilities offered by presence simulation.

Our sense of physical reality is a construction derived from the symbolic, geometric, and dynamic information directly presented to our senses. Sensory simulation is thus at the heart of virtual reality technology and, since vision is generally considered the most dominant sense, the development of efficient methods for generating high quality visual representations of simulated environments is of primary importance.

Real-time 3D exploration of digital elevation models (DEM), which are computerized representations of the Earth's relief, is now one of the most important features in a number of practical applications, that range from scientific simulators, to gaming systems, to virtual storytelling applications.

O. Balet et al. (Eds.): ICVS 2003, LNCS 2897, pp. 21–29, 2003.
© Springer-Verlag Berlin Heidelberg 2003

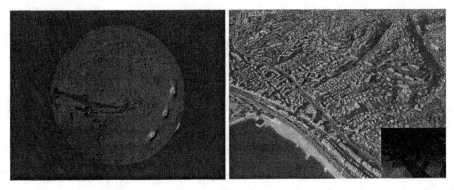

Fig. 1. Flying over reconstructed terrains at different scales: Left: Global reconstruction of Mars. Right: City scale exploration (Nice, France); textured terrain and same view with wireframe showing adaptive rendering tessellation.

Rendering large-scale high resolution terrains with high visual and temporal fidelity on a graphics PC platform is, however, a very challenging task, since it is necessary to meet the following requirements on the rendering subsystem:

- **high visual and temporal fidelity:** at least 30 frames per second, with about 1M pixels/frame with color defined at 16 to 24 bits per pixels;
- **large scale high resolution terrains:** texture mapped elevation data (DTM or DEM/DSM). Typical current database sites are represented by elevation grids of about 8Kx8K to 40Kx40K (this means up to billions of vertices per model). Color resolution is generally similar or 2 to 4 times larger;
- **graphics PC platform:** at the time of this writing, this means a one or two-processor machine with 32 bit architecture, large local disk, 1GHz or more Pentium class processor, DDR memory, and good quality commodity graphics board (AGP4X/8X, theoretical peak rendering speed in the order of tens or hundreds of millions of vertices per second).

The above requirements indicate that scene complexity is much larger that what can be handled by brute force methods. Since there is no upper bound on the complexity of a scene visible from a specific viewpoint, occlusion and view frustum culling techniques are not sufficient alone for meeting the performance requirements dictated by the human perceptual system. Achieving this goal requires the ability to trade rendering quality with speed. Ideally, this time/quality conflict should be handled with adaptive techniques, to cope with the wide range of viewing conditions while avoiding worst case assumptions.

Current dynamic multiresolution algorithms are, however, very processor intensive, and fail to provide adequate performance for large datasets. In particular, multiresolution rendering techniques were designed for the previous generation machines, and are generally too processor intensive. The potential of current GPUs is far from being fully exploited, and, on current platforms, performance is directly related to CPU processing power, which grows at a much slower rate than GPU's one. Current state-of-the-art techniques, based on hierarchical techniques (e.g., [4]) use only about 10%

to 20% of the available graphics power for large datasets and do not offer efficient means to preserve sharp features. Moreover, in most applications that need interactive terrain visualization, managing the terrain multiresolution structure is not the only task that must be accomplished by the system: dynamics simulation, AI of other agents, database queries, and other jobs have to be carried out in the same time. For this reason, using current multiresolution solutions, the size of the terrain representation that can be constructed/updated and rendered for each frame is severely limited by the CPU processing power and by far smaller than the GPU capabilities.

We recently introduced a technique, named Batched Dynamic Adaptive Meshes (BDAM), that is based on the idea to move the grain of the multiresolution models up from triangles to small contiguous portions of mesh in order to alleviate the processing load and to better exploit current graphics hardware. The technique is based on a paired tree structure: a tiled quadtree for texture data and a pair of bintrees of small triangular patches for the geometry. These small patches are TINs that are constructed and optimized off-line with high quality simplification and tristripping algorithms. A hierarchical view frustum culling and view-dependendent texture/geometry refinement can be performed, at each frame, with a stateless traversal algorithm that renders a continuous adaptive terrain surface by assembling these small patches. An out-of-core technique has been designed and tested for constructing BDAMs using a generic high quality simplification.

Thanks to the batched CPU/GPU communication model, the proposed technique is not processor intensive and fully harnesses the power of current graphics hardware. The remainder of this paper summarizes the method and discusses the results obtained in a virtual flythrough over a textured digital terrain model of the city of Nice, France.

2   Methods and Tools

Most of current multiresolution algorithms are designed to use the triangle as the smallest primitive entity. The main idea behind our approch is to adopt a more complex primitive: small surface patches composed of a batch of a few hundreds of triangles. The benefits of this approach are that the per-triangle workload to extract a multiresolution model is highly reduced and the small patches can be preprocessed and optimized off-line for a more efficient rendering. We summarize here the main concepts behind BDAM. Please refer to the original papers for further details [1,2].

In BDAM, the small patches form a hierarchy of right triangles (HRT) that is coded as a binary tree. This representation can be used to easily extract a consistent set of contiguous triangles which cover a particular region with given error thresholds. These small triangular patches can be *batched* (hence the name) to the graphics hardware in the most efficient way. Therefore, each bintree node contains a small chunk (in the range of 256..8K) of contiguous well packed tri-stripped triangles. To ensure the correct matching between triangular patches, BDAM exploits the right triangle hierarchy property that each triangle can correctly connect to: triangles of its same level; triangles of the next coarser level through the longest edge; and triangles of the next finer level through the two shortest edges.

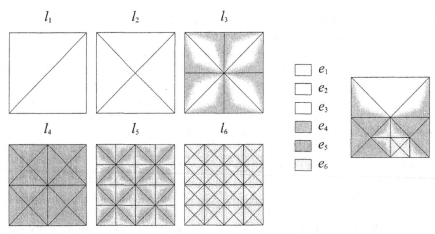

Fig. 2. An example of a BDAM: each triangle represents a terrain patch composed by many triangles. Colors correspond to different errors; the blending of the color inside each triangle corresponds to the smooth error variation inside each patch.

To guarantee the correct connectivity along borders of different simplification levels, triangular patches are built so that the error is distributed as shown in figure 2: each triangle of the bintree represents a small mesh patch with error e_k inside and error e_{k+1} (the error corresponding to the next more refined level in the bintree) along the two shortest edges. In this way, each mesh composed by a collection of small patches arranged as a correct bintree triangulation still generates a globally correct triangulation. This simple edge error property is exploited, as explained in the original paper [2], to design a distributed out-of-core high quality simplification algorithm that concurrently builds all patches.

In Fig. 2 we show an example of these properties. In the upper part of the figure we show the various levels of a HRT and each triangle represents a terrain patch composed by many graphics primitives. Colors correspond to different errors; the blending of the colors inside each triangular patch corresponds to the smooth error variation inside each patch. When composing these triangular patches using the HRT consistency rules, the color variation is always smooth: the triangulation of adjacent patches correctly matches.

Texture and geometry trees. To efficiently manage large textures, the BDAM approach partitions them into tiles before rendering and arranges them in a multiresolution structure as a tiled texture quadtree. Each texture quadtree element corresponds to a pair of adjacent geometry bintree elements. The roots of the trees cover the entire dataset, and both trees are maintained off-core using a pointerless structure that is mapped at run time to a virtual memory address range. During rendering, the two trees are processed together. Descending one level in the texture quadtree corresponds to descending two levels in the associated pair of geometry bintrees. This correspondence can be exploited in the preprocessing step to associate object-space representation errors to the quadtree levels, and in the rendering step to implement view-dependent multiresolution texture and geometry extraction in a single top-down refinement strategy.

Errors and bounding volumes. To easily maintain the triangulation coherence BDAM exploits the concept of nested/saturated errors, introduced by Pajarola[6], that supports the extraction of a correct set of triangular patches with a simple stateless refinement visit of the hierarchy [6, 4] that starts at the top-level of the texture and geometry trees and recursively visits the nodes until the screen space texture error becomes acceptable. The object-space errors of the patches are computed directly during the preprocessing construction of the BDAM. Once these errors have been computed, a hierarchy of errors that respect nesting conditions is constructed bottom up. Texture errors are computed from texture features, and, similarly, are embedded in a corresponding hierarchy. For the rendering purpose, BDAM adopts a tree of nested volumes that is also built during the preprocessing, with properties very similar to the two error rules: 1) bounding volume of a patch include all children bounding volumes; 2) two patches adjacent along hypotenuse must share the same bounding volume which encloses both. These bounding volumes are used to compute screen space errors and also for view frustum culling.

Large dataset partitioning. In order to handle the size and accuracy problems related to large dataset management, we partition input data in a number of square tiles, therefore managing a forest of BDAM hierarchies instead of a single tree. This effectively decomposes the original dataset into terrain tiles. It should be noted, however, that the tiles are only used to circumvent address space and accuracy limitations and do not affect other parts of the system. In particular, errors and bounding volumes are propagated to neighboring tiles through the common edges in order to ensure continuity for the entire dataset. The tiles have an associated (u, v) parameterization, which is used for texture coordinates and to construct the geometry subdivision hierarchy. The number and size of the tiles is arbitrary and depends only on the size of the original dataset. In particular, we make sure that the following constraints are met: (a) a single precision floating point representation is accurate enough for representing local coordinates (i.e. there are less than 2^{23} texels/positions along each coordinate axis); (b) the size of the generated multiresolution structure is within the data size limitations imposed by the operating system (i.e. less than the largest possible memory mapped segment).

Top-down view-dependent refinement and rendering. For each of the partitions that compose the dataset, we map its data structure into the process address space, render the structure using a stateless top-down refinement procedure, then delete the mapping for the specified address range. The refinement procedure starts at the top level of the texture and geometry trees of a given tile and recursively visits their nodes until the screen space texture error becomes acceptable or the visited node bounding sphere is proved off the viewing frustum. While descending the texture quadtree, corresponding displaced triangle patches in the two geometry bintree are identified and selected for processing. Once the texture is considered detailed enough, texture refinement stops. At this point, the texture is bound and the algorithm continues by refining the two geometry bintrees until the screen space geometry error becomes acceptable or the visited node is culled out. Patch rendering is done by converting the corner vertices to camera coordinates and binding them along with associated normals and texture coordinates to the appropriate uniform parameters, prior to binding varying vertex data and drawing an indexed triangle strip. With this method, each required texture is bound only once, and all the geometry data covered by it is then drawn, avoiding unnecessary context switches and minimizing host to graphics bandwidth requirement.

Memory management. Time-critical rendering large terrain datasets requires real-time management of huge amounts of data. Moving data from the storage unit to main memory and to the graphics board is often the major bottleneck. We use both a data layout aimed at optimizing memory coherence and a cache managed using a LRU strategy for caching the most recent textures and patches directly in graphics memory. Since the disk is, by far, the slowest component of the system, we have further optimized the external memory management component with mesh compression and speculative prefetching (see [2] for details).

3   Results

An experimental software library and a terrain rendering application supporting the BDAM technique has been implemented and tested on Linux and Win32 platforms. The results were collected on a Linux PC with dual Intel Xeon 2.4 Ghz, 2GB RAM, two Seagate ST373453LW 70 GB ULTRA SCSI 320 hard drives, AGP 8x and NVIDIA GeForce Fx Ultra graphics.

The test case discussed in this paper concerns the preprocessing and interactive exploration of a terrain dataset of the Nice metropolitan area[1]. We used a 8K x 8K elevation grid with 100 centimeter horizontal resolution. On this terrain, we mapped a 16K x 16K RGB texture with 50 centimeter resolution.

3.1   Preprocessing

The input dataset was transformed to multiresolution by our texture and geometry processing tools. For textures, we used a tile size of 256x256 pixels, which produced a 7 level quadtree and compressed colors using the DXT1 format. Texture preprocessing, including error propagation, took roughly two hours and produced a structure occupying 132 MB on disk. Processing time is dominated by texture compression. For geometry, we generated two 17 levels bintrees, with leaf nodes containing triangular patches of 32x32 vertex side at full resolution and interior nodes with a constant vertex count of 600. Geometry preprocessing, that included optimized tristrip generation and data compression, has been performed roughly in 3.5 hours, producing a multiresolution structure which occupies 321 MB. Size has been reduced by compression to about 60 % of the size of the original model. The full resolution model is made of 46M triangles. For the sake of comparison, Hoppe's view dependent progressive meshes [3], that, like BDAMs, support unconstrained triangulation of terrains, need roughly 380MB of RAM and uses 190MB of disk space to build a multiresolution model of a simplified version of 7.9M triangles of the Puget Sound dataset[2]. Preprocessing times are similar to BDAM times. By contrast, SOAR [5] geometry data structure, which is based on a

---

[1] dataset: courtesy of ISTAR high resolution cartographic database.

[2] The dataset at various resolution is freely available from
   http://www.cc.gatech.edu/projects/large_models/ps.html

hierarchy of right triangles, takes roughly 3.4 GB[3] on disk for the processed data set, but is much faster to compute since the subdivision structure is data independent.

3.2   View-Dependent Refinement

We evaluated the performance of the BDAM technique on a number of flythrough sequences. The quantitative results presented here were collected during a 100 seconds high speed fly-over of the data set with a window size of 800x600 pixels and a screen tolerance of 1.0 pixel. The qualitative performance of our view-dependent refinement is further illustrated in an accompanying video[4], that shows the live recording of the analyzed flythrough sequence (Fig. 5).

Figure 3 illustrates the rendering performance of the application. We were able to sustain an average rendering rate of roughly 60 millions of textured triangles per second, with peaks exceeding 71 millions, which are close to the peak performance of the rendering board (Fig. 3 left). By comparison, on the same machine, SOAR peak performance was measured at roughly 5.5 millions of triangles per second, even though SOAR was using a smaller single resolution texture of 2Kx2K texels. The increased performance of the BDAM approach is due to the larger granularity of the structure, that amortizes structure traversal costs over many graphics primitives, reduces AGP data transfers through on-board memory management and fully exploits the post-transform-and-lighting cache with optimized indexed triangle strips.

Rendered scene granularity is illustrated in figure 4 with the peak complexity of the rendered scenes reaching 1.7M triangles and 9.6M texels per frame. Since we are able to render such complex scenes at high frame rates (30 to 210 Hz for the entire test path, Fig. 4), it is possible to use very small pixel threshold, virtually eliminating popping artifacts, without the need to resort to costly geomorphing features. Moreover, since TINs are used as basic building blocks, the triangulation can more easily adapt to high frequency variations of the terrain, such as house walls, than techniques based on regular subdivision meshes.

4   Conclusions

We have presented an efficient technique for out-of-core management and interactive rendering of large scale textured terrain surfaces. The main idea behind the method is to move the grain of the multiresolution models up from triangles to small contiguous portions of mesh in order to alleviate the processing load and to better exploit current graphics hardware. The results demonstrate that, thanks to the batched host-to-graphics communication model, performance is limited by graphics processor speed. The technique is thus well suited for a range of interactive applications, including virtual storytelling systems requiring the interactive rendering of massive outdoor sets.

---

[3] The version of SOAR used in this comparison is v1.11, available from
   http://www.cc.gatech.edu/~lindstro/software/soar/
[4] The videos are available from http://www.crs4.it/vic/multimedia/

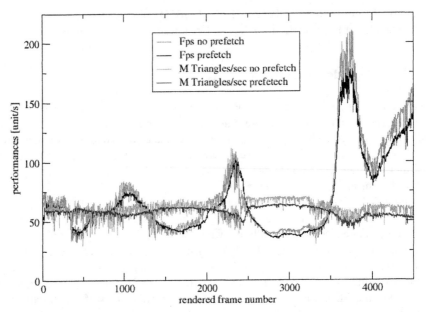

Fig. 3. Performance Evaluation. Rendering rates per frame with and without data prefetching. Note how the prefetch version presents a smoother behaviour.

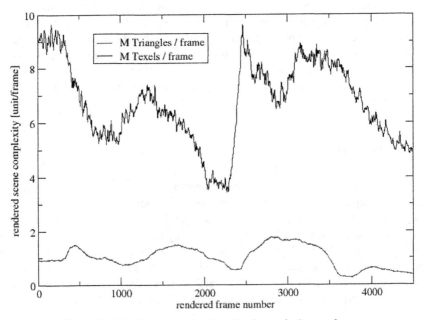

Fig. 4. Complexity evaluation. Rendered complexity per frame.

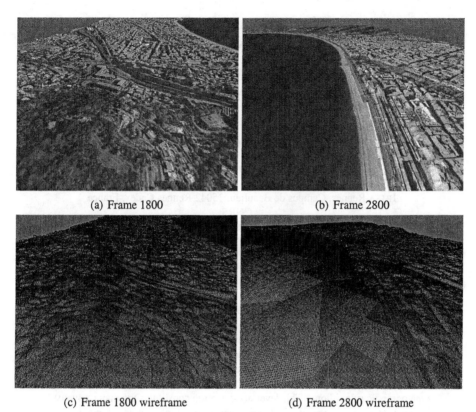

(a) Frame 1800   (b) Frame 2800

(c) Frame 1800 wireframe   (d) Frame 2800 wireframe

Fig. 5. Selected flythrough frames. Screen space error tolerance set to 3.0 pixels.

References

1. Paolo Cignoni, Fabio Ganovelli, Enrico Gobbetti, Fabio Marton, Federico Ponchio, and Roberto Scopigno. BDAM – batched dynamic adaptive meshes for high performance terrain visualization. *Computer Graphics Forum*, 22(3), September 2003. To appear.
2. Paolo Cignoni, Fabio Ganovelli, Enrico Gobbetti, Fabio Marton, Federico Ponchio, and Roberto Scopigno. Planet–sized batched dynamic adaptive meshes (p-bdam). In *Proceedings IEEE Visualization*, Conference held in Seattle, WA, USA, October 2003. IEEE Computer Society Press. To appear.
3. H. Hoppe. Smooth view-dependent level-of-detail control and its aplications to terrain rendering. In *IEEE Visualization '98 Conf.*, pages 35–42, 1998.
4. P. Lindstrom and V. Pascucci. Visualization of large terrains made easy. In *Proc. IEEE Visualization 2001*, pages 363–370, 574. IEEE Press, October 2001.
5. P. Lindstrom and V. Pascucci. Terrain simplification simplified: A general framework for view-dependent out-of-core visualization. *IEEE Transaction on Visualization and Computer Graphics*, 8(3):239–254, 2002.
6. R. Pajarola. Large scale terrain visualization using the restricted quadtree triangulation. In H. Rushmeier D. Elbert, H. Hagen, editor, *Proceedings of Visualization '98*, pages 19–26, 1998.

A Cinematography System
for Virtual Storytelling

Nicolas Courty[1], Fabrice Lamarche[2],
Stéphane Donikian[3], and Éric Marchand[1]

[1] INRIA
IRISA Rennes, Campus de Beaulieu, 35042 Rennes Cedex, France
Marchand@irisa.fr
[2] University of Rennes I
IRISA Rennes, Campus de Beaulieu, 35042 Rennes Cedex, France
[3] CNRS
IRISA Rennes, Campus de Beaulieu, 35042 Rennes Cedex, France
Donikian@irisa.fr

Abstract. In this paper we introduce a complete framework to automatically generate "cinematographic view" of dynamic scenes in real-time. The main goal of such a system is to provide a succession of shots and sequences (of virtual dynamic scenes) that can be related to pure cinema. Our system is based on the use of an image-based control of the camera that allows different levels of visual tasks and a multi-agent system that controls those cameras and selects the type of shot that has to be performed in order to fulfill the constraints of a given cinematographic rule (idiom). This level of adaptation constitutes the major novelty of our system. Moreover, it stands for a convenient tool to describe cinematographic idioms for real-time narrative virtual environments.

1   Introduction

Automatic cinematography can be seen as the ability to choose viewpoints (eventually animated) from which virtual environments are rendered, with narrative constraints. In this sense, a strong parallel with cinema can be drawn; camera shots and motions participate to the emotional commitment a user can get with narrative virtual environments. Since the beginning of the seventh art, film directors have implicitly established a set of rules and conventions that encode proper ways to tell stories in an accurate and explicit mode (see [2] for examples). Though, this set of rules is not sufficiently detailed to define a formal grammar which could be directly used in virtual storytelling applications. Indeed, given a complete three dimensional description of a scene that includes motion of various objects and characters, many possibilities exist to film with respect to the traditional way of filming. Moreover, we can assume that choosing among one of these possibilities depends on many factors (director's intentions, lighting purpose, disposition of the scene, etc.).

In the contrary of cinema, when dealing with interactive environments such as video games or interactive fiction, it is not possible to use storyboards to characterize pre-

O. Balet et al. (Eds.): ICVS 2003, LNCS 2897, pp. 30–34, 2003.
© Springer-Verlag Berlin Heidelberg 2003

cisely the way each shot will be taken. In fact, due to the user interactions, the placement of cameras and actors can not be precomputed and, consequently, shots can not be planned in advance. Though it is always possible to set up offline some camera positions and switch between them at runtime (pre-composed "cut scenes"), this technique has proved to lack of expressiveness and forbids utilization of particular shots like over-the-shoulder shots for instance. This emphasizes the need of an autonomous cinematographic system in order to adapt to the dynamic world.

2   Automatic Cinematography

Many works have been done to automatically generate complete camera specifications, but among those works it is possible to distinguish two different types of approaches, considering or not real-time constraints. Hence, getting the exact flow of actions before they happen allows to run a planning process, which corresponds to the real cinematographic one [8,4]. But, due to the user interaction, those approaches can not be used in real-time virtual environments as the flow of actions becomes unpredictable. This point constitutes the major difficulty in automatic cinematography, in the sense that the system has to generate a coherent and accurate viewpoint at each frame without knowing anything about the future of the actions. In [7], He *et al.* are the first to explore real-time automatic camera control. In [3], Bares uses a constraint-based approach for shots composition in a 3D interactive fiction. The FILM language[1] has two objectives: characterize the camera behavior of film idioms and adapt dynamically to the specific situation of any given shot. Funge [5] is one of the first to compare the camera system to an agent. Before the animation, a set of rules describing the camera behaviors are established, and during the animation its A.I. engine chooses between all those rules. Tomlinson [11] considered the camera as a creature, ruled by desires and intentions, that can act upon its environment (displacing lights for instance), in order to display the emotional content of the scenes.

3   Overview of the Cinematography System

The main goal of our system is to provide one camera configuration for the $3D$ engine at each iteration of the application. Let us note that provided that the application would propose several view-ports of the virtual environment, the camera manager should give an equivalent number of camera configurations. Choosing the best camera configuration for the camera manager is performed through the use of information provided by other modules devoted to scenario, characters and environment management. This information can also be the result of direct queries. Those aspects will not be discussed in this paper. The camera manager is composed of a multi-agent system which controls several cameras that act, independently and with different goals, in the virtual environment.

3.1   Camera Control

To perform positioning tasks and animation of the different camera, our system uses an image-based animation system, as proposed in [10]. Among other, this approach allows

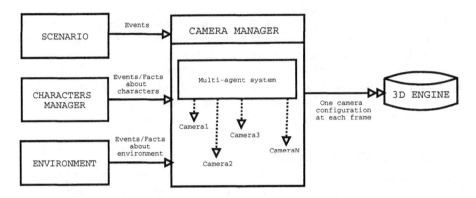

Fig. 1. Architecture of our system regarding to the other parts of the application

definition of multi-level tasks: a main task (or focusing task) that has to be respected at each frame, and some secondary tasks that can be executed providing that the main task is ensured. This feature allows flexibility in the control of the camera. Our camera module provides cinematographic primitives to control the camera. Several solutions may exist at the same time to solve a particular camera positioning task. Choosing between those solutions may depend on the desired effect as well as a particular context. Indeed, while evaluating the quality of a shot, the possible side effects due to the environment, like occlusions or lighting conditions, must be taken into account. Solutions to the detection of occlusions, and to possible strategies to avoid them exist [6, 10] and can be used efficiently in this context. Mainly, given an occlusion detection process, two possibilities are available: one can try to avoid the bad configuration, or if it is impossible (or if it results in a bad shot), the camera behaviors must adapt and choose for instance another shooting sequence. Using a camera control allowing different task levels is quite interesting in this context: while ensuring the nature of the shot (the image-based constraints), remaining degrees of freedom can be used to avoid bad configurations.

3.2   Modeling Idioms and Editing Purposes

The language of film is a common international reference and it can be viewed as a structured style for conveying stories that is familiar to viewers. Even if stories of several movies are different, the related style is so structured that certain situations are almost filmed from the same way. This stereotypical way to capture specific actions into a predetermined sequence of shots is called a film idiom. Idioms are cinematographic rules which represent a codified way of chaining different points of view depending on the nature of the filmed scene. Starting from this assumption, an idiom can be interpreted as an abstract agent chaining shots on different points of interest in the scene. Focusing on those point of interests can be achieved in several manners from different viewpoints. To adapt to the dynamic world, a multi agent system offering good synchronization properties [9] is used. The key concept of this architecture is to exploit redundancy of points of view satisfaction on a given scene in order to automatically select the best camera in respect with idioms description, knowing that each camera is described as an autonomous agent. The synchronization facilities offered by the multi-agent system are used to ensure consistency during the film, between the concurrent cameras but also between the running idioms.

4 Conclusion

In this paper a cinematographic system adapted to real-time applications such as virtual Storytelling is introduced. The camera control is handled with our image-based constraints framework, and provides a multi-level control of the cameras (through the use of different level of visual tasks at the same time), and is well suited to avoid bad configurations (like occlusions) that are very likely to happen in dynamic environments. Our multi-agent system allows to exploit redundancy that can exist in the different ways of filming scenes, thus performing a trade-over between traditional ways and existing rules of cinematographic productions and dynamic environments constraints. This constitutes one of the major novelty in comparison with prior works. Moreover, this system constitutes a fast and intuitive tool to design cinematographic behaviors (idioms) that conveys narrative information with respect to film language.

References

1. D. Amerson and S. Kime. Real-time cinematic camera control for interactive narratives. In *AAAI'00*, 2000.
2. D. Arijon. *Grammar of the Film Language*. Communication Arts Books, New York, 1976.
3. W.H. Bares, J.P. Grégoire, and J.C. Lester. Realtime constraint-based cinematography for complex interactive 3d worlds. In *Tenth National Conference on Innovative Applications of Artificial Intelligence*, pages 1101–1106, 1998.
4. D.B. Christianson, S.E. Anderson, L.W. He, D.H. Salesin, D.S. Weld, and MF.. Cohen. Declarative camera control for automatic cinematography (video). In *Proc. of the 13th Nat. Conf. on Artificial Intelligence and the Eighth Innovative Applications of Artificial Intelligence Conference*, pages 148–155, Menlo Park, August 1996.
5. J. Funge, X. Tu, and D. Terzopoulos. Cognitive modeling: Knowledge, reasoning and planning for intelligent characters. In *Proc. of SIGGRAPH 99, Computer Graphics Proceedings*, pages 29–38, Los Angeles, 1999.
6. N. Halper, R. Helbing, and T. Strothotte. A camera engine for computer games: Managing the Trade-Off between constraint satisfaction and frame coherence. In *Proc. of Eurographics'01*, pages 174–183, Manchester, UK, September 2001.
7. L.-W. He, M.F. Cohen, and D.H. Salesin. The virtual cinematographer: a paradigm for automatic real-time camera control and directing. In *Proc. of SIGGRAPH 96, in Computer Graphics Proceedings*, pages 217–224, New-Orleans, August 1996.
8. P. Karp and S. Feiner. Automated presentation planning of animation using task decomposition with heuristic reasoning. In *Proc. of Graphics Interface '93*, pages 118–127, Toronto, Ontario, Canada, May 1993.
9. F. Lamarche and S. Donikian. Automatic orchestration of behaviours through the management of resources and priority levels. In *Proc. of Autonomous Agents and Multi Agent Systems AAMAS'02*, Bologna, Italy, July 15-19 2002. ACM.

10. E. Marchand and N. Courty. Controlling a camera in a virtual environment. *The Visual Computer Journal*, 18(1):1–19, February 2002.
11. B. Tomlinson, B. Blumberg, and D. Nain. Expressive autonomous cinematography for interactive virtual environments. In *Proc. of the 4th Int. Conf. on Autonomous Agents*, pages 317–324, Barcelona, Spain, June 2000.

Narrativity and Authoring

Authoring Highly Generative Interactive Drama

Nicolas Szilas[1], Olivier Marty[2,3], and Jean-Hugues Réty[4]

[1] IDtension
1, rue des Trois Couronnes, 75011 Paris, France
nicolas.szilas@libertysurf.fr
http://www.idtension.com
[2] LSS / ENS-EHESS
48, bd Jourdan, 75014 Paris, France
olivier.marty@ens.tr
[3] LATTS / ENPC-UMLV
Cité Descartes, 77426 Marne-la-Vallée, France
[4] LINC – Laboratoire Paragraphe /IUT de Montreuil
140, rue de la Nouvelle France, 93100 Montreuil, France
jh.rety@iut.univ-paris8.fr

Abstract. Authoring non linear narratives is a difficult and challenging issue. In this paper we focus on the process of authoring with the IDtension system, an interactive drama system designed by one of the authors. We report an experiment of realizing a real-size scenario and start from this point to think about nonlinear narratives and the possibilities and limits of the IDtension writing tool.

1 Introduction

1.1 Definition of Interactive Drama

The term "Interactive Drama" (ID) could refer either to existing forms of interactive fiction, video games, participatory theatre, etc. or to futuristic immersive systems, like the Holodeck described in StarTrek. In this paper, we call Interactive Drama an experience on computer such as described in [1]. We propose the following definition of Interactive Drama:

Interactive Drama is a drama on computer where the user *is* a character. *Being* a character means being able to perform any action on the fiction world that the other characters can perform.

For instance, if one character gives some information to the user, she should be able to give it to some third character. This definition shows that ID does not exist yet: in existing interactive fictions or story-based video games, simulated characters perform actions that the player cannot perform; thus the user is not a character; rather, she guides a character through a limited set of actions.

1.2 Authoring

We distinguish three main issues in designing Interactive Dramas:

- How to build ID systems: What narrative principles can constitute the base for such systems? How is it possible to interact with a story? How to overcome the seeming contradiction between story and interactivity? What part takes Artificial Intelligence in this task?

O. Balet et al. (Eds.): ICVS 2003, LNCS 2897, pp. 37–46, 2003.
© Springer-Verlag Berlin Heidelberg 2003

- What is the role of the user: What does it mean for the user to be a character in a story? What is her narrative role in the story? How does she interact with the system? What existing experience is the closest from ID: book, video game, role playing, child playing, etc. [2].
- What is the role of the author: How does the user communicate her intention and values through the ID? Does the author "give up control" in ID? How to "write a story" given the fact that, eventually, the precise course of events in the story is in the hands of the user?

Let us note that these three issues are indeed not independent. We believe the first one to be the most critical. The question of interactive fiction – which is not new – has not been solved by writers themselves because it involves sophisticated computing systems. As long as no viable technical solutions exist for ID, one cannot conceive the kind of art or entertainment it could be. This is the reason why our previous publications on the subject [3,4,5,6] concern technical solutions for ID.

A prototype system – called Idtension – now exists. With this system in hand, the next step was to write a convincing story. This step has raised several questions that we discuss in sections 3 with the description of a concrete experience. The IDtension system is presented in section 2.

Other advanced ID systems describe ID as a combination of elementary scenes or beats [7,8,9,10,11]. In opposite, IDtension describes ID with a finer grain, similarly to [12]. With such a fine grain description of drama, authoring becomes even more difficult.

2   Overview of IDtension

We provide in this section a general description of the IDtension system. Further details can be found in [6].

2.1   The Simulation of Narrative

Many models of narrative describe a story as a temporal succession of events. Let us mention for instance the Propp model [13], the Heroe's journey or the screen writing handbooks [14,15,16]. We found that these models, sometimes called "plot models", are not suited to the level of interactivity we target because they are fundamentally linear: the order of events is almost predetermined. On the other hand, the field of ID being historically related to the field of believable agents, the simulation of characters evolving in a virtual world constitutes another basis for ID. However, we have shown in a previous paper [3] that simulating human beings with intelligent agents (as, for instance, in [17]) is not sufficient to generate a well constructed narrative, because fundamentally, narrative contains "inverse causality" [18]. Because of these two opposite approaches of ID, which reflect the traditional opposition between plot-based and character-based drama, there is a tendency to oppose plot-based approaches and simulation-based approaches, as if simulation was to be restricted to the simulation of living or non living matter [19]. IDtension extends simulation to the narrative itself. It is inspired from structuralism, which aimed at describing the narrative as the temporal unfolding of a non-temporal structure [5].

Let us sketch out what are the advantages of this approach over the plot-based approach by considering the reproduction of a visual scene. The plot-based approach is similar to a painting: to each zone in the scene corresponds a point in the painting. Conversely, the simulation-based approach of IDtension is similar to a 3D model: the deep structure of the narrative is modeled, and the story is the result of the simulation of this structure, as well as the deep structure of the simulated object is modeled, and what you see on the screen is the result of the simulation of the 3D model. The main advantage of simulation is that it facilitates interaction: The user can influence the simulation while the deep structure remains the same.

2.2 The Global Architecture

The IDtension structural model of narrative includes a rule based system which defines the possible actions in the story and how these actions can be chained together. The rules has been inspired from Bremond [20] and Todorov [21]. In addition to these Structuralist models, IDtension includes a user model for sequencing the actions [3,5]. Such user models are also present in other system for ID [7, 22].

The system is composed of the following modules (see Fig. 1):

- The Narrative Logic: this modules calculates the set of actions that are possible at a given stage of the narrative. It is composed of about 40 rules, which are generic for all narratives. Each rule implements a logical condition for an action to be possible. For instance, if a character A knows that a character B has accomplished a task t, then A could congratulate B for having performed t. Actions include *to inform, to encourage, to dissuade, to accept, to refuse, to perform, to congratulate, to condemn*, etc.

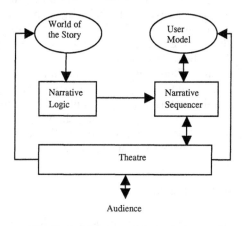

Fig. 1. Architecture of the narrative engine

- The World of the Story defines the basic entities of the story: characters, objects, places, goals, tasks, sub-tasks or segments, obstacles, states of characters (defined with predicates) and facts concerning the material situation of the world of the story (the fact that a door is closed, for example).
- The User Model stores the history of perceived actions, the perceived values of characters, the opened narrative sequences, etc. This enables to estimate the impact of actions on the user.
- The Narrative Sequencer is the "director" of the system. It receives possible actions from the Narrative Logic, and asks the User Model for the impact of each action, and sends to the theatre the actions to be played.
- The Theatre is responsible for displaying the action(s) and manages the interaction between the computer and the user. Currently, the theatre used in the system is a basic text generator, as output, and a selection among possible actions, as input. Future theatre will typically include a Real-Time 3D interface.

2.3 The Goal/Tasks Model

The tasks in a story are parts of the "performative landscape of the story", i.e. what characters can physically do into the story. With IDtension, this includes:

- Goals: states in the world of the story that characters wish to reach.
- Tasks: acts that characters can perform. Performing some tasks enables a character to reach a goal.
- Segments: sub-tasks (task are linear successions of segments)
- Obstacles hinder a segment (thus a task) to be performed. Obstacles play a central role in narrative, in particular in screenwriting (Field Egri) because they allow new developments, suspense, surprise, etc.

There is a subgoaling mechanism based on obstacles. Obstacles can be triggered out depending on conditions. Reaching goals may add or withdraw conditions. Thus, a character can try to reach a goal in order to release an obstacle.

This subgoaling mechanism is to be related to the planing structures used in other ID systems [22,17], although less formalized. Our structure is however more narrative oriented and less Artificial Intelligence oriented.

The IDtension model is not restricted to the performative level. An axiological level – i.e. a level of ethical judgement – is also present with a notion of *value*. A value is an author-defined axis, like "honesty", "honor", etc. Tasks can be assigned with values, and every character has its own sensibility to values. For instance, some task can be dishonest, so that a character sensible to honesty will be reluctant in performing it. Thus, two tasks can reach the same goal, while being differently evaluated. A task is said to be conflictual to a character if the task can reach one of her goals and if this task is negatively evaluated according to this character's sensibility.

The task model of IDtension allows for the modeling of various narrative phenomena, like external and internal conflicts, expected and unexpected obstacles, ethical opposition between characters, conflicts of interest between characters, etc.

2.4 The User Model

Thanks to the richness of the model described above, the Narrative Logic provides a set of actions which are potentially very interesting from a narrative point of view. The actual narrative interest however depends on the proper estimation of the impact on the user. We have identified six criteria to be satisfied in order to have a "good" story:

- motivational consistency: The action is consistent with the goals of the character.
- ethical consistency: The action is consistent with previous actions of the same character, with respect to the axiological system.
- relevance: The action is relevant according to the actions that have just been performed. This criterion corresponds to one of the Grice's maxims.
- cognitive load: The action opens or closes narrative processes, depending on the current number of opened processes. A process is a micro narrative sequence, as defined in [20].
- characterization: The action helps the user understanding the character's features.

- conflict: The action either directly generates some conflict (performing a conflict-ing task), or the action pushes the user towards a conflicting task (for example by blocking a non-conflicting task, if a conflicting alternative exists).

This set of criteria may be modified in the future. Other interesting criteria have been proposed in [7][23].

2.5 Results

A preliminary testing was conducted with a fairly simple story composed of three goals, four tasks and three obstacles ([6]). The test showed the large amount of choices proposed to the user, at each step. However, the example was too simple to show how the story was greatly influenced by user's choices. A new story is now being implemented by the authors of this paper.

3 Authoring with IDtension

3.1 Different Levels of Authoring

With the current version of IDtension, the author can write at three levels:

The structures: Complexity of the narrative structure is a very important issue. Every time an author is willing to design a non linear/interactive narrative (this happens with ID, hypertext literature or video games), there is some complexity level over which the author looses control over the actual structure of his writing because the graph of this structure becomes much too large. We have found that a particularly relevant level for understanding and writing the story is the "goal/tasks" structure (depicted in Fig. 2). Goal/tasks structures contain only one goal, and several tasks to reach this goal. Here, the complexity is broken down into a number of goal/tasks structures. The link between these goal/tasks structures lies into the notion of obstacle (see previous section). From the author's point of view, obstacles have a meaning in the model of the narrative she is designing out. This understanding helps the author gaining control over the whole structure by considering individual goal/tasks structures, i.e., without drawing out the whole graph of all the goal/tasks structures. For now, the goal/tasks structures are entered by direct coding into the system.

The surface text: To each generic action and to each specific entity of a story corre-spond a textual form. For example, the action "X INFORM Y that he wants to per-form the task t" could be expressed: "[X:name] tells [Y:name]: "I have decided to [t:infinitive]". Parts between brackets are then replaced by the textual forms given by the author for characters or tasks. This is a very basic form of text generation, whose main advantage is that the author has control over all the text. Note that there is no "dialog writing", because with IDtension so far, a dialog is only the result of an ex-change of verbal actions. We have chosen a spreadsheet to enter these textual forms, as depicted in Fig. 3, because it is sufficient for our goal and more usable for an au-thor than other formats.

The parameters: There are many parameters in the system which enable to control the narration. For example, one can modify the weighting of each effect, in the calculus of impact of each action. These parameters have the greatest influence on the results. However, it is hard to anticipate the effects of each parameter on the behavior of the story, especially for a non programmer. Thus, in the current stage, the parameters are not chosen by the author himself. They are rather used once the scenario is programmed, during testing.

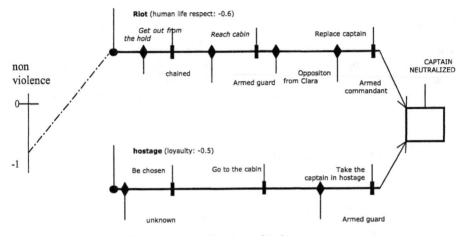

Fig. 2. An example of a goal/tasks structure

Type	Name	Form	Style	text (original text is in French)
Action				
	Inform			
		player_is_actor		
			neutral	
				You tell [addressee]: "you know, [content]".
		player_is_addressee		
			neutral	
				[actor] says : "[content]"
			crude	
				[actor] says "hey chap, [content]"
			polite	
				[actor] tells you :"[addressee:name], did you know that [content]?"
				[actor] says: "do you know that [content]?"

Fig. 3. Extract from the surface text table

3.2 First Experience Feedback

At this point, the IDtension project involved two actors. The computer scientist who built the software and the writer who was in charge of the story. Nicolas Szilas launched IDtension project and built the whole system. He then got in touch with Olivier Marty to help him writing a real size story. The process of imagining and writing the story took several months and presented a few difficulties.

Trying to forget about the techniques of linear novels writing, the author had to imagine a virtual landscape instead of a real story. The conception work was a spatial work instead of a temporal or linear one. The writer had to adapt himself to imagine a wide landscape and a set of actions, letting the control of time to the user of the ID system. Indeed, it is the user of the program who opens her own path in the author's virtual world, who draws her own lines of time within the static landscape.

The author only provides raw material out of which the user builds its own story. It happened that this raw material was shaped by the constraints of the model. A few patterns of writing, such as tasks or obstacles, were added because they matched with the model.

Lastly, it was not intuitive to design the goal/tasks structures from scratch. The writer would often begin by writing or imagining a fragment of story. He would then transform it to make it fit within the goal/tasks structure.

3.3 The Influence of the Tool on Authoring

The author uses structures such as the one shown in Fig. 2 to take an overview of the virtual world he is conceiving. Indeed, the exponential possibilities of the story oblige him to imagine an impressive landscape so huge that it is hardly possible to mentally overlook it without the IDtension device. Therefore the goal/tasks structures are used to write the main lines of the stories, they let details of each sequence to the surface text tables (see Fig. 3).

Instead of the usual word processor, The author had to enter the dialogs into the data base thanks to a spreadsheet. The writing with a spreadsheet looks like the construction of a table more than the writing of a normal text based on a linear oral speech. This leads to a methodic, symmetric and almost fractal way of writing. The author first puts a title to columns and then declines the dialogs lines after lines, obeying to the constraints of each column. This writing methodology typically corresponds to a computer scientist view of literary production, because it splits the text between structure and form, while they are intrinsically interwoven for a literary author [24].

The use of these structures and tables is a new step in the way techniques determine our thoughts ([25]). As a matter of fact, the use of these softwares tends to prevent the author from thinking in a linear way. It obliges his mind to spatial thoughts and symmetric constructions. He is no longer writing a continuous story –that would draw a single line between a beginning and an end. He is now forced to imagine a spatial area within which many stories can take place. Therefore, the writing tool he uses determines his thoughts and his production.

3.4 The Linearization/Delinearization Cycle

We found it difficult, in our early experience with IDtension, to write at the abstract level. It should be noted that any writing activity implies two levels: an abstract level (the concepts of the story) and a concrete level (the "text" itself). For example, in screenwriting and drama writing, the author usually defines a subject, the characters, the values and conflicts, and then writes the story itself [15,14].

By looking closer at the writing process of non interactive drama, one realizes that the process of abstract writing for those media is not straightforward. For example, it is usually advised to write the backstory of characters, that is what happened to the characters before the beginning of the story, in order to get better characters. In order to construct a representation of characters in their mind, authors start from a story, even if it is a different story from the one that has to be told. Similarly, the drama writer has to "know his characters", to the point where the character "start talking to" her [14 p.41], or to the point where the author and the characters "have chatted about this and that" [16 p.32]. For an author, the most efficient way to build a character is to imagine a situation where he or she is talking to him.

These practices suggest that it is actually not natural to write a story from an abstract perspective only. In non interactive writing, there is a bi-directional process between the abstract description of the story and fragments of stories. The final result is a story. In interactive narrative however, the final result remains abstract.

Thus, we draw out from our experience a methodological framework of the design of interactive narratives. This framework involves trajectories between three kinds of representations, as represented in Figure 4:

- The abstract representation: it is the abstract description of the story, necessary for making it interactive. In the case of IDtension, it is mainly composed of goal/tasks structures depicted in Fig. 2.
- The "fragments of stories" are produced by the writer (either in her head or with paper and pencil) in order to imagine what could happen during the interaction. It can be linear or a graph of interconnected fragments. this seems to be the natural way of thinking about a story. Because IDtension, like other ID systems, goes beyond linear or multilinear stories, this level of representation is obviously insufficient for describing the story itself.
- The interactive experience: it is the interactive performance that the audience is experiencing while playing with the system.

The flow of information depicted in Fig. 4 can be decomposed into two main design cycles: (1) the conceptual cycle, between the abstract story and the fragments of stories: the author imagine or simulate with paper and pencil the interactive story in order to build the abstract structure; (2) The computer cycle: the abstract structure is coded then executed, which gives feedback to build and modify the abstract structure.

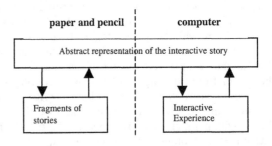

Fig. 4. Four representations involved in the design of an ID. Arrows represent how one representation modifies another representation

The computer cycle is the most accurate, because the authors can experience the final result of the story. But it is costly, because it involves programming.

5 Conclusion

The goal/tasks structures help the author to design non linear narratives. However, there still is a gap between the abstract descriptions of Interactive Drama and the current and natural practices of authors. The linearization/delinearization cycle is the way the author tries to fill up this gap by simulating fragments of story on paper or in her mind. The research of tools that would give to the author a representation of the complexity of non linear narrative structures is crucial but is not likely to eventually provide a complete answer to the problem. We believe that the linearization/delinearization cycle will always exist to some extend. Thus, tools should be designed to assist the flow of information between the different representations of narrative the author is working with.

References

1. Bates, J. Virtual Reality, Art, and Entertainment. In Presence: The Journal of Teleoperators and Virtual Environments. Vol. 1. No. 1. MIT Press. (Winter 1992)
2. Ryan, M.-L.: Narrative as Virtual Reality. John Hopkins University Press (2001)
3. Szilas, N.: Interactive Drama on Computer: Beyond Linear Narrative. In Papers from the AAAI Fall Symposium on Narrative Intelligence, Technical Report FS-99-01. AAAI, Press Menlo Park (1999) 150-156. Also http://nicolas.szilas.free.fr/research/aaai99.html
4. Szilas, N.: A New Approach to Interactive Drama: From Intelligent Characters to an Intelligent Virtual Narrator. In Proc. of the Spring Symposium on Artificial Intelligence and Interactive Entertainment (Stanford CA, March 2001), AAAI Press, 72-76.
5. Szilas, N.: Structural Models for Interactive Drama. In the proceedings of the 2nd International Conference on Computational Semiotics for Games and New Media (Augsburg, Germany, Sept. 2002)
6. Szilas, N.: IDtension: a narrative engine for Interactive Drama. In Göbel et al. (eds) Proc. TIDSE'03. Frauenhofer IRB Verlag, (2003)
7. Weyhrauch, P. Guiding Interactive Drama. Ph.D. Dissertation, Tech report CMUCS-97-109, Carnegie Mellon University (1997)
8. Stern A., Matteas M.: Integrating Plot, Character and Natural Language Processing in the Interactive Drama Façade. In Göbel et al. (eds) Proc. TIDSE'03. Frauenhofer IRB Verlag, (2003)
9. Donikian, S. HPTS: a Behaviour Modelling Language for Autonomous Agents. In : Fifth International Conference on Autonomous Agents, ACM Press, Montreal, Canada (2001)
10. Machado, I., Paiva, A., and Brna, P. Real characters in virtual stories – Promoting interactive story-creation activities. In Proceedings of the First International Conference on Virtual Storytelling (ICVS 2001). Lecture Notes in Computer Science 2197, Springer Verlag (2001) 127-134
11. Majerko, B., John Laird. Building an Interactive Drama Architecture. . In Göbel et al. (eds) Proc. TIDSE'03. Frauenhofer IRB Verlag (2003)
12. Sgouros, N. M.: Dynamic, User-Centered Resolution in Interactive Stories. In Pollack, M. (ed.) IJCAI'97 Proceedings of the 15th International Joint Conference on Artificial Intelligence. Morgan Kaufmann Publishers, San Francisco (1997)
13. Propp, V.: Morphologie du conte. Seuil, Paris (1928/1970)
14. Field S.: Screenplay – The Foundations of Screenwriting. 3rd edn. : Dell Publishing, New-York (1984)
15. Jenn, P.: Techniques du scénario. FEMIS, Paris (1991)
16. Egri, L.: The Art of Dramatic Writing. Simon & Schuster (1946)

17. Cavazza, M., Charles, F., Mead, S. J.: Characters in Search of an author: AI-based Virtual Storytelling. In Proceedings of the First International Conference on Virtual Storytelling (ICVS 2001). Lecture Notes in Computer Science 2197, Springer Verlag (2001) 145-154
18. Genette, G: Figures II. Seuil, Paris (1969)
19. Frasca, G. Simulation versus Narrative: Introduction to Ludology. in Mark *et al.* (Eds.) Video/Game/Theory. Routledge, (2003, in press)
20. Bremond, C.: Logique du récit. Seuil, Paris (1974)
21. Todorov, T. Les transformations narratives. *Poétiques,* 3 (1970) 322-333
22. Riedl, O., Micheal Young. Character-focused Narrative. Subm. to *Virtual Reality* (2003)
23. Bailey, P. Searching for Storiness: Story-Generation from a Reader's Perspective. In Proc. AAAI Fall Symposium on Narrative Intelligence (North Falmouth MA, 1999), AAAI Press
24. Davis; M., Michael Travers. A Brief Overview of the Narrative Intelligence Reading Group. In Papers from the AAAI Fall Symposium on Narrative Intelligence, Technical Report FS-99-01. AAAI, Press Menlo Park (1999) 11-16
25. Goody, J. La raison graphique, Editions de Minuit, Le sens commun (1995)

Character-Focused Narrative Generation for Execution in Virtual Worlds

Mark O. Riedl and R. Michael Young

Liquid Narrative Group, Department of Computer Science, North Carolina State University,
Raleigh, NC 27615, USA
moriedl@ncsu.edu, young@csc.ncsu.edu
http://liquidnarrative.csc.ncsu.edu/

Abstract. Because narrative plays such a key role in the understanding of events in our daily lives, the ability to generate narrative can be of great use in virtual reality systems whose purpose is to entertain, train, or educate their users. Narrative generation, however, is complicated by the conflicting goals of *plot coherence* – the appearance that events in the narrative lead towards the narrative's outcome – and *character believability* – the appearance that events in the narrative are driven by the traits of the story world characters. Many systems are capable of achieving either one or the other; we present a new approach to narrative generation in the Actor Conference system, which is capable of generating narratives with both plot coherence and character believability. These narratives are declarative in nature, readily lending themselves to execution by embodied agents in virtual reality environments.

1 Introduction

Narrative as entertainment, in the form of oral, written or visual stories, plays a central role in our social and leisure lives. There is also evidence that we build cognitive structures of the real events in our lives represented as narrative to better understand what is happening around us [4]. This "narrative intelligence" is central in the cognitive processes that we employ across a range of experiences, from entertainment contexts to active learning. Interaction within a virtual world, especially one created by an interactive 3D virtual reality system, provides an engaging environment in which a system's user can readily view unfolding action as narrative. In narrative-oriented virtual reality systems, the effectiveness of interaction is enhanced when the actions of the system-controlled characters – intelligent computer agents embodied as graphical avatars – are controlled and coordinated with one another to provide a coherent storyline.

The ability to structure system characters' action sequences so that they can be understood as elements of a story's narrative is of importance to systems that wish to effectively use narrative for entertainment, training, or education. Most existing narrative-oriented virtual worlds are built using pre-scripted action sequences; characters play out the same elements of the same story each time the system is run. In contrast, a system that generates a novel narrative structure for each user session can tailor its narratives to the individual preferences or needs of the user instead of relying on scripted sequence prepared in advance. Automatic narrative generation presents many

O. Balet et al. (Eds.): ICVS 2003, LNCS 2897, pp. 47–56, 2003.
© Springer-Verlag Berlin Heidelberg 2003

technical challenges, however, one of which is the ability to balance the trade-offs between *plot coherence* and *character believability*. A plot (or action sequence) is coherent when a user can understand the way in which the events of a narrative have meaning and relevance to the outcome of the story. A character is believable [3] when the actions taken by the character can be seen to come from the character's internal traits. While narrative coherence is essential for an audience to make sense of what they are seeing, character believability is important in a virtual reality medium where characters are expected to be expressive and entertaining.

The research presented here considers the importance of the trade-off between plot coherence and character believability. In general, narrative generation systems that generate highly coherent narrative structures often neglect issues of character and believability. Likewise, systems that capitalize on the use of highly believable characters tend to promote poor narrative structure. In this paper, we present the narrative generation system, the Actor Conference (ACONF), which attempts to address the weaknesses and capitalize on the strengths of the various existing approaches to automated narrative generation.

2 Related Work

In order to comprehend the relevance of related work to our own research, we present a framework for categorizing narrative generation systems. The classification framework ranks narrative generation systems along two continuous dimensions: plot coherence and character believability. The ideal situation is to be able to generate narratives that are both high in plot coherence and character believability.

Story-generation systems can also be categorized as *author-centric*, *story-centric*, or *character-centric* [8] (adapted from [2]). Author-centric systems model the thought processes of an author. Story-centric systems model linguistic and grammatical properties of story texts, such as in [12] and [2]. Character-centric systems model the goals, beliefs, and plans of characters in the story-world with the intention that story emerge as characters pursue autonomous goals and interact with each other. The two taxonomies are tightly coupled; we believe that character-centric systems tend to result in stories with strong character-believability but weak plot coherence, while author-centric systems result in stories with strong plot coherence but weak character believability. We do not consider story-centric systems further because they often do not utilize strong notions of plot or character, focusing instead on discourse structure of storytelling. The classification framework is shown in Figure 1.

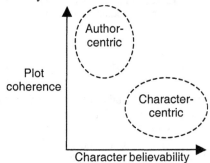

Fig. 1. Classification framework for narrative generation systems.

Character-centric systems rely on the concept of emergent narrative [1], which postulates that narrative emerges from unstructured interaction of autonomous agents. Narrative arises from the interaction between agents, similar to the way story can emerge through free improvisation or through structured activities such as game playing. Because emergent narrative relies on interactions, these systems can capitalize on the use of animated agents that contain a rich repository of behaviors and emotions. One of the risks of emergent narrative, however, is that narrative may not emerge [1]. This fragility is weighed against believability of the experience; when narrative emerges, the user will be engaged with a rewarding experience. Tale-spin [9] explicitly represents characters as collections of beliefs, needs, and interpersonal relationships. An inference engine determines how the characters could behave in order to achieve their needs and narrative emerged from the interactions chosen by the inference engine. The Oz project [7;3] situates a user in a virtual environment populated by autonomous, animated agents. Each animated agent has a set of goals and beliefs and autonomously works towards achieving its personal goals. In order to ensure an interesting experience for the user, an external module – a drama manager – attempts to discretely manipulate the autonomous agents' desires in order to force narrative to emerge. Interactive narrative – a focus of the Oz project – is a special sub-problem in narrative generation, but [14] demonstrates a similar approach to narrative generation that does not involve an interactive user.

In contrast to character-centric systems, author-centric systems involve computational theories for generating narratives. These systems algorithmically piece together a narrative as a sequence of events that are related through some form of logical structure. Since author-centric systems generate narrative through a structured, rational methodology they are not plagued by failure in the same way that character-centric systems are. However, by focusing on the logical structure of a narrative, character actions making up the events in a narrative will be chosen to fit the narrative's structure and not necessarily chosen because that is the natural course of action for a believable character to take. The Universe system [5;6] uses a planner to select a sequence of actions for the characters in the story world to perform. The planner in Universe only incorporates actions into the narrative sequence that contribute to the system goals although system goals may be described at a high level of abstraction, such as "keep lovers apart" (Universe operates in the domain of soap-operas). Defacto [13] uses a rule-based approach to narrative generation. A knowledge base is populated with rules about character relationships, goals, social norms, as well as rules about intention and the attempt to perform actions. The rules are encoded in a format which enables the system to reason logically about character intentions and actions. The result of narrative generation is a list of temporally ordered attempted actions that are assigned success or failure in order to achieve an outcome that is satisfying and suspenseful.

3   The Actor Conference System

The Actor Conference (ACONF) system is explicitly designed to take advantage of the strengths of both the character-centric and author-centric techniques and thus achieve both strong plot coherence and strong character believability. ACONF is itself an author-centric system and, like the Universe system [5;6], uses a decompositional, partial-order planner to assemble a sequence of actions, comprising the narrative. The actions in the plan represent the behaviors that the characters are going to perform as part of the narrative. Using a planner for narrative generation is advantageous for two reasons. First, planners operate by identifying causal relationships between actions which naturally map to the domain of narrative [16]. Secondly, the output of a planner is a temporally ordered sequence of discrete operations. These operations can be directly executed by agents in the virtual world [17;11].

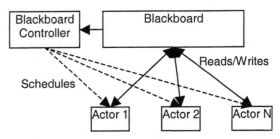

Fig. 2. The Actor Conference architecture.

Partial-order planners, however, are not alone adequate for the task of narrative generation. Consider the fact that a partial-order planner chooses only those actions that are necessary to achieve a certain world state. Thus, in a narrative, characters whose actions are planned by a partial-order planner will perform behaviors that will bring about that state but not necessarily perform behaviors that are consistent with the audience's expectations. Believable characters have idiosyncrasies and are expected to perform behaviors that are motivated by individualistic beliefs and desires instead of narrative structure, which they, arguably, would not be aware of.

In order to capture personalized character behaviors during conventional partial-order planning, we introduce expert systems for each of the characters that exist in the story world. Each expert system – referred to as an "Actor" – is instantiated with a full understanding of a single story world character, the actions it can perform, and the ways it will react to situations and interact with other characters. The expert system is not the character itself, but understands its assigned character as if it were an actor in a play who is tasked with giving life to its character. The responsibility of constructing a coherent narrative is thus distributed among the experts. Using a blackboard architecture, a single planning problem is broken up into smaller planning problems and handed off to each Actor so that it can plan a sequence of behaviors that achieve a particular goal in a believable fashion. The smaller planning problems are reassembled onto the blackboard and the process iterates. Actor expert systems are limited in their planning processes to only considering actions for the character that it represents. This limitation prevents one Actor from making decisions about other characters' actions and also provides convenient boundaries with which we can split up and distribute the narrative plan structure. A diagram of the ACONF architecture is shown in Figure 2.

3.1 Narrative Planning in Actor Conference

Since ACONF uses decompositional planning to model the narrative authoring process, narrative is represented as a partial-order, causal link plan where each step in the plan is an abstract or primitive action that a character in the story world will perform. The blackboard contains structures called hypotheses – guesses about the solution – that contain (possibly) incomplete narrative plans and sets of associated annotations. The blackboard provides an architecture for control and coordination, but narrative generation is in the hands of the experts. The experts – Actors – are autonomous agents that represent individual characters in the story world and encapsulate the ability to plan actions that their characters perform in the story world. At the core of each Actor is the Longbow decompositional, partial-order planner [15].

Actor Conference builds a narrative as a single plan, consisting of actions performed by all characters in the story world. A single plan that will control the performance of every character is useful for generating narratives with strong plot coherence because the plan actions will be guaranteed to be causally relevant to the outcome of the narrative [11]. The two issues that our research addresses are: (a) how a single narrative plan can be distributed among many agents and then reassembled, and (b) how multiple Actor agents can utilize the well-established paradigm of partial-order planning for highly characterized action planning.

3.1.1 Cast Calls

Deferring for now the issue of how Actor agents can plan character-specific actions, we address how the single narrative plan can be broken down and distributed to Actor agents and reassembled. An Actor receives a hypothesis from the blackboard, containing a narrative plan. The narrative plan is incomplete when it contains one or more flaws, such as an action with unsatisfied preconditions or an abstract action that has not been expanded into less abstract actions. Plan flaws are resolved through iterations of the planning algorithm [10;15]. For now, let us assume that an Actor, A, representing story world character, Kate, has been scheduled to refine a hypothesis containing an incomplete plan. Actor A is tasked with resolving flaws in the narrative plan by placing actions into the plan structure that best illustrate Kate's character.

Unless ACONF is generating a one-man play, an Actor is invariably going to have to incorporate the actions of other characters into its plan. To handle the situation of character interaction, we employ modifications to the standard planning process. First we encourage the use of highly hierarchical plan structures. This gives us two advantages. The first advantage is that hierarchical plans can be constructed at different levels of abstraction that help define the structure of narrative and can guide the Actor as it refines the plan. The second advantage is that, at a sufficiently high level of abstraction, characters do not exert idiosyncratic behavior. Suppose that Actor A inserts the action, talk-about(Joe, Kate, sports-cars) – in which the character, Joe, will speak to Kate about sports cars – into the narrative plan. Talk-about, as an abstract description of a communicative act, captures the essence of the interaction between Kate and Joe without concern that Joe might have a tendency to be long-winded when speaking on the subject of sports cars.

The planning algorithm used by the Actor agents, however, has been modified in the following way: it is prohibited from decomposing abstract actions that are to be performed by other characters. That is, when Actor A comes across a flaw that requires it to expand an abstract action that is not performed by Kate, Actor A is forced to leave the flaw unresolved, leaving a gap in the completeness of the plan. To continue the previous example, Actor A is able to insert the action, talk-about(Joe, Kate, sports-cars), into the narrative plan (assume that talk-about establishes some condition later in the plan that Kate understands sports-cars), but, because it describes an action to be performed by Joe, Actor A leaves the abstract action unexpanded. We refer to these gaps as *cast calls* because they are points in the narrative plan where other Actors can script themselves into the story. When an Actor posts a hypothesis to the blackboard containing a further refined, yet still incomplete plan, it is analyzed by the blackboard controller for cast calls. One or more Actors are scheduled to respond to the cast call, retrieve the hypothesis from the blackboard, and begin refining the plan contained within. Presumably any Actor that responds to the cast call identifies with the character described in the cast call and can therefore expand the abstract action left by the previous Actor.

The question remains of who gets to respond to the new hypothesis once it is posted to the blackboard. Certainly the Actor representing Joe is a candidate to refine the hypothesis. However, as far as the creator of the hypothesis, Actor *A*, is concerned, the flaw need only be resolved by a character that fills the same role that Joe plays, e.g. some character knowledgeable about sports cars. Therefore, when the cast call is created, the plan is annotated with a description of a character role, and not a specific character name. The role is determined by analyzing the preconditions and constraints of the unexpanded action.

3.1.2 Actor Planning

Narrative planning occurs in manageable chunks inside the Actor expert systems. Each actor is an expert on a single character in the story world and is motivated to choose the behaviors for that character that best illustrate the character's traits within the constraints of the unfolding plot. Since an Actor performs planning as a response to a cast call, all actions that are planned are either to be performed by the character represented by the Actor or are high-level descriptions of interaction between characters. Character expertise in the Actor agent is captured in two different ways. First, each Actor agent has its own action library that defines the actions and decomposition rules that a single character can perform. Second, each Actor captures character through a customized plan search heuristic function.

The Actor's private action library can be thought of as a knowledge-base describing how an individual story world character behaves and interacts with the world. The action library contains a complete set of actions that the character can perform. Each action has a specification of the conditions that need to be true for the character to perform the action and the way in which the action affects the state of the story world once it is performed. Most Actors will share some similarity in the actions in their action libraries; however characterization relies on the ability of actions to differ in their preconditions and effects. For example, violent actions in a moral character's action library may require that the character believe the victim of the violence to be deserving of the outcome.

Furthermore, some actions are designated as primitive and others are designated as abstract. The planner attempts to expand abstract steps, under the restrictions described in the previous section, by applying decomposition rules to instantiated abstract actions. One can think of these decomposition rules as schemata for how the character will behave. Decomposition rules also allow for idiosyncrasies to be expressed because decomposition rules can describe subsequences that contain actions that are not rationally motivated. It is possible, and even desirable, for there to be more than one decomposition rule for every abstract action the character can perform. However, there does not have to be abstract actions for every possible circumstance that a character might find herself in. When an Actor lacks an abstract action to capture a circumstance, it can rely on the basic planning algorithm to insert plausible sequences of customized, primitive actions into the plan.

Besides customized action libraries, Actors capture character expertise through the use of customized plan-space search heuristics. The Longbow planner uses search heuristics to utilize domain knowledge to perform a best-first search through the space of possible plans [15;10]. In ACONF, the planning process is distributed among the Actor agents and for each Actor the planning domain is the story world character itself. The heuristic function for each Actor captures its character's preferences about the types of actions it likes to perform and the elaborateness of the sequence.

3.2 From Plan Space to Hypothesis Space

Actors search for plans within the space of all possible, sound plans [10;15]. The ACONF system, as a collection of collaborating agents, searches for a complete hypothesis in the space of all possible hypotheses. As an Actor searches for an incomplete but sound plan, it necessarily leaves regions of the plan space unexplored; an Actor cannot explore the entire plan space due to complexity trade-offs and due to prohibitions from considering actions for characters other than the one it represents. However, there may be many possible candidate plans that the Actor can find. This is especially true if the Actor is expanding an abstract action and has more than one applicable decomposition rule in its action library. If the Actor commits to a plan, it is committing to a particular structure for the narrative and this commitment will guide how the other Actors in the system refine and construct their own hypotheses. This raises the issue of plan space backtracking. Each Actor is only solving a localized portion of the overall problem; what may seem valid in the local scope may have severe repercussions to the system as a whole as other Actors could be left unable to refine the solution. Since each Actor searches the plan space independent of the others, one can think of each hypothesis as having its own plan space. There is no way for one Actor to backtrack to a part of the overall plan space that another Actor chose not to explore. This separation of plan spaces is shown in Figure 3.

In Figure 3, there are three hypotheses in the hypothesis space on the blackboard: X, Y, and Z. Actor A posts hypothesis X to the blackboard and, during the process of creating hypothesis X, explores a portion of the plan space. The plan space is shown as the tree structure inside the hypothesis. Each smaller circle is a plan node in the plan space. Circles that are crossed out represent inconsistent plans. The dashed triangles represent branches of the plan space that have not been explored. The double-lined circle represents the plan that Actor A commits to (a plan is sound and complete except for decomposition of abstract steps to be performed by other characters). Actors B and C both attempt to refine hypothesis X but cannot, for whatever reasons, find plans that resolve the flaws that Actor A left behind. If there are no alternatives to hypothesis X, narrative generation will fail! It is possible that another plan exists in the unexplored regions of hypothesis X's plan space, but Actors B and C are helpless to explore these regions because it is part of a different Actor's decision-making process. Because the hypothesis space is unrelated to plan space, we are threatened by the possibility that narrative generation in ACONF is incomplete.

Incompleteness for this reason is unacceptable. Therefore, we have modified the blackboard controller to allow hypotheses to be *revisited*, that is, for an Actor to discard the plan it previously committed to and search for a new partial solution in a previously unexplored region of the plan search space. Revisitation should not be confused with backtracking in the hypothesis space. Backtracking in hypothesis space means to choose an alternative hypothesis to expand. For example, when hypothesis Y is found to be inconsistent in Figure 3, ACONF backtracks to try an alternative: hypothesis Z (which is also found to be inconsistent). However, it is clear that the only hope of finding a complete narrative in the example in Figure 3 is to revisit hypothesis

X and to expand regions of the plan space contained within. Just as a partial-order planner maintains a queue of unexplored plans in plan space [10], the blackboard controller maintains a queue of unexplored hypotheses in hypothesis space. In order for hypothesis revisitation to work, when a hypothesis is explored, it is not removed from the queue. Instead it is re-ranked (we assume the blackboard controller is searching the hypothesis space in a best-first manner) and reinserted into the queue. With revisitation, the hypothesis search problem in ACONF is as complete as the partial-order planner used by the Actors in the system.

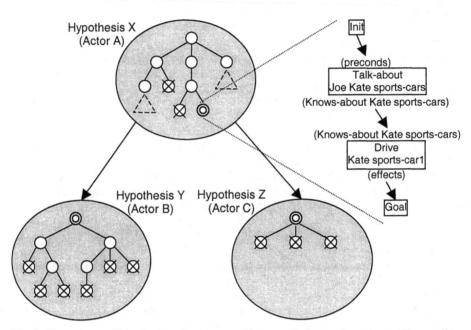

Fig. 3. Plan spaces within the hypothesis space. The gray circles are hypotheses. The smaller, embedded, circles are nodes in the narrative plan search space. Each plan space node contains a (possibly flawed) plan, one of which is shown expanded to the right.

4   Narrative Plan Execution and Interactivity

ACONF is a purely generational system and does not handle the execution of its narrative plans. Instead, ACONF can be coupled with an execution engine, such as Mimesis [17;11], that is specifically designed for execution of partial-order plans in a 3D graphical virtual world. The Mimesis architecture consists of a narrative generation component, responsible for dynamic generation and repair of narrative plans, and an execution substrate, responsible for performing the narrative plan through systematic control of animated avatars in a 3D virtual world. In this case, the narrative generation component encapsulates the ACONF system.

Complications to the plan execution process arise in two ways. The first is due to a mismatch in the characterization of actions used by a partial-order planner, such as ACONF, to produce plans and the code used by the virtual world to implement them. The story plan is a sequence of discrete actions whose effects happen instantaneously. In contrast, most of the corresponding character behaviors in the virtual world require a relatively long period of time to complete. This is especially true when actions must be coordinated with slower graphical character animations. To preserve the temporal semantics of the plan's structure, the Mimesis execution substrate launches sentinel threads for each action to be performed [17]. These sentinel threads monitor the environment until the effects of the action have been achieved or the action has failed.

The second complication dealt with during plan execution arises when a user assumes the control and identity of a story-world character through its avatar. Given that the user is not constrained to follow the narrative plan and may be only partially aware of the narrative plan, that character is now capable of performing actions within the story world that interfere with the structure of the story plan [11]. Because each action that the user performs might change the world state in a manner that would invalidate some unexecuted portion of the narrative plan, the Mimesis execution substrate monitors the user's action commands and signals an *exception* whenever the user attempts to perform an action that would change the world in a way that conflicts with the causal constraints of the story plan. Exceptions are handled by replacing the current narrative plan with a contingency plan. Contingency plans are pre-computed by Mimesis through repeated calls to ACONF with varied initial conditions. The way in which exceptions are handled within the Mimesis architecture is described further in [17] and [11].

5 Conclusions

Actor Conference is a narrative generation system that utilizes techniques from author-centric and character-centric narrative generation systems in order to balance the conflicting concepts of plot coherence and character believability and generate narratives that are both apparently understandable and character-driven. The system generates narrative plans – partially-ordered sequences of story world character actions – with rich temporal and causal structure. The causal nature of the narrative plans ensures plot coherence because character actions establish the conditions necessary for the narrative goals of the story. Character believability is achieved by distributing the partially built narrative plan structures to expert agents that represent characters in the story world. With a slightly modified planning process, highly customizable action libraries, and heuristic functions than rank the believability of a sequence of actions, the expert "Actor" agents are able to illustrate the traits of the characters they represent, despite the rational nature of planning.

ACONF uses blackboard architecture coordinates the efforts of the numerous Actor agents, effectively making its narrative generation process a search through the space of hypotheses, or partial narratives. Each hypothesis in the search space contains a fragment of the overall narrative plan search space. Heuristics inform the process of search through the hypothesis search space, allowing for the possibility of revisiting previously explored hypotheses so that planning completeness is assured.

References

1. Aylett R. Narrative in virtual environments – towards emergent narrative. In: *AAAI Fall Symp. on Narrative Intelligence*. Mateas M, Sengers P eds. 1999.
2. Bailey P. Searching for storiness: story generation from a reader's perspective. In: *AAAI Fall Symp. on Narrative Intelligence*. Mateas M, Sengers P eds. 1999.
3. Bates J. The role of emotion in believable agents. In: *CACM* 1994; 37; 122-125.
4. Bruner J. *Acts of Meaning*. Harvard University Press: Cambridge, MA 1990.
5. Lebowitz M. Creating characters in a story-telling universe. *Poetics* 1984; 13; 171-194.
6. Lebowitz M. Story-telling as planning and learning. *Poetics* 1985; 14; 483-502.
7. Mateas M. (1997). An Oz-centric review of interactive drama and believable agents. *Technical Report CMU-CS-97-156*. School of Computer Science, CMU, Pittsburgh 1997.
8. Mateas M, Sengers P. (1999). Narrative intelligence. In: *AAAI Fall Symp. on Narrative Intelligence*. Mateas M, Sengers P eds. 1999.
9. Meehan J. Tale-spin, an interactive program that writes stories. In: *Proceedings of the 5th International Joint Conferences on Artificial Intelligence*. 1977.
10. Penberthy J, Weld D. UCPOP: A sound, complete, partial order planner for ADL. In: *Proceedings of the 3rd Int. Conference on Knowledge Representation & Reasoning*. 1992.
11. Riedl M, Saretto C, Young, R. Managing interaction between users and agents in a multi-agent storytelling environment. In: *Proceedings of the Second International Conference on Autonomous Agents and Multi-Agent Systems*. 2003.
12. Rumelhart D. Notes on schema for stories. In: *Representation and Understanding: Studies in Cognitive Science*. Bobrow D, Collins A eds. 1975.
13. Sgouros N. Dynamic generation, management and resolution of interactive plots. *Artificial Intelligence* 1999; 107; 29-62.
14. Theune M, Faas S, Nijholt A, Heylen D. The virtual storyteller: Story creation by intelligent agent. In: *Proceedings of the First International Conference for Interactive Digital Storytelling and Entertainment*. 2003.
15. Young R, Pollack M, Moore J. Decomposition and causality in partial-order planning. In: *Proceedings of the Second International Conference on Artificial Intelligence and Planning Systems*. 1994.
16. Young R. Notes on the Use of Plan Structures in the Creation of Interactive Plot. In: *AAAI Fall Symp. on Narrative Intelligence*. Mateas M, Sengers P eds. 1999.
17. Young R, Riedl M. Towards an architecture for intelligent control of narrative in interactive virtual worlds. In: *Proceedings of the Int. Conference on Intelligent User Interfaces*. 2003

Managing Authorship in Plot Conduction

Daniel Sobral[1], Isabel Machado[1], and Ana Paiva[2]

[1] INESC-ID, Rua Alves Redol 9, 1000 Lisboa, Portugal
{daniel.sobral, isabel.machado}@gaips.inesc.pt
[2] IST – Technical University of Lisbon, Av. Rovisco Pais 1, P-1049 Lisboa, Portugal
ana.paiva@inesc.pt

Abstract. The increasing complexity of interactive applications and crescent demand for educational systems aggravates the urge for a balance between interactivity and scripted content. Approaches to this problem have ranged from a focus on interactivity and emotional engagement to linear narratives, with limited interactive capacities. The introduction of non-linearity frequently imposes a heavy burden to the authoring process. We argue that the definition of a domain ontology is the foundation that bonds all intervenients in the creative process. Furthermore, we propose a framework with which to cope the different issues involved in the development of interactive narrative applications. Going through a concrete example, we argue that these concepts and tools can contribute to a work methodology with which to attain good results within a feasible time frame.

Keywords: Interactive Educational Narratives; Autonomous Agents; Narrative Paradox

1 Introduction

To have interactivity in storytelling we need flexibility in the way the story flows allowing the user to influence such story. On the other end, authors of stories need to keep some structure and some pre-defined flow of narrative, guaranteeing the climax of the story. These two, clearly opposite goals, lead to the *Narrative Paradox* [1] which is a recurrent trap which most Interactive Narrative Environments (INE) are unable to avoid. Furthermore, when we aim at INEs for educational purposes, new requirements imply an extra burden to the creation of these systems. For example, guaranteeing that certain events occur for pedagogical reasons.

In general, for creating INEs we can succinctly identify two main approaches: plot-based and character-based. Whilst the latter approach is often associated with the presence of autonomous agents, which can act in a fairly free way, and thus failing to transmit a purposeful meaning, the former is more associated with authored scripts. However, even if a Human authored plot may be essential to the conduction of the narrative, the amount of parameters that would need to be twitched could cause serious difficulties [5] [7] in building interactivity to these plot based systems. Further, most plot-based narrative systems divide the story into pieces and use explicit links to connect them. This imposes an exploding amount of effort to the author. Nonetheless, although some effort has been made to minimize [2] or even eliminate [5] explicit linking, such attempts are

O. Balet et al. (Eds.): ICVS 2003, LNCS 2897, pp. 57–64, 2003.
© Springer-Verlag Berlin Heidelberg 2003

still far from alleviating the unmanageable authoring effort constantly imposed to the author.

So, to handle these two often opposite goals, we argue that a feasible INE must support a flexible authoring process, minimizing the exponential work that characterizes most of the authoring of interactive (non-linear) narratives. The author should not have to directly control the characters' behavior in the story. Instead, only contexts should be provided where agents can perform their roles *in character* [3].

This also aims to minimize the conflict between *Creatives* (Writers and Designers) and *Programmers*. Although there is a current wave towards programming-savvy creatives and artist-friendly programming languages, the complexity of projects nowadays demand ever-growing teams and greater managing resources. This often causes a clash between the two mostly opposing roles, whose conflict can reduce the relevance of each one's role in the final product, which, after all, is being effectively implemented by the programmers.

Thus, we argue that the author's main responsibility should remain the establishment of constraints (artistic or educational) which the narrative, as a subjective perception process, must fulfill.

But, how can that be achieved? We argue that the building of a domain ontology is an essential process to create a common ground where the system can grow. Our approach is based on a generic framework with several components which will enable us to tackle on each of the issues that INEs must face.

2   The Context

To contextualize the approach presented, we will use cases from an European project, Victec[1] that aims to apply synthetic characters and emergent narrative to Personal and Social Education (PSE) for children aged eight to twelve. The project is focusing on the issue of bullying, and the building of empathy between child and character is not only a way of creating a novel experience, but the main educational requirement.

The final product of the project consists on a 3D real-time virtual environment, where children are faced with bullying episodes, inspired by what really goes on in the schools. Each session with the child consists on a sequence of episodes, where each episode depicts a certain dramatic situation in the bullying context. For example, a character being hit and then teased by a bully and a set of other children/characters. Between each episode, the user (child) will evaluate the situation, and *suggest* a possible course of action for the character the he or she is helping, influencing what will happen in subsequent episodes.

3   The ION-Act Framework

One of the difficulties in building INEs resides on the level of abstraction where the plot representation should be managed [4]. As long as sufficient ontological support

---

[1] http://www.victec.org
Project funded by the EU Framework 5 programme

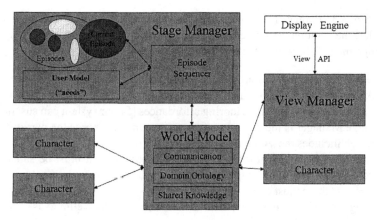

Fig. 1. The ION Framework and the Narrative Component

is given, the author can assume the characters (either scripted, autonomous or human-controlled) will perform according to certain patterns of behavior. For example, in the bullying domain, we can identify roles such as *Victims, Bullies, Helpers, Neutrals* with a very specific semantics associated. Also, some typical acts for these roles include *Hit, Ask to be Friend, Tease, Insult, Ask for Help*. Moreover, bullying is clearly episodic, and a series of stereotypical situations can be described. For example, episodes can represent *Conflicts* between characters, offer some *Empowerment* opportunities for the main character to deal with problems and can also represent situations where the *Resolution* of the bullying situation can happen. These notions of *Role, Actions* and *Types of Episodes* constitute the main knowledge that is used to establish a common ontology that defines the domain under which the author can define the narrative constraints.

Therefore, we identified the need to create a separation between authored constraints and the characters' architecture. From these requirements we have devised an Architecture for a Framework (**I**nteractive **O**bject E**n**vironment) that enables us to tackle each issue independently. Figure 1 presents a brief schematization of the developed architecture, with a particular emphasis on the narrative (**Act**) component.

The Architecture is composed by several modules (generically referred as *Agents*), following an Agent-based paradigm. Among the components are:

- The **World Model**. This component is the central knowledge source for the system. It also acts as a facilitator in the communication between the agents.
- The **View Manager**. We devised this component to obviate the frequent dependency between the characters' architecture and a specific display system. It's main responsibility is to transform the agents acts into calls to a generic visual API for a *Display System*. We have implemented a visualization system that implements the display API to a 3D environment (Figure 1 b)). It also transmits the user interaction to the rest of the system.
- The **Characters**. These implement the characters that play each of the roles. As we have said, we are not bounded by any specific architecture, as long as the role is correctly played. For example, the *Bully* should usually *Hit* or *Insult* the *Victim* when they are alone.

– The **Stage Manager**. This component has the responsibility to represent and manipulate the authored narrative knowledge. Therefore, it defines a sequencing policy through the satisfaction of the encoded constraints.

As we have mentioned, this architecture will enable us to disregard the inner details of each Agent, rather relying on a *correct* behavior within the domain. Therefore, we can emphasize our focus on the authoring affordances [5] our system can sustain.

The Stage Manager is the central narrative component. It keeps the narrative information, which includes the *user's needs* [7] and a set of *episodes*.

The user's needs represent the main set of constraints that must be satisfied, including generic dramatic knowledge and specific pedagogical requirements. A generic constraint is that there must occur at least one action every n seconds. In the more specific bullying scenario, for example, the user should advise the victim to ask for help (a global pedagogical goal).

Episodes define additional contextualization which will contribute to the satisfaction of these generic objectives. As we have seen, this makes no assumption on the characters architecture, but assumes a certain behavior pattern, ie., there is no absolute certain that the constraints that are annotated in the episode are effectively true. For example, an episode could be described as follows (internally this is translated to restrictions in variables and logical propositions): "John (the victim) and his new friend are in the schoolyard, and in front of them comes Luke (the bully). Some other children are also there". This episode qualifies as a *conflict* situation, but does *not* guarantee the occurrence of a conflict (acts like *Hit, Insult, Tease*).

At each step, the Stage Manager uses a sequencing algorithm to select the next episode. Each episode is annotated with a set of preconditions, necessary for their selection, which allows a pre-filtering of available episodes. Next, the episode information is used to infer its potential (if the episode is a conflict situation, which characters are present, where is it located). Furthermore, a set of post-conditions can also be set. These define the conditions that are *expected* to be satisfied at the end of the episode. Besides being helpful in defining the episode potential, this is particularly useful to concretize the conditions under which the episode should end, freeing the system from the rather abstract notion of an episode.

The episode chosen is one that will maximize the satisfaction of the user's needs. For example, the episode presented above should be selected in earlier stages of the interaction because the user must presence a conflict in order to help the main character.

4   The Authoring Process

The first step in the development of our system is the creation of the ontology. An ontology is a description of the concepts pertaining a specific domain and their relationships. In our case, we are interested in defining an ontology applied to the bullying domain which includes some of the concepts mentioned in previous sections. There is no single correct method for defining an ontology, rather being oriented towards the uses that are expected. Since there are many different perspectives involved in the project (psychological/educational and technical) and the topic is often victim of misjudgments and

Fig. 2. A screen from an authoring tool developed in the project

prejudices, the ontology comes as a formal basis for understanding between the several perspectives.

Although essential for the whole process, the definition of the ontology, *per se*, does not constitute the authoring in our system. The author's main activity is, given the solid context (terminology and formal definition of properties and relationships) provided by the ontology, the design of episodes and establishment of global objectives and user *needs*. For this, we are developing authoring tools (Figure 2) to define the narrative constraints which are globally referred as *stories*.

Each story is defined by specialists (psychologists and educators, which are the *creative* authors in our system) according to the context in which they are to be applied. Specific stories exist to depict location or gender-specific situations. Each story contains a set of characters, locations and objects with specific characteristics that are relevant to the situation. Furthermore, a set of episodes are also defined, offering the implicit narrative content.

The need for *user needs* have already been clearly noted by Szilas [7]. In our case, not only is important to define the empirical notion of a satisfying experience, but the user needs are crucial to formally impose and evaluate pedagogical requirements. Therefore, needs are the source for narrative control. Currently, needs cannot be controlled by the author, but are directly encoded in simple rules which are verified by the stage manager. For example, the episode is terminated if no act is performed within a configurable time frame. Another need is that the user should advice the victim to ask for help. As most needs, these do not influence directly the characters, but rather which episode is chosen next, giving new contexts to the characters. Nevertheless, character's behavior in the new context depend on what have happened before.

We argue against the explicit control of the characters, favoring an independent development of characters and plots. Nevertheless, the reality of schizophrenic behavior

Fig. 3. A first prototype

[6] which frequently daunts truly emergent narratives may force an increasing control. Our framework supports this in a seamless way, through the use of the World Model, where explicit ontological knowledge may be expressed. We believe that the establishment of a balance between freedom and control will enable good results in a reasonable amount of time.

Not every notion defined within the ontology is implemented in the system, whether in the character's architecture or in the guidance system represented by the stage manager. The pair ontology/system also allows the exploration of the tradeoffs between implicit (coded in the agents, *emergent*) and explicit (coded in the needs and the stage manager) domain model.

5   First Experiments

A first prototype has been created with a 3D virtual interface (Figure 3) which tests the visualization process by simulating one sample episode (with scripted characters), depicting a situation created by specialists in bullying from the Victec team. These simple simulations are important in a process of evaluating some aspects of the architecture, character design, interaction facilities and usability. Some first studies have been performed with this prototype [8] which showed the large potential of these technologies in the educational context, particularly in conceiving believable, true to life (although safe) environments.

The episode depicted in this prototype is a *conflict* episode which happens within the *classroom*. The episode includes a *bully*, a *victim* and some *spectators* (for technical reasons these are simplified as a single entity and are not visually represented). The episode's action flow can be summarized as follows:

bully: Provoke(victim) Each act has many possible interpretations. This act is performed through the action *Push(books)*. In this case, we knew the books (belonging to the victim) would be there and explicitly associated the act with this action. Some pattern matching mechanisms are necessary to ensure a correct execution within a more generic environment.

victim: React This act is performed according to the previous one, in this case explicitly through *Pick(books)*.
bully: Hit(victim) Performed by *Push(victim)*.
bully: Gloat
neutral: Gloat Performed as a simulation of multiple spectators.
victim: Cry This final act culminates the conflict, revealing the coping difficulties of the victim as a consequence of the situation. It is relevant to note that, although scripted, this response intends to simulate a real situation, in which crying follows a severe humiliation, particularly if it involves a third party (*spectators*).

Due to the scripted nature of the episode, we were able to include certain dramatic motifs, as specific camera movements and action of the *invisible observers*. Truly autonomous characters will make this task much harder and probably with a much lesser performance.

Very little interaction is possible in this prototype. At the end of the episode, the victim asks for help, being indicated a set of possible answers. Following this prototype, we are considering several interaction modalities, which are being studied. These include the ability to interact with the environment in real-time and also in a limited form of communication through writing. The use of scripted characters and well defined scenarios will allow us to assess on the feasibility of these methods. The extensive use of the *Wizard of Oz* methodology have provided invaluable knowledge and will be essential in further assessments.

6   Conclusions and Future Research

Creating autonomous behavior have been a prolonged headache for scientists in the field of interactive narrative. By enabling a certain independence between the characters and the narrative assessment system we can thoroughly test the latter with scripted characters, which will bring greater confidence in latter stages of the application, where we expect to include really autonomous agents (which are being developed in parallel). This independence is largely achieved through the definition of a common ontology for which a constant interaction with the specialists in bullying was necessary to extract the associated terminology and concepts. Nevertheless, constant iterative updates are necessary during the project. The building of formal representations of ontologies through the use of existing tools are not absolutely necessary but may contribute for a stronger agreement about the concepts being described.

The authoring process in most INEs, especially in games, consist in an iterative process of communication (often frustrating) between writer and programmer. This limits the (clearly fundamental) role of the author in the development of the system. We believe that the author has the responsibility to provide material to guide the system and should not be forced to control every detail of it. Our architecture enables the creation and integration of tools for the author and a certain independence to the programmer.

Acknowledgements

This work is partially supported by the European Community under the Information Society Technology (IST) RTD programme, contract VICTEC IST-2001-33310. We would like to thank all the Victec team for invaluable comments.

References

1. Aylett, R.: *Emergent Narrative, Social Immersion and Storification.* In Proceedings of Narrative and Learning Evironments Conference (NILE00), Edinburgh, Scotland, 2000
2. Brooks, K.: *Metalinear Cinematic Narrative: Theory, Process and Tool.* PhD Thesis, 1999
3. Hayes-Roth, B. et al.: *Acting in Character.* In R. Trapple and P. Petta, Creating Personalities for Synthetic Actors, 1997
4. Louchart, S. and Aylett, R.: Narrative Theory and Emergent Interactive Narrative. In: Proceedings of 2nd International Workshop on Narrative and Interactive Learning Environments, 6th - 9th August, Edinburgh,Scotland, 2002
5. Mateas, M.: *Interactive Drama, Art, and Artificial Intelligence.* PhD Thesis, 2002
6. Sengers, P.: *Anti-Boxology: Agent Design in Cultural Context.* PhD Thesis, 1998
7. Szilas, N.: IDtension: a narrative engine for Interactive Drama. In: Proceedings of the 1st International Conference on Technologies for Interactive Digital Storytelling and Entertainment (TIDSE 2003), March 24-26, Darmstadt (Germany), 2003
8. Woods, S. et al.: What's Going On? Investigating Bullying using Animated Characters. IVA 2003

Authoring Edutainment Stories
for Online Players (AESOP):
Introducing Gameplay into Interactive Dramas

Barry G. Silverman, Michael Johns, Ransom Weaver, and Joshua Mosley

Ackoff Center for Advancement of Systems Approaches (ACASA)
University of Pennsylvania, 220 S. 33rd Street, Philadelphia, PA 19104-6315
barryg@seas.upenn.edu

Abstract. The video gaming industry has experienced extraordinary technological growth in the recent past, causing a boom in both the quality and reve-
nue of these games. Educational games, on the other hand, have lagged behind
this trend, as their creation presents major creative and pedagogical challenges
in addition to technological ones. By providing the technological advances of
the entertainment genres in a coherent, accessible format to teams of educators,
and developing an interactive drama generator, we believe that the full potential
of educational games can be realized. Section 1 postulates three goals for reaching that objective: a toolset for interactive drama authoring, ways to insulate authors from game engines, and reusable digital casts to facilitate composability.
Sections 2 and 3 present progress on simple versions of those tools and a case
study that made use of the resulting toolset to create an interactive drama.

Keywords: videogame generator, role-playing games, interactive drama, training, stealth learning, agent approach

1 Introduction and Goals

We envision a future where many games exist that help people to cope with their
health issues, child rearing difficulties, and interpersonal traumas. Further, these
games will be so compelling and easy to revise that many players will feel compelled
to contribute their own story to the immersive world – a contribution that is both self-
therapeutic and that helps others who see some of their own dilemma in that story.
This will be an industry that is consumer grown, since they will be the creators of new
games for other consumers. A few of many possible examples include: (1) parents
will experience what other parents of handicapped children have struggled with and
overcome, (2) children who are bullies will learn what their bullying does to other
kids, and (3) people with chronic health issues (overeating, diabetes, heart disease,
etc.) will learn what happens when self-denial and poor diets prevail. We envision
that a single underlying game-editing environment and alterable cast of digital characters can be used to facilitate such a variety of games with therapeutic value.

At present there are many obstacles to this vision: (1) the videogame industry offers addictive, immersive entertainment and provides most of the seeds for this industry to grow from; however, their games have little education focus and they provide

O. Balet et al. (Eds.): ICVS 2003, LNCS 2897, pp. 65–73, 2003.
© Springer-Verlag Berlin Heidelberg 2003

few if any tools directly re-usable in this niche; (2) the computer-based education field does produce interactive training tools; however, these are heavily corporate and government training-based and have almost no entertainment value and hence aren't spontaneously fueling much consumer interest; (3) the field of movies and TV show writing creates compelling characters that consumers care deeply about, but this medium offers no chance of interactivity that is vital to self-discovery and skill development; (4) the field of human behavior modeling offers innumerable models based on first principles of physiology and psycho-social dynamics, yet outside of a few experimental military simulators, these are rarely inserted into autonomous characters in videogames and interactive dramas; and (5) the successful edutainment offerings to date (e.g., Math Blaster, Reader Rabbit, Oregon Trail, etc.) are monolithic, non-alterable creations of their proprietors. We need a next generation of environments that takes the best from each of these fields and provides the needed capability. The elements of this environment mostly exist, but they haven't been properly put together yet.

We believe one could take the important elements that exist today and synthesize them into the desired capability for Authoring Edutainment Stories for Online Players (AESOP). Provided the game authoring toolbox (what we call AESOP) is usable and useful, then game authors will be able to 'write about' their situations and game players will benefit from being immersed in the problems that others have had to deal with. There is evidence that games can provide transferable knowledge [1], and furthermore, games allow for the creation of situations that thrust the player into the role of a teacher, another proven method of education. *The first goal* of this research is thus to explore ways for a game generator to help authors introduce entertainment and free play into dramas that utilize stealth learning, learning by teaching, and self-discovery for training and behavior change purposes.

This goal is compounded since learner-oriented game design is one of the most difficult areas in developing videogames. First off, although training requires players to progress through stories (pedagogically valuable scenarios), at its heart game play is not about interactive fiction, though there are those who buy interactive fiction games. Drama is all about storytelling from the author, while gameplay is much more about story creation by the player – and these competing aesthetics need to be resolved if pedagogical games are to achieve their potential in general.

A *second goal* of our research is to provide a high- level graphical user interface for the generator, and by that to insulate authors from having to learn the details of a game engine. As already mentioned, we are seeking to set up a generator that can expose constructs and parameters of a storyworld so that new interventions may be more readily authored that promote free play and entertainment within a narrative structure. To support this research, we are attempting to produce a cast of animated puppets and sets (introduced in what follows) in a way that they can be reused for many stories (*third goal*). This is the idea of a composable and reusable storyworld, including digital sets, cast members, and Campbellian archetypes that can be adapted and extended for further sequels not even yet anticipated. Our ideas for reusable casts and archetypes follow from works such as [2, 3, 4] as well as how they are used in franchise games, comics, and serials. As shown below, we include characters of different ages, genders, and backgrounds/ethnicities, and in the roles of hero, sidekick, allies, opponents, tricksters, lovers, and so on. Our hopes for reuse by many nontechnical authors have driven us to keep most things simple (art, animations, behaviors, etc.).

It is worth pointing out that, for now, we made a conscious decision to base this cast and sets around 2-D, hard-edged cel-based animations since research has shown that subjects with health behavior change issues often allocate little cognitive processing to health messages, and feel greater confidence about being able to process and conquer message sets introduced in cartoon formats [5]. However, the underlying technology also supports 3-D animations, as are used in our Unreal Tournament version for military training.

In addition, we chose a finite state machine (FSM) approach as the basis for our dialog model and our scriptwriting application, where nodes contain both dialog and animation instructions for the avatar and Non-Player Characters (NPCs) to carry out, and edges represent the various dialog choices available to the user after a given node finishes. The AESOP generator is currently implemented to help authors with this simple FSM approach and so that it can encapsulate and deliver the interactive game to other devices that display and track game play. Section 2 will explain this structure in more detail. Elsewhere we explore migrating to more complex FSM models and to agents that are in effect infinite state machines as in [6].

2   The AESOP Generator

AESOP is intended as a front-end authoring aid that includes plot and dialog editing GUIs, storyworld templates, pallets of reusable parts, digital cast members, autonomous behavior modules, and reusable art/animation assets. Figure 1 overviews the high level architecture of the ssytem, and the discussion that follows provides further details.

The lead author of this paper serves as principal investigator of both the AESOP generator [7] and the Heart Sense Game (HSG) role-playing drama [8]. This application connects AESOP to an engine written in Director. Another project called Athena's Prism is just getting started that will utilize portions of the AESOP environment as well, but which will invoke a locally produced game engine. This article focuses primarily on the HSG and Director version of the AESOP generator.

Figure 1 shows two boxes labeled Editor Suite and Engine. Various tools were placed into these boxes and evaluated/improved over time, as subsequent sections of this article suggest. For example, the plot map (acts, scenes, etc.) and character back-stories started as text-only descriptions, evolved to a manually filled-in multimedia set of webpages (http://www.seas.upenn.edu/~barryg/heart/index.html), and we now believe that the information they convey can serve as the basis for an interactive editor that will assist in merging learning objectives with story writing goals. The following sections detail our current approach.

At times we have included autonomous emotive agents in earlier versions of HSG, agents capable of emergent behavior [6, 8], while our other applications make substantial use of such autonomy. These are NPC agents that operate with their own behavior goals, standards, and preferences, and that can react to and effect the drama and the player. The current article omits discussing these characteristics, but we have numerous papers on this topic: e.g., see [6, 7] among others, and we continue to work on the challenges of integrating author- vs. agent-driven story elements.

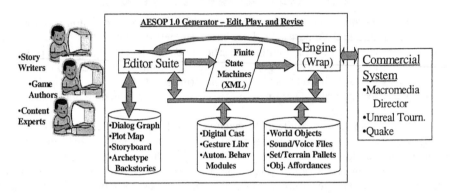

Fig. 1. Architecture of the AESOP generator to insulate commercial engines and help authors create interactive dramas

2.1 Finite State Machine Editor

Our finite state machine editor is a modified version of Visual Graphs for Java, developed at Auburn University. To facilitate our particular needs, the second author of this paper added custom dialog boxes for the data we manipulate, and added support for the XML output required by our game engine.

In our graphs, nodes contain uninterruptible segments of storytelling, and edges correspond to the choices given to the user after each node plays out (see Figure 2). Within each node is a set of behaviors assigned to various characters, arranged as a tree. There are eleven possible behaviors, the most common being: 1) *SOUND*, which causes the specified character to lip-synch a line of text either defined by a wav file or, failing that, a text-to-speech generator; 2) *ACTION*, which causes the character to perform some specific animation; or 3) *MOVE*, which causes the character to physically move from one position on the screen to another. When one behavior finishes, all of its direct children are executed in parallel. This allows for authors to specify the timing of various components of a scene without knowing specific details about the art or voice assets that will eventually be put in place.

Once the FSM is created, one can save the graph out to XML format which will be used by the game engine.

2.2 Gesture Builder

The fourth author of this paper, and his Digital Media Design (DMD) and Fine Arts students, have created all the artwork for the reusable casts as well as the sets and terrain objects for the HSG version of AESOP. The Flash artwork was developed in tandem with the story development using a stylus pen and Adobe Illustrator. Each body part was drawn on a separate layer to aid the construction of the Flash-animated "puppets." To provide the maximum flexibility, it was essential to build the animations so they could be run independently and simultaneously.

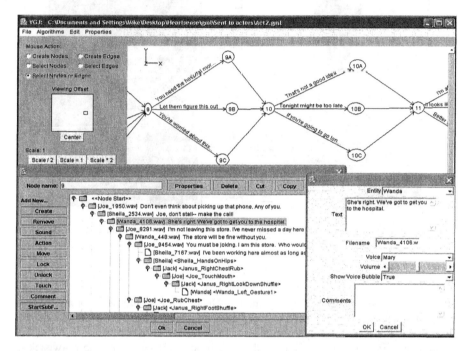

Fig. 2. Select screens of the FSM Editor for branching dialogs and for adding choreographic and MultiMedia instructions to FSMs

In addition, they created a Director-based demonstrator in order to test how the Flash animation segments would flow into each other and in order to build gestures. The third author then used this as a starting point to build a browser application that would output, as XML files, sequences of animation that could be utilized in the FSM Editor by the scriptwriters. A simple example might just be "Jack blinks." A more complicated gesture, such as "Jack looks angry" might include a change of facial expression, a shift of weight and movement of arms, forearms, and hands so they raise to the hips.

This structural approach is fairly common to the game industry; however, in this particular case it was necessary to provide a simple interface and upgradeable characters that could accept new animations on a need-by-need basis as the story development team authored stage direction. Macromedia Flash was a simple and inexpensive 2D animation tool well understood by the undergraduate DMD students. Motion capture, and post-capture editing, would be another technique of generating animation fragments that could integrated with this animation editor.

Fig. 3. Overview of the Flash macro editor for building gesture procedures and movies

2.3 Engine/Wrapper

A traditional approach to creating a game like Heart Sense would be use a multimedia development program such as Macromedia Director. The final product would be a self-contained application, royalty free and not requiring Director to run, and suitable for running from a CD or placing on the web in an html wrapper. The drawback is that the creation of subsequent games would require access to the expensive Director software, as well as access to an (even more expensive) programmer knowledgeable in Director's powerful and sophisticated internal scripting language, Lingo.

The third author foresaw that Director could be used to create an "engine" that alone is not a game, but instead is designed to accept instructions for assembling and presenting a game. Consequently, the two major software components developed were 1) the creative tool (FSM Editor) in Java and 2) the presentation tool (Engine) in Macromedia Director. Director was the first choice for this due to the ease of producing executable programs for Windows and Macintosh, and browser-embedded applets that are platform independent.

The heart of the Engine is an algorithm that translates the instructions created by the FSM Editor into code native to Director. Specifically, it coordinates the behavior of multiple characters (enforces turn taking, cueing, etc), assigns resources and procedures from libraries (voice files, animation movies, etc.) to puppets, and handles input from the user. The content that it manipulates is created entirely in the FSM Editor. By separating all game-specific details out of the Engine, we created an environment in which an author needs to know nothing about Director in order to create or modify games. One needs only to understand the FSM Editor, which was custom-designed for games of this type, in order to create new games that can be run by the Engine.

3 Results to Date

The AESOP generator has been developed in parallel with the creation of the HSG, and with the goal of supporting the authoring of that game. No game is likely to succeed if its appeal cannot be summarized in a few sentences. To initiate the process, the first author of this paper came up with a short description of the intended game and a paper-based version. Specifically, for HSG, this description is (after some massaging from HSG co-investigators): *Heart Sense Game is a role- playing game in which you help the hero try to solve a crime and simultaneously rescue his career and find romance. However, as the hero, some of the many characters you might get clues from need your help to deal with heart attacks before they or others can help you. Since, for their own reasons, they often don't believe they are having a heart attack or don't want to take care of it promptly, there are significant obstacles to helping these characters to help themselves. And if you prefer to harm these characters, you are free to do so, but watch out; your own future will be effected as well!*

The three-act, character-driven soap or adventure story is a proven formula both in the movies and on TV. The writers immediately recognized this format and could relate to its conventions to drive the player and his or her avatar through the story summarized above. Likewise, the training content developers could identify with a hero's journey. Jointly, writers and content experts began to make passes over the story to preserve its engagement aesthetic. The various authors provide brainstorming ideas and interactively deepen the script. The writers tend to form narrative descriptions of the scenes and the training developers begin to allocate their learning objectives to these quests and scenes. A negotiation goes on where the dramatically inclined attempt to limit the learning objectives in any given scene, while the trainers try to assure their full set of goals is covered somewhere in the overall journey.

The extent of the training objectives determines in part the length of the story, and the number of quests that must be included. Thus, for example, in the heart attack domain there are multiple types of heart attack presentations, and three main categories of behavioral delay. After brainstorming, the goal of limiting the length to that of a TV show (one hour for once through) eventually ruled the day and limited the journey to three quests in total. Further, writers insisted that each scene should move along quickly and not sacrifice dramatic pace for the sake of training detail. Since persuasion theory supports this idea (peripheral cues are of high value), the negotiation landed on the side of less-is-more. In either gaming or storytelling, it's vital that each line of dialog potentially has three purposes: move the plot along, reveal some aspect of the speaker's backstory, and set up any local effect (e.g., joke, action, lesson, etc.). To make this happen, each character in a scene needs to have a well defined, story-pulling role, and this required a number of discussions and rewrites about dialogs, plots, scenes, and beats.

The result of a negotiation between writers and trainers often omits the concept of gameplay since neither is trained in this aesthetic. This case study was no exception. While the first version of the drama was interactive, the story was essentially linear and the player could only choose which of about three possible phrasings to reply with for each situation. The player had no sense of being in control, of being able to alter the outcomes, or of thinking there was a reason to play again. Conflict involves true tradeoffs – something must be sacrificed for gains in another dimension. This is entertaining and it gives the player real choices to make in the drama, not just phrasings of verbiage. With this as background the authors of this paper worked with the writers to try and get them to shift their approach to a non-linear scriptwriting effort.

In the end we found three strong storylines, and got the writers and training content specialists to go along with them so the players could have a sense of controlling the outcome. Also, in each storyline there were contagonists modeling proper cues and providing feedback, rewards (things to collect like career options, family relationships, etc.), and antagonists meting out punishments or threatening things that might be lost. For each of these three main storylines, the lead author tasked the writers to create several dialog strategies.

In general, the writers were uncomfortable in authoring their three story versions on anything other than a word processor. Not wanting to destroy their creative processes, we supported this effort, and then had a secretary move the dialogs to the FSM Editor after they were finalized. The authors and content experts then verified the results both via printouts and via play testing. The end results included about 100 pages of script which translates into 346 state nodes, 480 edges, 691 dialog acts, and 1346 gesture commands invoking 461 unique gesture macros. Overall, this authoring effort required about one person-year broken down in round numbers as 500 person-hours from the dialog writers to author the script, 80 person-hours for the secretary to enter the script into the trees, 400 combined person-hours from the two graduate research assistants to add the choreography to the trees, and perhaps six person-months equivalent across all the faculty co-investigators (content developers, story critics, and play testers).

One particularly successful aspect of our approach has been its robustness in a high turnover environment. The development of Heart Sense relied heavily on student labor for writing, artwork, and some programming, and consequently we could not afford to use a system that required a long period of training. Furthermore, since these students tended to work at home or during scattered hours, there was little opportunity for direct communication outside of scheduled meetings. The clear separation between the various components of the workflow for this project, however, contributed substantially to the feasibility of creating a finished product. The majority of the content contributors to this project knew little about the pieces that were not their own, and in many cases, they were able to use familiar tools.

4   Discussion of Results and Next Steps

Our research up to this point has revealed some surprising facts. First, there are no environments one can turn to for rapid authoring of pedagogically-oriented interactive drama games. While games from other genres are beginning to arrive packaged with sophisticated editing tools, the educational gaming community generally is forced to create non-modifiable games on a per-subject, per-audience basis. There exist a growing number of tried and true guidelines for creating fun games. There exists a huge body of work on the subject of effective methods of education. And narrative has its own effectivity metrics. But, at present, most games are designed from the start with entertainment as the primary goal, with any learning on the part of the player as a beneficial side effect. Pedagogical games, on the other hand, begin with rigid learning objectives that must be satisfied, which place severe constraints on the design of the game. This tension has created a deep gap between the creators of educational games and the creators of entertainment games, and consequently, little mutual benefit is generated from work in either community.

We believe that the solution to this problem lies in the creation of a system that provides the building blocks of interactive storytelling by implementing the basics of a variety of gaming devices as composable parts, with their actual arrangement and content determined by the educators. Dialog, character movement, puzzle manipulation, resource models, conflict, and other mechanics would be weaved generically into a unified game engine, with the educators able to simply choose which ones suit the story, pedagogical goals of the game, and needs of the target audience. While a game like Heart Sense is inherently dialog-oriented with its focus on persuasion and interpersonal relationships, one would also want the generator to support a wide array of genres. Such a unified engine is becoming an increasingly realistic possibility, with many recent games beginning to blend elements from a variety of others, causing genres, and more importantly game engines, to converge. Given an environment such as this to work within, designers can harness the state of the art in the technical aspects of interactive storytelling while staying focused on content creation.

In terms of the three goals stated at the outset of this paper, there has been some forward progress, and with it has come the realization of new challenges. To date, we have tried explicitly to keep the cast and generator simple, and in turn, to limit the features that authors need to conquer. The field needs to move beyond this, to step forward on this generator front, and to rise to the challenge if we are to achieve the goal of many games to help people to learn to cope with the array of health and personal issues that confront them.

Acknowledgements

We gratefully acknowledge the National Heart Attack Alert Program, the National Library of Medicine PO # 467-MZ-902060, and the Beck Fund. Also appreciated is the help of the HSG team (Drs. Holmes, Kimmel, Green, and Holmes) and numerous student helpers.

References

1. Green, G.S., Bavelier, D.: Action Video Game Modifies Visual Selective Attention. Nature. **423** (2003) 534-537
2. Campbell, J.: The Hero with a Thousand Faces. Bollingen Series/Princeton University Press, Princeton (1973)
3. Decker, D.: Anatomy of a Screenplay, First Annual Theory of Story Conference (Storycon), Palm Springs: CA, (September, 2002) www.anatomyofascreenplay.com/book.htm
4. Propp, V.: Morphology of the Folktale. University Texas Press, Austin (1968)
5. Green, M., Brock, T.C.: The Role of Transportation in the Persuasiveness of Public Narratives. Journal of Personality and Social Psychology. **79** (2000) 701-721
6. Silverman, B.G., Johns, M., Weaver, R., et al.: Using Human Behavior Models to Improve the Realism of Synthetic Agents. Cognitive Science Quarterly. **2** (2002) 273-301
7. Silverman, B.G., Johns M., Weaver R. Satisfying the Perceived Need for Free Play in Pedagogically Oriented Interactive Dramas, Conference on Animated and Social Agents Proceedings. IEEE Press, New York (2003)
8. Silverman, B.G., Holmes, J., Kimmel, S., et al.: Modeling Emotion and Behavior in Animated Personas to Facilitate Human Behavior Change. INFORMS' Journal of Healthcare Management Science. **4** (2001) 213-228

From the Necessity of Film Closure
to Inherent VR Wideness

Nelson Zagalo[1], Vasco Branco[1], and Anthony Barker[2]

[1] Department of Communication and Art, University of Aveiro, Campus
Universitário de Santiago, 3810-193 Aveiro, Portugal
{ntz,vab}@ca.ua.pt
[2] Department of Languages and Cultures, University of Aveiro, Campus
Universitário de Santiago, 3810-193 Aveiro, Portugal
abarker@dlc.ua.pt

Abstract. Film is a "closed" medium, so narrative closure is a necessity; VR is
a "wideness" medium, so narrative completeness is not vital. In this paper, we
would like to analyse the purposes of narrative film closure in terms of the
viewer and explore VR "wideness" effects within user emotions, to demonstrate
that "wideness" eliminates the necessity of closure through continuous engagement and gratification. From this exploration we allege that VR narrative
forms must grant less attention to closure and focus most on their new capacity
for "wideness".

1 Introduction

We assume film to be a "closed" medium, because film structure is made of rigid and
resolute time and space. Entertainment film narratives have a beginning and an ending
determined by the amount of time needed to convey their messages. Yet there are
some types of narrative where the author strives to create an illusion of not ending,
explicitly avoiding closure of the narrative. About this avoidance, Metz [6] says that
"what these fake finals project to the infinite is the imaginary information of the
reader, not the materiality of the narrative sequence". On the subject of film space,
Bazin [1] argues that film is like a slice or mask of reality, stating that the universe
presented is unlimited or continuous beyond the screen. We concur with Bazin, but as
Metz says about film temporality, in this case, the universe beyond the screen only
exists in the viewer's mind, it's not in the "materiality" of the screen. As a result, film
narratives are conveyed in "closed" temporal and spatial sequences.

In the Virtual Reality (VR) media it is not the "world" creator who determines the
temporality dimension, but the user who will establish the amount of time he spends
in there, so we are not limited by a temporal sequence where a concrete beginning and
an ending must exist. In spatiality, it is the user, once again, who decides where he
wishes to explore, where he wants to look; he is not conditioned by a frame or even a
mask of reality, he moves and looks freely. This is what we will refer to as VR
"wideness", the unlimited time and space to convey narrative.

O. Balet et al. (Eds.): ICVS 2003, LNCS 2897, pp. 74–77, 2003.
© Springer-Verlag Berlin Heidelberg 2003

2 The Purposes of Closure

According to Andrew [5] the study of narrative in film theory "arises not simply because it has been the historically dominant mode of cinematic production, but because it is above all a tool for contextualizing, a logic for delimiting meaning". We can conclude from this that without closure we can't produce narratives. Closure supposes that narrative presents an already completed sequence of events and that the structure of events must be logical and predetermined. The fact that the structure is based on logical and already completed events is what allows meaning creation from narrative in the final analysis. Thus closure is a consequence of the temporality boundaries of film

The control of film over the watcher is so unconditional that Bordwell [3] characterizes narrative film as working "quite directly on the limits of the spectator's perceptual-cognitive abilities". Closure is extremely important in order to generate cognitive experiences throughout the film narrative. Carroll [4] defined suspense as "an emotional response to narrative fiction" and that the condition necessary for suspense to occur is the "uncertainty" of what will happen. Vorderer [8] talks about predictability and says: "the limited predictability of what will happen next is of crucial importance to the enjoyment of the user" - the watcher will feel suspense only when he "has anticipations of what will happen and preferences for what should happen". So in order to produce uncertainty and limited predictability in the watcher, it is necessary to create a structure of logical events that can conduct the watcher from the beginning to the end and at the same time give him only the necessary information to stimulate his own preferences. That's the reason why most films use narratives to convey messages and mostly with strong closures in order to attain higher levels of emotion.

3 Wideness Effects

In VR, reality is not so enclosed; it is actually "wide". The user has open space and unlimited time. Wideness creates a proper mood in the user for the introduction of all kinds of experience. The fact that the user is completely unfocused opens doors easily to emotions created by a sense of *estrangement* from place. Murray [7] goes further and says "once the illusory space is created, it has such psychological presence that it can almost divorce itself from the means of representation".

Hence what engages the user is a constant *descriptive* discourse of the virtual world in contrast to film, where the engagement comes from a *narrative* discourse. The description discourse can change at any time and leave the user experiencing what Bridges [2] calls "open-criterions narratives". The purpose of these narratives is "not to relate events "as they actually happened", but rather to render intelligible the present state of desire in relation to its ultimate object". No one can be certain of the structure of those narratives nor know how they will end, because they are happening right now, and they depend on the user to evolve and so to be structured. This is literally opposed to Metz's categorization of film narratives: "one event must in some way have ended before its narration can begin".

The VR discourse needs the self-insertion of the user into the virtual world; it has as a prerequisite his explicit intention to embody himself in this world. This self-delivery will be then reinforced by the creation of affections between the user and other beings through "morality depictions" [4]. These feelings toward others will generate communitarian engagement within a virtual world.

Thus, "wideness" depends on the author's skills and capacity to create beautiful and eye-catching worlds, on production houses to continue enhancement through new patches and additions to the worlds but the most important challenge of wideness is the imperative to stimulate human communication, more specifically the interpersonal interaction systems formed inside the worlds. Human interaction systems were defined by Watzlawick [9] as "open" systems with properties like: "time as a variable, system-subsystem relations, wholeness, feedback, and equifinality". Consequently, interaction systems properties must underlie the elaboration of cognitive experiences inside virtual worlds in order to attain the greatest wideness possible.

4   Differences and Similarities

Storytelling in film evolves via the limited units of time and space, which are the necessary conditions for the establishment of "uncertainty" and "limited predictability". With the conditions established, engagement is then created through narrative discourse directing spectator anxiety through a desire to know the resolution. At the same time these limitations and conditions inside film storytelling cut off any form of control coming from the spectator. The spectator is allowed to interpret and assimilate the ideas he is seeing in the manner he likes, but he has no choice or control over the facts presented before his eyes. The behaviour of storytelling through VR is completely different. Time and space will progress without limits, creating the necessary setting to engage the user in this world. Based on a descriptive discourse, the "world" directs the user to the true knowledge of the story structure dissolving the need for an end. Control and choice are here fundamental to the user because they will form the real meaning of the story and also because unlike film, in VR the user is always in the position of the first person of the telling.

In the area of similarities, film and VR share the creation capacity of visual worlds, representations of the world that we can interpret in the case of film or even control in the case of VR. These representations are in general based on the creation of social simulations in order to engage people. For film, these simulations serves to increase conflict, for VR they serve the complexification of the structure. Both film and VR claim to substitute the real world by creating an artificial one. Furthermore it is from that substitution need or simulation characteristic that we can view VR as the natural evolution of film media. We can say that VR embodies perfectly the realization of André Bazin's "myth of Cinema Total" [1].

5   Conclusions

From this analysis we came to the conclusion that VR in one sense will draw upon many aspects of film art and from another angle it will partially supersede film media. VR "wideness" will help make up for the deficiencies of film in simulating social experiences. Who hasn't felt the disappointment of seeing a film and thinking "so what?"; in most film social simulations it seems that we have only viewed a slice of life of that particular person. It remains with us, it may make us think and evolve intellectually, but at the same time we feel this need, this desire, to continue to accompany that character. VR will then use its own forms of film closure, less final "inner" closures, in order to get to the higher levels of arousal that presently only film art can give us. But the great improvement will then come from a wideness that avoids endings, like in the real world, in our daily lives, every event has some type of closure, but the flow of life continues. Virtual storytelling is then a representation of the capacity that the user has to choose, the capacity he has to control situations and not merely to submit to endings.

Virtual storytelling is based on the continuous elaboration of the structure that will sustain social event simulations, mostly experienced in a sort of interpersonal communication. In a way VR can be seen as a new virtual interpersonal form of communication, mostly because of its significant differences from film, that is, the concrete perspective of the first person in the story and at the same time the fact that the user is no longer merely witnessing depicted events, but also experiencing face-to-face communication, with human interactions and contexts.

Thus, from a VR point of view, the "story" should not be seen as an end but as a form of evolution of the whole virtual storytelling ecosystem. The user will benefit from the apprehension of the structure instead of merely comprehending the moral lesson given.

References

1. Bazin, André, O que é o Cinema? , 1958, Livros Horizonte, Lisboa, 1992
2. Bridges, Thomas, "The Narrative Construction of Civic Freedom", Philosophy and Civil Society, 2002, [06.08.2003], <http://www.civsoc.com/nature/nature6.html>
3. Bordwell, David, Narration in the Fiction Film, Routledge, London, 1985
4. Carroll, Noel, "The Paradox of Suspense", in Beyond Aesthetics : Philosophical Essays, Cambridge University Press, 2001
5. Dudley, Andrew, Concepts in Film Theory, Oxford University Press, New York, 1984
6. Metz, Christian, "Observaciones para Una Fenomenología de lo Narrativo", 1968, in Ensayos sobre la Significación en el Cine (1964-1968), Paidós Comunicación, trans. Carles Roche, Barcelona, 2002
7. Murray, Janet, Hamlet on the Holodeck: The Future of Narrative in Cyberspace, MIT Press, Massachusetts, 1998
8. Vorderer, Peter, "Interactive Entertainment", in Media Entertainment – The Psychology of its Appeal, Ed. by Zillmann, D. and Vorderer, P., Lawrence Erlbaum Associates, Publishers, New Jersey, 2000
9. Watzlawick, P. Beavin, J., Jackson, D., Pragmática da Comunicação Humana, 1967, Trans. Álvaro Cabral, Editora Cultrix, São Paulo, 1999

Virtual StoryTelling: A Methodology for Developing Believable Communication Skills in Virtual Actors

Sandrine Darcy, Julie Dugdale, Mehdi El Jed, Nico Pallamin, and Bernard Pavard

UPS-IRIT-GRIC
Groupe de Recherche en Ingénierie Cognitive
118, Route de Narbonne
31062 Toulouse Cedex
{darcy,dugdale,eljed,pallamin}@irit.fr, pavard@cict.fr
http://www.irit.fr/ACTIVITES/GRIC

Abstract. Until recently virtual applications rarely incorporated any deep social, cultural or emotional capabilities exhibited in normal human interaction. In this paper, we present a methodology to develop virtual actors with believable communications skills who may provide a sufficient feeling of immersion to reproduce an efficient simulation of human activities. We focus on the relationship between gestures and verbal activities during communicative acts. We will show that an approach based on video analysis is valuable for the design of a system allowing realistic interactions between the avatars and/or the avatars and the environment. Although the analysis is still in progress, we present some preliminary results from our experiments.

1 Introduction

The design of interactive scenarios in virtual reality is a major socio-technical stake. Up until now, virtual applications rarely incorporated any deep social, cultural or emotional capabilities exhibited in normal human interaction. The approach thus lacks believability for the users and cannot be applied to many complex situations where design choices or decision-making are strongly influenced by these dimensions.

The aim of this research is to develop virtual actors with non-verbal communications skills who may provide a sufficient feeling of immersion to reproduce an efficient simulation of human activities. In this paper, we will address the methodology used to develop these virtual actors. We are interested in the relationship between gestures and verbal[1] activities during communicative acts. We will show that a video based analysis is valuable for the design of a system allowing realistic interactions between the avatars and/or between the avatars and the environment.

2 Methodological Approach

The design of an interactive virtual reality device cannot be undertaken without a precise definition, at the right level of granularity, of the non verbal communication activities required to reproduce realistically human-like interactions. The dialog be-

---

[1] Verbal activity refers to the speech but also includes para-verbal activities such as tone, pitch and pace of the voice

O. Balet et al. (Eds.): ICVS 2003, LNCS 2897, pp. 78–81, 2003.
© Springer-Verlag Berlin Heidelberg 2003

tween humans is largely regulated by gestures (e.g. turn-taking management, gaze direction). It is therefore essential to take into account this interactivity in the virtual reality environment. To identify and incorporate appropriate communication skills we have adopted a methodological approach based on video analyses of field studies. The stages in the methodology are complementary and are undertaken in parallel to provide continuous feedback that allows an iterative system development.

2.1 Contribution of Gestures and Verbal Expression to Human Interactions

The first step of this stage was to identify how gestures and speech contribute to human interactions. This consisted of reproducing in the most reliable way a virtual duplicate of short video extracts showing the interaction between humans recorded in natural field settings.

Table 1. On the left of each picture is the real person, on the right is the avatar. Example of the virtual characters with different level of realism

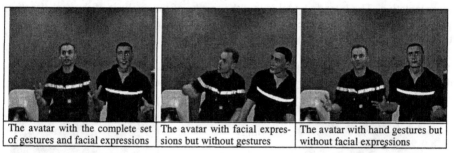

The avatar with the complete set of gestures and facial expressions	The avatar with facial expressions but without gestures	The avatar with hand gestures but without facial expressions

The second step then consisted of artificially deleting certain categories of gestures (e.g. facial expressions, torso movement) and evaluating the impact of these changes on the comprehension of the scenario.

This stage highlighted the difficulty of ensuring a good coherence between gestures and overall body posture when the same gesture (e.g. opening of hands) was applied to different body postures (e.g. kneeling or standing).

2.2 Identification of Non-verbal Communicative Acts and Associated Rules

An analysis of various video sequences of humans interacting in real situations was performed using Anvil [4] to identify the main non-verbal communicative acts and the associated rules. This analysis was performed in two phases. In the first phase all of the non-verbal acts were identified and classified according to the following categories: deictic, iconic, emblematic, metaphoric [1]. Based on this categorization, a more detailed analysis was conducted to identify the different ways to perform such a gesture as a function of different body postures (e.g. standing, crouching) and among these the most general and frequently occurring ones were chosen to be reproduced as animations. The outcome of the analysis is a set of gestures that allows a fluent transition from the different original body configurations. In the second phase the analysis focused on the actual conditions in which these gestures are performed taking into consideration the speech transcript, the position of the characters and objects in the scene and also the gestures performed by the other actors. The outcome of this second analysis is a set of simple rules which will be used to execute the gestures during the interactions between avatars.

2.3 Validation of the Environment

The last stage is based on an ethno-methodological analysis [(see [3] for an example of this approach). At this stage, our focus shifts from the execution of the actions to the interpretation that a user has of those actions. We adopt an ethno-methodological perspective to test the credibility of our avatars. This approach focuses more on the meaning of the actions performed by the persons than on the visual details. In our experiment we analyse short sequences of interaction between humans and then reproduce the same sequences in virtual reality. The basic rules and gestures identified in the previous stages will be implemented in a virtual environment created with Virtools™ [5]. An ethno-methodological analysis will then be performed on the virtual representation. The intended goal is that the results of the analysis of the real situation will be favorably comparable to those obtained from the analysis of the virtual situation.

Table 2. Example of a part of the ethno-methodological comparison. The real situation is on the right-hand side, the virtual representation is on the left-hand side

	A rises his hand to express his intention to communicate with B	

3   Results

This research follows an iterative methodology and we are conducting further experiments to understand better the various and complex communication factors involved in human interactions. Thus, it is difficult to provide guidelines as the analysis is incomplete. However, some trends appeared confirming previous work. The first stage of the methodology highlighted the importance of the congruence of gestures and body posture. In particular, it showed that the interpretation of a gesture is not static: various gestures may be associated with a verbal expression and similarly, depending on the context, a same gesture may be interpreted differently. However, the results showed that the feeling of realism is drastically reduced when gestures are not considered natural due to the incongruence in the articulations of the different body parts (e.g. positions of chest, arms, hands.). It is therefore not so important to produce a specific gesture associated with a specific term, but rather to ensure that the gesture appears natural according to the situation and the body posture. This leaves some freedom for the modeling of the avatars' communicative features. In addition, this stage also highlighted the importance of choosing a software platform which can apply realistic gestures according to the avatar's overall body gestures.

The outcome of the analysis conducted with Anvil (section 2.2) enabled us to begin creating a library of different upper-body animations among which the system will choose the adequate ones according to the rules of an emotional-cognitive engine.

We also observed through the various analyses the importance of gaze direction and deictics gestures. Like previous studies, we observed that gaze directions are often used to disambiguate the addressee or to stress new information [2]. Deictics have proved to be particularly used in all the tasks involving spatial information and unambiguous identifications of elements in the environment.

4 Conclusion

In this paper we introduced a methodology strongly based on video analysis. The methodology is flexible enough to be applied to different fields and to identify and validate generic communication features to be implemented in virtual characters. Such features drastically contribute to increase the credibility and emotional impact of the avatars.

The rules and gestural features that we are currently identifying may be difficult to implement (e.g. rule conflicts, management of priorities, etc.). The next step is to find the optimal architecture to achieve the best level of interactivity.

References

1. Cassell J.(1998) A Framework For Gesture Generation and Interpretation in Cipolla, R. and Pentland, A. (eds.), Computer Vision in Human-Machine Interaction, pp. 191-215. New York: Cambridge University Press.
2. Cassell, J., Torres, O. and Prevost, S. (1999). "Turn Taking vs. Discourse Structure: How Best to Model Multimodal Conversation." In Wilks, Y. (ed.), Machine Conversations, pp. 143-154. The Hague: Kluwer
3. Heath, C. and J. Hindmarsh (2002) Analysing Interaction: Video, ethnography and situated conduct. In May, T. (ed.) *Qualitative Research in Action.* London: Sage. pp. 99-121.
4. Kipp M. (2002) Anvil 3.5 User Manual. Animation of Video and Spoken Language. Graduate College for Cognitive Science. University of the Saarland. Germany. http://www.dfki./de/~kipp/anvil
5. http://www.virtools.com/

Mediation and Interface

Stories in Space: The Concept of the Story Map

Michael Nitsche and Maureen Thomas

Digital Studios for Research in Design, Visualisation and Communication
University of Cambridge
1 Bene't Place, Lensfield Road, Cambridge CB2 1EL
mn236@cam.ac.uk, micnit@yahoo.com

Abstract. While 3D space has become almost ubiquitous in computer games that apply narrative techniques, theoretical frameworks and practical experiments about the use of virtual space are underdeveloped compared to the number of works that deal with literary textual pieces such as MUDs. Offering one element to fill this gap, the notion of a *Story Map* is introduced in this paper. The interactor's experience of space and of the events in a Real-Time 3-Dimensional Virtual Environment (RT 3D VE) form a constant discourse and *Story Maps* are seen as a form of the interactor's comprehension of this discourse. The *Common Tales* research project exemplifies the development of this theory before the value of the *Story Map* for MMORPG's will be outlined.

1 Introduction

1.1 Approach

This paper operates from two premises:

1) Events take place. Whether in novels, film, or RT 3D VE most (but not all) narratives unfold in space. These media create fictional spaces, in which stories are understood and situated by the reader/ audience/ user.

2) Space needs to be understood. Visitors to a building/ movie audiences to a film projection/ readers of literary texts/ users of RT 3D VE's have to make sense of the spatial data provided. The results are individual cognitive maps of the understood space and its ingredients.

This paper argues that both effects intertwine in RT 3D VEs and that this combination can be used to generate effective narrative in virtual worlds. The user's cognitive map of the virtual space combined and filled with meaning by the events unfolding during the interactive experience of the RT 3D VE is what this paper defines as *Story Map*. The model gives designers a point of reference how users comprehend virtual worlds and offers a tool to improve the content structure of RT 3D VEs.

1.2 Discussion of Approach

Narrative Spaces in Literature and Film

Various researchers have discussed connections between space and narrative in literary and hypertextual structures. Murray discusses space in the form of a literary pre-

O. Balet et al. (Eds.): ICVS 2003, LNCS 2897, pp. 85–93, 2003.
© Springer-Verlag Berlin Heidelberg 2003

sented labyrinth structure in a textual Multi User Dungeon (MUD) where 'the story is tied to the navigation of space' [21]. Based mainly on literary texts, Ryan points towards the 'text-as-world' metaphor in a model of the textual space as a 'three-dimensional environment to be lived in, an area for travel, a landscape and a geography to be discovered in time. It is mapped by the bodily movements of characters from location to location' [23]. But the closest literary concept to *Story Maps* is Herman's 'storyworld' theory. He defines 'storyworlds' as 'mental models of who did what to and with whom, when, where, why, and in what fashion in the world to which recipients relocate – or make a deictic shift – as they work to comprehend a narrative' [14]. Herman describes the connection between narrative and his 'storyworlds': 'narrative can also be thought of as systems of verbal or visual cues prompting their readers to spatialize storyworlds into evolving configurations of participants, objects, and places'. The 'storyworlds' are seen as the cognitive results of the process of comprehending the story cued by the author and completed by readers. Structural elements of architectural cognitive maps can be traced in them in a way parallel to the concept of *Story Maps* for virtual story spaces proposed here.

The difference between Herman's 'storyworlds' and the *Story Maps* lies within their creation. Herman focuses on the creation of space through a linear literary-based system that evokes a spatial 'storyworld', while *Story Maps* evolve during a non-linear interactive exploration of a virtual spatial environment. Space and spatial understanding in 'storyworlds' is the achievement of the literary discourse – space in *Story Maps* is part of the discourse itself, as virtual space is not purely imagined, but is itself an expressive element. Herman concentrates on the creation of space through a narrative, but he does not investigate spatial systems and how they in fact generate narrative.

Film generates a screen space as a consistent 'visible space within the frame' [4] made up of edited shots/ frames. Although the projection of each frame creates a 2D picture, it is read as the presentation of a 3D space [5]. Within this space the story unfolds. While watching the film, the audience assembles the screen spaces from many shots and interprets the information to create a fictional world. They combine the visible, and cinematically interpreted space with an anticipation of how the surrounding space – 'off-screen' and therefore invisible – might look. Only small parts of the story-world space are visible at any one time on the screen, and the audience adds/ imagines the missing parts that are 'out of frame'. A film's diegetic world consists of more that just the presented screen space, is encourages the audience to form some idea of the overall space of the story and strives to evoke certain readings [1] of the fictional space. Finally, the cinematic mediation and the implied perspective position the audience in relation to what is depicted [13].

The effects and implementations of visualizations of cinematic space are manifold, and their narrative role can be enhanced to the extent that the graphically depicted space functions only as a vehicle for narrative [3]; space becomes subordinated to the narrative. Such a space does not have to be coherent in itself anymore – it might be incomprehensible outside the specific narrative for which it was created, and cannot be explored in any other way than from within the fictional narrative world.

RT 3D VEs can generate spaces accordingly, as each view of a designed virtual space has to be generated by a virtual camera – leading to a mediated form of spatial experience. This signifies camera-work and editing techniques as basic elements of spatial experiences in RT 3D VEs.

Coherent Space in Architecture and RT 3D VEs

Real-time rendered virtual spaces offer a flexibility comparable to that of cinematic space. But there is an important difference between a film set and a virtual world: Film sets – in contrast to RT 3D VEs – do not have to be coherent and closed spaces, whereas RT 3D VEs provide the interactor with the impression of such a spatial closure. If the audience were to step into the architectural space of the film set and take control over the camera, they would see a modern film studio at the point where the set ends. The space would have no coherence and the illusion created by the fictional world would be broken. In contrast, it is a defining part of RT 3D VEs that they allow this step into the precisely defined represented space – this positions RT 3D VEs nearer to architectural spaces.

Solid architectural space is read by the visitor as being coherent as opposed to the fragmented fictional spaces of literature and film. But architecture also operates through a form of fragmentation as it relies on the reception of parts of the whole that can be experienced by a visitor only over a period of time and in the form of movement. Architectural space is time-dependent, as it relies on the fragmented reception of parts of the whole spatial structure that cannot be perceived in its totality by the observer (see e.g. Corbusier's principle of the 'architectural promenade'). Although immersed in the space, the visitors cannot perceive the space's totality in one glance and have to explore it gradually. Numerous approaches have been made to analyze architectural space: from basic geometric shapes and their arrangement [7], interconnected patterns of use [2] [15], to cognitive maps as ways to comprehend spatial context [20]. This paper refers to Lynch's analysis of structural elements of cognitive maps to develop the model of *Story Maps* further.

As elaborated above, cinematic mediation is crucial to RT 3D VEs. However, the feature of interactive access to the virtual space separates virtual story worlds from a pure cinematic comprehension and refers to architectural space. Navigating in a RT 3D VE depends on the creation of a cognitive map of the space just as it does in the physical world [22], which is why Lynch's theories about the creation of these cognitive maps have repeatedly been applied to virtual worlds [25] [9] [26] [8] [24]. The research focused on optimized navigation in virtual world that was applied, for example, in data visualization or military training – not on narrative.

1.3 Related Work

The importance of cognitive maps in the exploration of RT 3D VEs is an accepted phenomenon but their narrative potential still largely unexplored by academics. Friedman combines narrative and the concept of mapping [11]. Unfortunately, it is not always clear whether Friedman refers to cognitive maps or environmental maps [10].

Champion combines vistas and encounters in virtual space to 'memento maps', which are themselves combined with the spatial cognitive maps. The functionality of 'memento maps' covers the user's memory of past events and Champion argues for a 'virtual heritage' [6] based on these past events. Past events, indeed, form an important part of the *Story Map*, but *Story Map* include expectations and intentions by the user reaching into possible future events, and deliver their elements in a clearly mediated (and thereby interpreting) form. Story Maps are not aimed to improve spatial navigation (as Champion points out as main feature of his model) but at the development of a narrative in the comprehension of the content through the interactor.

Among the researchers who explicitly step away from literary texts and towards RT 3D VEs, Fuller and Jenkins outline parallels between travel-journals that mainly deal with the description of the travels between two locations, and Nintendo games that offer comparable navigation between virtual locations [12]. Although simplifying all Nintendo games into one genre weakens their approach, they point out the importance of a spatial structuring of content within a spatially explorable immersive RT 3D VE, as opposed to a textually described world. Their comparison also suggests that cognitive mapping of the virtual space is necessary, as only an understood space can be translated into a travel log. Further exploration of space as a narrative element is undertaken in Jenkins' later work, where he approaches computer games as 'spatial art' [17] inspired by various aesthetic principles. Narrative finds its way into these worlds through the spatial design. 'Game designers don't simply tell stories; they design worlds and sculpt spaces' [16].

This very much mirrors the approach of this paper, but lacks the necessary inclusion of the cinematic means that depict these sculpted spaces to the interactor. To repeat the basic elements of the *Story Maps* are: the connection of event and navigable space, the cinematic mediation of space and event, and the cognitive mapping of these events and the dramatic setting in space. The Story Map is the result of the latter comprehension process that can be influenced through evocative means of event-, space-, and mediation-structure. How these features can be combined towards a shaping of individual *Story Maps* will be described in reference to the practical research project *Common Tales*.

2   The Common Tales Project

2.1   What Is Common Tales?

The Common Tales project was a collaboration between Sony Computer Entertainment Europe (SCEE), National Film and Television School (NFTS) and the Digital Studios (Cambridge University) conducted 1999-2000 at the Sony Development Studio Cambridge. The overall goal of the project was to combine cinematic storytelling with Playstation console games – not to create a new game, but to try out visual and narrative elements. The project used a basic narrative design that applied serial structures to game consoles and focused on the two main heroes both under the player's control. The heroes' characters were deepened and their relationship towards each other elaborated over the course of the series and in dependency to the player's actions. The design philosophy was that of a character-driven serial. How do the principles of the *Story Map* apply to such a setting?

2.2   Elements of the Story Map Applied

The Maze-Sequence
The first example applies a breaking of spatial and cinematic consistency to create a desired dramatic and narrative effect. *Common Tales* included a sequence set in a

small underground maze. In order to make this maze appear larger and less legible, pre-defined camera positions were set inside the labyrinth and the positioning of these cameras was used to complicate the generation of a cognitive map of the space through cinematic means. The rules of cinematography include the law of never crossing the line. The given camera set-up repeatedly broke this rule. By breaking this cinematic law, the visualization creates a disorientating effect, because it uses the established cinematic understanding and reading of visual camera-work of the interactor but does not follow the expected cinematic tradition. The camera set-up in simulates confusion, intensifying the player's experience of the maze. Cinematic mediation made small maze appear more complicated than it actually was.

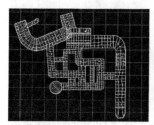 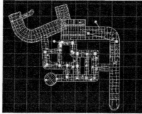 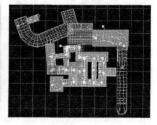

Fig. 1. Camera set-up in the Common Tales maze: basic spatial structure, the concentration of cameras in the central labyrinth part, the interactive triggers for the various cameras

Event-structuring was used to heighten the stakes of the maze-sequence further by including an antagonist in the maze, who chased the user-avatar through the labyrinth. Breaking the laws of spatial logic, this space was further intensified. While the interactor experiences the maze as a coherent space explorable through linear navigation, the movements of the pursuing antagonist were unpredictably non-linear. Whenever out of view from the interactor, the antagonist's avatar was able to teleport to various locations within the maze, breaking any possible spatial anticipation by the user. Instead of following a linear path, the antagonist could surprise the interactor at any time through spatial inconsistencies. Technically, this was implemented though trigger-zones activated through the user-avatar's movements. In this case, no camera work is needed to explain the spatial teleportation – but instead *not* revealing the antagonist's new spatial position provided for a dramatic effect.

The generation of a *Story Map* of the events in the maze is deliberately complicated through cinematic means, event structure, and spatial design in order to emphasize the dramatic tension of the scene – once the tension is resolved, the complex camera-work is disabled and the view switches to a simple following camera that allows for easy navigation and functional further exploration of the maze.

The Library-Sequence

At other points of the Common Tales prototype a specific reading of the events had to be supported in order to keep the events comprehensible and consistent. Here, various means were applied to direct the interactor's generation of the *Story Map*. For example, pre-defined cut-scenes were used as one way to signify the importance of a special event in space. One key moment in Common Tales sees the user-controlled character in the midst of a burglary stealing a precious sword from a virtual library. In order to signify the moment of the theft as important story event, the control was taken away from the user and a short cut-scene was staged at the moment of the theft itself. The inserted scene keeps the game events continuous but limits interactive access [18]. This specific scene included a structured directed event-structuring through a change in the interactive access. A defining interactive feature of *Common Tales* is that it grants interactive access to two virtual heroes. Interactors' control can switch – or be switched by the system – from one hero to the other. The moment of the theft introduces this feature as the cut-scene ends with the controls not returning to the first hero who conducted the theft, but to the second who witnesses the theft from a distance.

Fig. 2. Screenshots from the *Common Tales* theft scene; at the first frame control is taken at the last frame control it is switched to the second main character (the woman in the foreground)

Change of interactive access and event-structuring, change of the camera's point of view, and the accentuation of the key moment through the cut-scene are combined to provide a cluster of evocative elements that make the events and the interactor's comprehension of them in the *Story Map* comprehensible and significant in the special location of the library.

The Cube Club-Sequence
Consisting of a set of data, space in a RT 3D VE can be divided into different subspaces. These different locations can be stored as separate elements that have to be uploaded by the engine when generating the space of the VE. There is no spatial connection between these data files, only a mathematical one, which allows a designer to interlink them in any way. Visiting users do not experience these spaces as separate from each other, as their user-avatars are 'teleported' between these separate spaces and this teleportation and the fragmentation of space can be hidden with basic camera cuts corresponding to familiar cinematic language. When teleporting an user-avatar to another location, the camera cuts to a new view of this avatar, hiding the spatial teleport effect. In this way, cinematic techniques can enhance the spatial coherence of RT 3D VEs and edit the fragmented space into one perceived entity using continuity editing techniques that reinforces spatial orientation [4].

However, the *de facto* connections between different spaces, hidden by cinematic means, can defy the nature of architectural space. This quotes the specifics of cinematic space, which is assembled from fragments over a period of time into an understandable – or sometimes deliberately confusing – configuration. David Lynch's *Lost Highway* (USA/FRA, 1997), for example, creates architecturally illogical spatial but cinematically valid spaces through editing. Branigan names these '"impossible" spaces', that cannot be logically justified in the diegetic world-space. These spaces lead to perceptual problems 'that force the spectator to reconsider prior hypotheses about time and causality' [5]. They disorientate and destabilize the audience as the spatial connections are broken. Such destabilization is provides a powerful effect for narrative and dramatic impact in film as well as in RT 3D VEs.

This strategy is experimentally implemented in the *Cube Club*-sequence of *Common Tales*. The virtual *Cube Club* level consists of several separate structures including the library where the above examined theft event is staged. Each individual structure is connected to another via invisible 'teleporter zones' and teleporting effects are camouflaged through camera cuts. Consequently, the interactor experiences the structure as one coherent spatial location. In practice, user-avatars are 'teleported' from one location to another when, for example, stepping through a door or emerging from a tunnel into a new area. The resulting spatial jumps are disguised by camera cuts, which obey the rules of cinematic continuity editing, to the next location entered by the user-avatar.

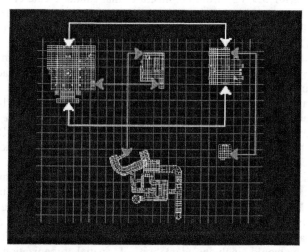

Fig. 3. The *Cube Club* level and the connection of separate spatial units – the bright arrows indicate the illogical spatial assembly

This combination of cinematically created and architecturally understood space allows spatially illogical constructs during the spatial explorations. In the example of the *Cube Club*-sequence, two opposing doors from one virtual room lead to similarly opposing doors in a different room (see the bright light arrows in the graphic). Leaving one room through the northern door sees users entering the seemingly adjacent room also through the northern door in terms of the virtual model. The change of the camera's point-of-view hides this effect and creates a 'spatial impossibility' that cannot be recreated in any physical setting.

The effect, here, is used to enhance the magical character of these rooms, which are symbols for the main conflict of the narrative staged around the basic conflict of fictional characters mingling with real human beings in the world of the RT 3D VE. The basic narrative premise of the *Common Tales* adventure consists of a combination of two inherently incompatible worlds: fiction and fact. The illogically connected rooms embody this theme in their spatial (dis)arrangement and represent a spatially defined narrative element in the expressive vocabulary of the title.

3 Conclusions and Future Work

As the *Common Tales* prototype illustrates: space, the mediation of it, and the events within it are highly interconnected in the shaping of the comprehension of the narrative RT 3D VE into a *Story Map*. Cinematic mediation has the power to complicate the comprehension of virtual space, but can also allow for impossible spaces; staged events and structured interactive access can signify certain moments of a user experience; spatial design can follow non-spatial logic. These features combined provide clearly evocative elements for an evolving *Story Map* based on cinematic mediation, spatial structuring, and event structuring. These three elements differ from other traditional separating RT 3D VEs from architecture (that cannot create cinematic space), film (that cannot create interactive explorable consistent space), and from literature (as events in RT 3D VEs are told through space, not space through events). *Story Maps* in RT 3D VEs are specific to interactive spatial storytelling.

While the above elaborated features outline a variety of evocative means that can influence *Story Maps* they do not necessarily prove that they exist. As each *Story Map* is highly unique it is difficult to prove their general form. However, their effect – the better understanding and generation of meaning from the experience by combining space and events – can be traced in MMORPGs like *Ultima Online* [Origin, US 1997]. In contrast to single-player titles such as *Common Tales*, MMORPGs provide spatial worlds but no pre-arranged line of events. But within these worlds users share stories that locate past events in special times and spaces. These myths and stories [19] mirror underlying *Story Maps* as they prove the assembly of events and spaces into interpretations towards one whole. It is a paradox that seemingly clearer-structured single-user titles have to learn storytelling techniques from the freedom and spatial assembly of online titles. What is missing in MMORPGs, on the other hand, is the awareness and use of the cinematic mediation. Therefore, two promising fields for further research would include adaptation of spatial organization and event-structuring from MMORPGs to single-player titles and adaptation of cinematic mediation as developed for single-user titles for MMORPGs.

References

1. Affron, C., Affron, M.J.: Sets in Motion. Art Direction and Film Narrative. Rutgers University Press, New Brunswick (1995)
2. Alexander, C., Ishikawa, S., Silverstein: A Pattern Language. Oxford University Press, New York (1977)
3. Bordwell, D.: The Classic Hollywood Cinema: Film Style and Mode of Production. Routledge & Kegan Paul, London (1985)
4. Bordwell, D., Thompson, K.: Film Art. An Introduction. McGraw-Hill Inc., New York (1993)
5. Branigan , E.: Narrative Comprehension and Film. Routledge, London (1992)

6. Champion, E.: Applying Game Design Theory to Virtual Heritage Environments (unpublished draft submitted to Graphite Annual Conference). (2003)
7. Ching, F.: Architecture: Form, Space, and Order. Van Nostrand Reinhold, New York (1979)
8. Darken, R.P., Peterson, B.: Spatial Orientation, Wayfinding, and Representation. In: Stanney, K.M. (ed.): Handbook of Virtual Environments. Lawrence Erlbaum Assoc. Inc., New York (2002)
9. Elvins, T.T., Nadeau, D.R., and Kirsh, D.: Worldlets - 3D Thumbnails for Wayfinding in Virtual Environments. In: Robertson, G., Schmandt, C. (eds.): Proceedings of the SIGCHI Conference on Human Factors in Computing Systems. ACM Press, New York (1997) 163-170
10. Friedman, T.: Electric Dreams: Cyberculture and the Utopian Sphere (unpublished draft)
11. Friedman, T.. Making Sense of Software: Computer Games and Interactive Textuality. In: Jones, S.G. (ed.): CyberSociety: Computer-Mediated Communication and Community. Sage Publ., Thousand Oaks (1995) 73-89
12. Fuller, M., Jenkins, H.: Nintendo® and New World Travel Writing: A Dialogue. In: Jones, S.G. (ed.): Cybersociety: Computer-Mediated Communication and Community. Sage Publications, Thousand Oaks (1995) 57-72
13. Heath, S.: Narrative Space. In: Screen. Vol. 17, **3** (1976) 68-112
14. Herman, D.: Story Logic: Problems and Possibilities of Narrative. Frontiers of Narrative Series. University of Nebraska Press, Lincoln London (2002)
15. Hillier, B.: Space Is the Machine: A Configurational Theory of Architecture. Cambridge University Press, Cambridge Melbourne New York (1996)
16. Jenkins, H.: Game Design as Narrative Architecture. In: Wardrup-Fruin, N., Harrington, P. (eds.): First Person: New Media as Story, Performance, and Game. MIT Press, Cambridge, MA (TBP)
17. Jenkins, H., Squire, K.: The Art of Contested Spaces. In: King, L. (ed.): Game On: The History and Culture of Video Games. Universe, New York (2002) 64-75
18. Juul, J.: Time to Play – an Examination of Game Temporality. In: Wardrup-Fruin, N., Harrigan, P. (eds.): First Person: New Media as Story, Performance, and Game. MIT Press, Cambridge, MA (TBP)
19. Koster, R.: Talk given at: Entertainment in the Interactive Age, Annenberg Centre, University of Southern California. (2001)
20. Lynch, K.: The Image of the City. MIT Press, Cambridge, MA (1960)
21. Murray, J.H.: Hamlet on the Holodeck. The Future of Narrative in Cyberspace. MIT Press, Cambridge, MA (1997)
22. Péruch, P., Gaunet, F., Thinus-Blanc, C., and Loomis, J.: Understanding and Learning Virtual Spaces. In: Kitchin, R., Freundschuh, S. (eds.): Cognitive Mapping. Past, Present and Future. Routledge, London; New York (2000) 108-125
23. Ryan, M.-L. : Narrative **aans** Virtual Reality. Immersion and Interactivity in Literature and Electronic Media. Parallax: Re-Visions of Culture and Society. The John Hopkins University Press, Baltimore London (2001)
24. Steck, S., D., Mallot, H., A.: The Role of Global and Local Landmarks in Virtual Environment Navigation. Presence, Vol. 9., **1** (2000) 69-83
25. Strohecker, C., Barros, B., Slaughter, A.: Mapping Psychological and Virtual Spaces. International Journal of Design Computing, Vol. 1. (online journal) (1998)
26. Vinson, N.G.: Design Guidelines for Landmarks to Support Navigation in Virtual Environments. In: Williams, M.G., Altom, M.W. (eds.) Proceedings of the SIGCHI Conference on Human Factors in Computing Systems. ACM, New York (1999) 278-85

Mediating Action and Background Music

Pietro Casella and Ana Paiva

Instituto Superior Técnico
Intelligent Agents and Synthetic Characters Group
Instituto de Engenharia de Sistemas e Computadores
Lisboa, Portugal
{pietro.casella,ana.paiva}@gaips.inesc.pt
http://gaips.inesc-id.pt

Abstract. An efficient use of background music is a very powerful tool to achieve high levels of immersion and to induce moods within interactive settings. Although this property is clear, the way in which action and music should be connected, so as to have such an efficient emotion delivery tool, is still to be fully understood.
An action-music mediation framework is proposed which facilitates the investigation of this relation which is supported by a tool that allows musicians to create and test new models of action-music interaction, and which ultimately will lead to further investigation on the "narrative-music" theoretic aspects of emotion induction.

1 Introduction

One old recipe to achieve high levels of immersion is the use of background music. Paradigmatic examples of this usage appear in opera, cartoons, films, theater and even in ancient tribal rituals. While opera is, by definition, story telling with music, cinema first appeared as being an exclusively visual art. The apparent emptiness of silence and difficult incorporation of certain emotions led to the use of music as a tool for emotion delivery. The evolution of the techniques of film music had its peak when the interaction between the composer and the film director became so tight that the way stories where being told had now completely absorbed music as part of the medium. One commonly mentioned example of this is Hitchcock's work with Herrman. Another example of using music to tell stories is its use in cartoons. The so called "Mickey Mousing" effect consists of using musical constructs to highlight every action on the screen, thus greatly improving the dramatic power of the animation[5].

With all this evidence of emotive power, music became an attractive tool also for the increasingly emotion demanding intelligent virtual environments. However, until recently, little attention has been given to computer music under this perspective, which has led to sometimes counter-producing examples of music as an emotion delivery tool. Not despising other cases of "bad musical results" such as those originated by poor sound quality, the case of music working against the narrative is the most relevant to the present work. This occurs either when the user gets the wrong emotional clue from music, or when the user predicts the flow of the action because of pattern recognition caused by repetitive music selection.

O. Balet et al. (Eds.): ICVS 2003, LNCS 2897, pp. 94–101, 2003.
© Springer-Verlag Berlin Heidelberg 2003

1.1 Approaches

To avoid the above mentioned problems two possible approaches where identified:

- Dynamic Music Generation - Creation of music in realtime or quasi-realtime using some technique.
- Action/Music Mediation - A better management of the music selection mechanisms in response to the environment's action[1].

Most previous research efforts fall into the first of these categories. The major such effort was what is now commonly called on the Computer Game Community as *Adaptive Music*. Some commercial sound engines provide primitives that facilitate the incorporation of random elements in music selection or pseudo-generation process. (ex. [4]).

Despite the fact that the resulting music is indeed more interesting and diverse, numerous reports [2] point to the fact that the integration of these sound primitives with the game is mostly hardwired and embedded in the action and graphics code, leaving little flexibility for the music composer to explore the realms of music and action interaction. In fact, most musicians are not even aware of the full power of this interaction[2].

Mixed efforts exist which fall in between the two possible mentioned approaches. The MAgentA architecture [1] is a system which uses generic composition algorithms to generate music in realtime based on emotional information from the environment. The work of Downie [3] in the void* system consists of a reactive AI based music selection agent which transforms and combines pre-composed musical elements, in response to perceptions about the action. This music character works as a part of the action.

The approach presented on this article, which fits on the second above mentioned possible solution, is one of providing a high level rule based action-music mediation framework. This facilitates the external specification of a music selection behavior, which responds to actions on the environment, thus centralizing the behavior of musical support to the narrative.

2 Mediation Framework

This section describes the proposed action-music integration framework. The main idea is that instead of having the the music control code as part of the environment action code, we have an independent *environment* which communicates action events to a *mediator* module, which infers what "music actions" should be taken and communicates them to the *output* module. The next subsections describe this process in more detail.

---

[1] In this context, action is the sequence of events that occur in the environment.

[2] Most computer game companies contract "super musicians" which are also programmers. Otherwise the musicians have to engage in a complicated negotiation process with the programmers, leading to suboptimal usages of the full potential.

2.1   Execution Model

The system assumes that the environment outputs an identifier of every relevant action.
The steps of the main loop can be described as follows:

1. An action occurs on the environment.
2. Environment sends an action identifier X on to the system.
3. The arrival of the symbol X triggers the generation process. An augmented grammar model is used to compute a sequence of symbols. The initial rules for the inference are those of the form $X \rightarrow ?$ which are active.
4. Once a symbol sequence is output from the generation process, it is interpreted from left to right.
5. The interpretation of each symbol depends on its type. Internal symbols represent internal actions and are used to update the internal state, External symbols are sent to the output module, and originate actions on that module.

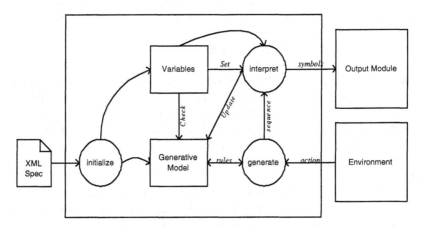

Fig. 1. System Architecture

Having described the general framework, we now focus on the description of the Mediator and Output Modules.

2.2   Mediator Module

The mediator module is where all the reasoning about action and music integration is processed, and thus the most relevant to the present paper.

This module works on a previously specified model of behavior, which is built using the graphical tool described bellow. The architecture provides a mechanism for storing variables and primitives for manipulating them. These variables are used on run time to compute the action sequence. The model of behavior consists of an augmented probabilistic context free grammar. The augmentations assume the form of preconditions on the variables for activation of the rules.

The main procedure that is triggered upon arrival of an environment' message is shown on Figure 2.

```
NewAction(MSG)
1. select rules with left side = MSG
2. restrict selected rules to those with precondition satisfied
3. use generative procedure to generate a sequence of symbols
4. for each symbol in sequence
5.     if symbol is internal
6.          interpret the symbol
7.     else
8.          send the symbol to the output module
```

Fig. 2. Main Procedure

The generative procedure (step 3) used is a simple Probabilistic Context Free Grammar generation algorithm, with the modifications to comprise the augmentations that where made to the formalism, namely the verification of the rules' preconditions which leads to an extra control on the dynamic distribution of the grammar, and the related language (e.g. by setting values of variables, one can inhibit certain rule groups, whose preconditions and consequent applicability depend on those variables)[3].

Another aspect is that the primitives for manipulating variables are treated as symbols themselves, so the grammar model works as a sort of program generator.

The symbols that are sent to the output module must be interpretable by that module. These symbols represent actions on that module. On the case of a music module, these symbols can be music or sound identifiers, playback parameter settings, etc.

Model Language. The underlying behavior specification language consists of a way to formally express the grammar of the mediator run-time behavior. One uses this language to specify a model which is loaded upon initialization on runtime. This behavior is a consequence of both the static model, and the associated generation algorithm, described on Figure 2.

The following list resumes the available primitives.

- *Variable manipulation primitives* - primitives for setting, incrementing and decrementing the value of variables.
- *Variable testing primitives* - primitives for testing the value of variables against thresholds.
- *Variable declaration* - When declared, a variable includes a name, an initial value and an optional trigger. The trigger has an associated value, a behavior type (which specifies if the trigger is run when the variable's value is under, over or equal to the value of the trigger) and a sequence of symbols (which are treated as if they where generated with the generative process). The triggers are tested each time the variable value is altered.

---

[3] Note that the grammar is context free, as the applicability of the rules does not depend on the sequence being generated. However, successive generations for the same initial symbol may use different grammar, as the sentences generated previously may have changed the grammar, and its distribution.

- *Symbols* - Each symbol has an associated identifier and an output token.
- *Rule declaration* - Rules are composed of a name and a weight plus a precondition, a left side and a right side. The precondition is a *Variable testing primitive*, the left side is a *symbol*, and the right side is a *sequence of symbols*.
- *Rule manipulation primitives* - primitives for changing attributes of rules such as the weight.

2.3 Output Module

The output module must have an interface that supports the arrival of action symbols from the mediator. These symbols are interpreted independently from the mediator. The semantics and the mechanics however must be fully understood by the musician.

The currently implemented Output Module works as a kind of real-time mixing facility and has some inertia properties which solve the problem of too much requests simultaneously. Each request has an associated behavior which may be 'enqueue', 'play immediately', 'play if possible' and 'play solo'. The synchronization issues related to playing musical loops are solved in two ways, namely it is possible to instruct the system to cross-fade two sounds, or it is possible to have the system play the second sound only after the currently playing loop is finishes. The rationale for this rich output module is similar to mind-body metaphor used when building for example human-like intelligent virtual agents, where the body has some coherence properties which are imposed by the physics of the body rather than the mind.

2.4 Example

The following pseudo code specification exemplifies how one can script different behaviors externally from the environment.

```
1 .// Variable declaration
2 .CHARACTER_STRENGTH
3 .     init: 0
4 .     trigger: > 10 -> PLAY_SOUND_IFEELGOOD
5 .// Rules
6 .LOCATION_STREET -> STOP_ENV_SOUND PLAY_STREET_SOUND
7 .CHARACTER1_ENTERS -> PLAY_CHARACTER1_NORMALMOTIF
8 .     pre: CHARACTER_STRENGTH < 5
9 .CHARACTER1_ENTERS -> PLAY_CHARACTER1_STRONGMOTIF
10.     pre: CHARACTER_STRENGTH > 4
11.CHARACTER1_ISMORESTRONG -> INC_VAR(CHARACTER1_STRENGTH)
12.CHARACTER1_ISMOREWEAK -> DEC_VAR(CHARACTER1_STRENGTH)
```

First we declare a variable to store the level of strength of character 1. This variable includes a trigger which fires the action PLAY_SOUND_IFEELGOOD whenever the value is over 10. The last two rules control the level variable on response to the corresponding events on the environment. The rules on line 7 to 10 specify different behaviors for the action CHARACTER1_ENTERS, depending on the level of strength.

2.5   Exploration Tool

A tool was developed that supports the creation and exploration of mediation models such as the one described on the example above. Figure 3 shows the graphical interface of this tool. This tool avoids explicit scripting by the musician. It is complemented with a simulator of runtime events (a gui with buttons that the user clicks to communicate symbols to the mediator, which sends actions to the output module, etc.), so that the output behavior can be observed.

The tool starts by inspecting the environment, mediator and output modules, via a well defined programming interface, so as to retrieve a list of the available symbols. For example the environment returns a list of all the actions that may occur on run time, the mediator returns a list of available operations (mainly variable manipulation operations), and the output module returns a list of symbols (mainly sound files) and operations (such as loop, play once, fade, etc.). New non-terminal symbols may be added at will.

Once the right model is created, it is saved to a file, which is then loaded by the architecture upon initialization. This file includes the declaration and initialization of the variables and corresponding triggers, plus the specification of the rules and their properties.

The typical configuration process is iterative, in particular when new symbols are added to the environment this tool should be used to revise the model so as to include the proper behavior for such events.

Figure 3 shows tool after the example above has been inserted. Note the symbols on the left hand side, and the rule insertion screen on the right hand side.

3   Conclusions

One optional mechanism for parallel emission of symbols, so as to provide a way of playing sounds in parallel, consists of a different type of terminal rule, which groups the right hand side symbols. The generation process marks these symbols so that the interpretation process emits them using a different procedure. This and other modifications may be added to the architecture by extending its interfaces for each process.

Symbols are implemented as objects. These objects can be extended and treated by the modules in very different ways. The inference mechanism uses the object's class' compare function for non terminal symbols.

One issue that is being worked on is the implementation of first order symbols (i.e. symbols with parameters) as another level of complexity. With this feature, the whole architecture will be seen as a mediator for generic objects in a functional perspective. Note that the mediator module is independent of the output module, so the mediation does not have to be action-music, and thus can be used to mediate other non musical behaviors.

One of the future developments will be the replacement of the output module by an algorithmic composition system that was previously developed by the authors (please refer to [1] for further details on this system).

Another noteworthy aspect, is the musician's approach to action music research. First, the musician should fully understand the nature of the symbols that are output

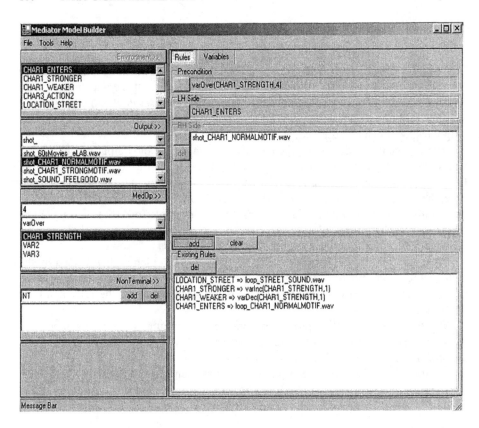

Fig. 3. Mediator Model Builder

form the environment. These symbols reflect the music's view of the narrative, therefore they should be planned to have the right and relevant level of detail. Secondly, the musician will work with a specific output module which has a limited set capabilities and a specific control language. Consequently, investigation into new models of execution for such module should be pursued focusing on the needs of the musician, rather than the opposite. Finally, it should not be assumed that the model of mediation presented in this paper is the right one for expressing action-music mediation, and as such, all modules were constructed having future modifications in mind, which will map the reasoning processes of the musician more naturally, for example by including new rule-selection algorithms, rule augmentations or completely different formalisms.

The architecture is being integrated on the FantasyA virtual environment, currently being developed at GAIPS-INESC. Upon finishing this integration, a performance evaluation will be made, followed by a usability evaluation, where music composers will be asked to try and model some imagined behavior, using the GUI for model building, and then interviewed, leading to an improved conceptual model of the available functionality. Ultimately, composer specific framework and best practices will become a medium for ever focused research on the interaction between action and music.

References

1. Pietro Casella and Ana Paiva. MAgentA: An Architecture for Real Time Automatic Composition of Background Music. IVA01, Madrid, Spain. Springer
2. Gamasutra, Audio Section. `http://www.gamasutra.com`
3. Mark Downie. Behavior, animation, music: the music and movement of synthetic characters. MSc Thesis. MIT, 2001.
4. Microsoft DirectMusic. `http://www.microsoft.com/directx`
5. Roy M. Prendergast. Film Music: a neglected art - a critical study of music in films. W. W. Norton & Company, 2nd Ed. 1992

The Effects of Mediation
in a Storytelling Virtual Environment

Sarah Brown, Ilda Ladeira, Cara Winterbottom, and Edwin Blake

Collaborative Visual Computing Laboratory,
Department of Computer Science, University of Cape Town,
Private Bag, Rondebosch 7701, South Africa
{sbrown,iladeira,cwinterb,edwin}@cs.uct.ac.za
http://www.cs.uct.ac.za/Research/CVC/

Abstract. This paper presents a study that explores the use of mediation in virtual environments (VEs) used for cultural storytelling. A VE was created in which a traditional San story was told. Two forms of mediation were used: visual and audio. Four versions of the VE were implemented, differentiated by the types of mediation included. An experiment was conducted, during which measurements of presence, story involvement and enjoyment were taken. Audio mediation was found to have a positive effect on presence. Visual mediation was found to increase story involvement, which is valuable in conveying a narrative successfully. Both audio mediation and the interaction between the mediations increased enjoyment. Overall, the use of subtle mediations that appear natural in the VE setting was shown to be effective.

1   Introduction

Passing traditional folklore from generation to generation has always played an important role in cultural preservation. In addition, museums are frequently challenged to present culture in a dynamic and animated way. To this end, the use of virtual reality (VR) to portray traditional storytelling experiences holds great potential for museums and cultural preservation in general. It is therefore important to investigate ways in which user understanding and appreciation of the experience may be enhanced.

This paper presents a large scale experiment (77 subjects) that investigated the effects of mediation on user presence and enjoyment in a storytelling VE as well as user involvement in the story being told. In this research, mediation may be understood as those features of a VE that are intended to facilitate interaction between the users and the system, and thereby increase user understanding of the VE.

This study illuminates the potential of simple mediations for enhancing presence in a storytelling VE, despite the use of material to which users are likely to be unaccustomed, namely San[1] narrative. Unfortunately, the San traditional culture has become increasingly difficult to preserve in the modern world. Vivid portrayals of this culture would be highly beneficial to preserving South Africa's cultural heritage. The effects of

---

[1] The San people are hunter-foragers indigenous to southern Africa. They have a rich tradition of oral storytelling that is difficult to capture with the written word[16].

O. Balet et al. (Eds.): ICVS 2003, LNCS 2897, pp. 102–111, 2003.
© Springer-Verlag Berlin Heidelberg 2003

Fig. 1. A San storyteller and companions, sitting around a fire. The storyteller (far left) makes animated gestures as he tells the story.

adding simple visual and audio mediations to a VE, both in isolation and in combination are evaluated. The VE created to tell the San story and investigate the mediations is displayed in Figure 1.

In Section 2, relevant background information is presented, Section 3 describes the experiment and the results are presented and discussed in Section 4. Our conclusions and possibilities for future work are presented in Section 5.

2   Previous Work

2.1   Presence

Presence is a central concept in VR research. It is a term used to describe the degree to which users perceive a mediated experience to be non-mediated[9]. The goal of most VR systems is to provide the user with the illusion that the VE is real (non-mediated). That is, to induce a sense of 'being there' in the VE.

In order to create VR applications that are attractive and useful to users, it is important to understand how presence may be enhanced. In light of such knowledge, effective applications can be developed by focussing on those aspects that enhance presence. There are numerous definitions of presence in VR literature. For our purposes, we have used the definition that appears most often[14, 4, 18, 11, 15], namely a subjective sense of being in the VE.

2.2   Mediation in Virtual Reality

Mediation covers all those experiences that are created using technology[9]. The aim of mediated experiences is often to give the user the illusion that his or her experience is direct, real and not in fact mediated. A number of studies have investigated different ways of mediating a VR experience. Huong Dinh *et al.*[4] found that the addition of tactile, olfactory and especially auditory mediation to a VE increased the user's sense of presence. Furthermore, it was found that increasing visual detail and vividness did not lead to an increase in presence. They postulated that this was because virtual reality is, in essence, about visual display. Therefore, even a low quality environment still contains visual mediation, whereas other sensory mediations are either present or not.

In a review of the causes and effects of presence, Lombard and Ditton[9] found that increasing the number of sensory mediations increased user presence. However, the mediations had to be consistent with each other and with the virtual environment in order to be effective. Inconsistent mediations emphasised the artificiality of the environment and so lessened presence. Lombard and Ditton also found that image quality, size and viewing distance were all important for effective visual mediations. Quality and dimensionality were found to be important aspects of audio mediation[9].

2.3   Storytelling and Narrative

There has been a great deal of interest in investigating narrative and storytelling in computer-based environments[13, 17, 3, 12]. Kevin Brooks[2] identifies three questions which are important to consider when storytelling and VR are merged: how can computer mediation support the development and portrayal of stories; what mediations can affect different portrayals of a story and so deliver different experiences; and what part does the user have in this process. Our study explores possible answers to these questions.

It is important to note that narrative and narration are two distinct concepts. According to Clarke and Mitchell[3], narrative refers to the events of the story and narration refers to the process of storytelling. One of the key distinctions between VR and other storytelling media (e.g. film) is that VE users have a great deal more control over what they see and experience. This freedom poses a challenge in storytelling environments. Clarke and Mitchell suggest that the more freedom users have to determine the narrative, the weaker the influence of the author becomes over the narration experience[3]. They also believe that interactive narratives curb the development of empathy with the characters and engagement in the plot. Thus, it might be argued that in order to present an engaging storytelling experience, the narrative should be told by a storyteller who is charismatic and maintains some control over it[13]. In light of the above, we decided to make use of an engaging San storyteller who fosters minimal interaction with the user. In this way, the San narrative would not be altered by interaction and the user would still be engaged by the storyteller. Users are able to interact with the VE by moving around and altering their point of view.

2.4   Culture and Virtual Reality

According to Anstey, Pape & Sandin[1], VR provides a distinctive means for presenting cultural exhibitions. Jackson *et al.*[7] argue that cultures themselves are dynamic entities and thus should not be portrayed statically. VR has the ability to represent cultures as dynamic and vibrant, rather than as collections of artifacts. Yet, according to Roussou[13], the use of VR as

> an artistic, educational and cultural medium is largely overlooked and unexplored.

For museums worldwide, there has been a growing interest in the possibility of using VEs to create meaningful and educational exhibitions of different cultures[13, 10, 8]. For instance, in Greece, a VR reconstruction of the ancient city, Miletus, is used to educate visitors on ancient times and lifestyles at the Foundation for the Hellenic World[13]. A further example is a VR heritage project developed by Ireland's North Gate Centre. Here, VR was used to represent the North Main Street area in Cork City, Ireland as it was in the 17th century and as it is at present. This project was developed to increase interest in local history and foster exploration of local ruins[10].

3 Methodology

The aim of our study was to show that either audio or visual mediation would increase user presence in a storytelling VE. It was predicted that the inclusion of both forms of mediation would be more effective in this respect than either mediation alone. Furthermore, the inclusion of visual mediation was expected to increase the user's involvement in the story. This was expected, since the visual mediation related directly to the story that was told. We postulated that this would increase user interest and therefore, story involvement. Lastly, any form of mediation was expected to increase user enjoyment in the VE.

3.1 The Virtual Environment

In order to test the above hypotheses, a VE was created in which a traditional San story is told. This VE was created using the Genesis3D games engine[5]. The scene is set in a highly detailed cave at night time. Inside the cave there is a blazing fire, surrounded by three figures. Digital photographs of caves in the Cederberg mountains[2] of the Western Cape, South Africa, were used to texture the rocks. The three agents were conceptualised as San hunters, one of whom is the storyteller. They are shown in Figure 1. Photographs of San men were used to texture the agents, in order to achieve the correct appearance. The user is not embodied within the VE, i.e. no avatar representations were provided. Initially the user is placed outside on rough, barren terrain and is able to see the mouth of the cave. The user is then invited to sit around the fire and listen to the story with the San hunters. All sound in the VE was partially spatialised, having both direction and location.

Two types of mediation were implemented: audio mediation in the form of subtle environmental night sounds, such as a fire crackling and crickets chirping; and visual mediation in the form of San rock paintings[3] related to the story that is told. The rock

---

[2] San people once inhabited the Cederberg mountains of South Africa, and rock paintings have been found in many caves in this area.

[3] Rock paintings were an integral part of the San lifestyle[16].

paintings were created by copying elements of real San paintings, thereby increasing their authenticity. Figure 2 shows four of the eight San rock paintings used as visual mediation. These were placed on the cave wall nearest to the storyteller, where they were clearly visible. The user was able to approach the paintings to examine them more closely. In accordance with Lombard and Ditton's findings, we ensured that the visual and audio mediations were consistent with the environment and each other[9].

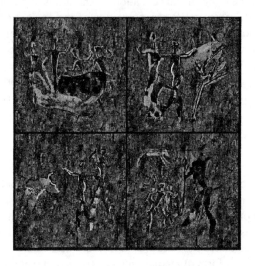

Fig. 2. Four of the San rock paintings, used as visual mediation. The paintings show scenes from the story that was told in the VE. The story refers to Kaggn the trickster, who pretends to be a haartebeest and frightens some children. At the end, they run home to their fathers for protection.

Therefore, within the basic framework, four versions of the VE were created, differentiated by the type and amount of mediation included in each: Paintings and Sound (P/S); No Paintings and Sound (NP/S); Paintings and No Sound (P/NS); and No Paintings and No Sound (NP/NS).

3.2   The Experiment

Equipment. Typically, VR has not been accessible to the general public, due to expensive equipment requirements. We aimed to create a VE that was more easily accessible, in terms of cost. Therefore, this study made use of a desktop-based VE that was relatively inexpensive to run. Two high-performance personal computers with Nvidia GeForce2 MX400 graphics cards and 17" monitors were used. Input was effected through mouse and keyboard; headphones were used to output the VE soundtrack. The system's frame rate varied between 15 and 20 frames per second, depending on the user's perspective view.

Experimental Subjects. The experiment was conducted with 77 test subjects, who were paid for their participation. This large group ensured the statistical validity of the experimental results. All participants were first and second year university students. The subjects were randomly divided into the four experimental conditions, as evenly as possible. Each subject only experienced one of the experimental conditions and was not aware that there were multiple VEs.

Procedure. The experiment took place in a dedicated room. Subjects were given a short introduction to the format of the experiment and were then allowed to become familiar with the required navigation controls. This took place in a separate VE. This ensured that lack of familiarity with the technology would be less likely to interfere with the experiment. The subjects were then primed with a short description of San lifestyle and mythology. This served to create an awareness of the San culture and provide a context for the main VE[11]. Thereafter, the participants were placed in the San VE. Following this VR experience, each subject completed questionnaires, which are discussed in Section 3.3.

3.3   Measures and Collection

Experimental Variables. The following three dependent variables were used in the experiment: Presence in the VE; Involvement in the story being told (SINV); and Enjoyment of user in the VE (ENJ). The independent variables were Audio mediation (S/NS) and Visual mediation (P/NP).

Questionnaires. While there is no standard method for measuring presence, most researchers use questionnaires to allow retrospective self-report by users. We decided to use the Igroup Presence questionnaire (IPQ)[6], since the authors' definition of presence corresponds with our own. The IPQ was constructed by combining previous questionnaires and new questions. This 14-item questionnaire has been thoroughly tested and statistically validated[14, 15]. Each item consists of a 7 point scale, yielding a possible presence result of 7 (minimum) to 98 (maximum).

Data for the story involvement and enjoyment variables were gathered from two additional questions, where subjects rated their involvement in the story and enjoyment of the VE on a scale from 1 to 7. Subjects were also asked to give any other comments concerning the San storytelling environment, or the experiment in general.

4   Results and Discussion

The relationships between the variables were analysed using a 2x2 factorial Analysis of Variance (ANOVA). A summary of the descriptive statistics from the ANOVA is displayed in Table 1.

Presence. As can be seen from Table 1, those subjects who experienced audio mediation (S) achieved the highest presence levels on average. The subjects who experienced no audio mediation (NS) achieved the lowest presence levels. This result is confirmed by the results of the factorial ANOVA. A significant main effect was found for audio

Table 1. Summary of descriptive statistics from factorial ANOVA conducted with audio and visual mediation as the independent variables, and presence, story involvement and enjoyment as the dependent variables. S/NS refers to audio mediation, where S means mediation is included and NS means mediation is not included. Similarly, P/NP refers to visual mediation and Interaction refers to the possible interactions between mediations. SINV refers to story involvement and ENJ refers to enjoyment.

	Level of Factor	Level of Factor	N	Presence Mean	SINV Mean	ENJ Mean
Total			77	56.69	4.26	5.13
S/NS	S		39	61.31	4.31	5.38
S/NS	NS		38	51.95	4.21	4.87
P/NP	P		39	58.08	4.74	5.36
P/NP	NP		38	55.26	3.76	4.89
Interaction	S	P	20	62.95	4.90	5.90
Interaction	S	NP	19	59.58	3.68	4.84
Interaction	NS	P	19	52.95	4.58	4.79
Interaction	NS	NP	19	50.95	3.84	4.95

mediation on presence ($F = 138.8$, $p < 0.002$). Introducing audio mediation to the virtual environment increases average presence in users by 17%. These results indicate that background audio mediation is important for increased presence in a VE. The ambient, spatialised sound creates a 3D effect that places the user more firmly in the VE. However, the addition of visual mediation did not appear to have any effect on presence. The VE that was created was already visually compelling and adding additional visual items had no significant effect on presence. This corresponds with results reported in previous experiments [9]. This suggests that there is a threshold beyond which visual mediation does not enhance presence.

Story Involvement. Table 1 shows that both groups which experienced visual mediation achieved higher story involvement levels than the groups which did not. Once again, this result is confirmed by the results of the factorial ANOVA. A significant main effect was found for visual mediation on story involvement ($F = 9.49$, $p < 0.003$). Introducing visual mediation to the VE has a similar effect on story involvement as audio mediation has on presence. It increases the average story involvement in users by 23.7%. The fact that audio mediation had no significant effects here could be partly due to the fact that the San paintings related directly to the story, while the environmental sounds did not.

Enjoyment. Table 1 also displays the results for enjoyment (ENJ). The group that experienced both mediation types achieved the highest average enjoyment. The scores for all of the other groups were fairly similar. Two significant effects were found in the factorial ANOVA: a significant interaction between audio and visual mediation ($F = 5.87$, $p < 0.02$) and a significant main effect for audio mediation ($F = 4.01$, $p < 0.05$).

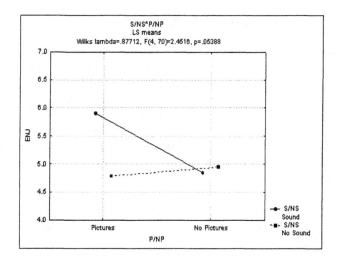

Fig. 3. Means plot of the significant interaction between audio mediation and visual mediation on enjoyment. When audio mediation is present, visual mediation increases enjoyment by 20.4% and when visual mediation is present, audio mediation increases enjoyment by 22.9%. However, adding a single mediation without the other does not increase enjoyment.

In order to understand the interaction of the mediations on enjoyment, a series of one-way ANOVA tests were conducted using enjoyment as the only dependent variable. These showed that the effect of visual mediation on enjoyment was significant only when those users who experienced audio mediation were considered ($F = 11.11, p < 0.002$), and vice versa ($F = 11.41, p < 0.002$). These results are displayed graphically in Figure 3.

As Figure 3 shows, if the VE contains audio mediation, adding visual mediation increases enjoyment by a large amount, and vice versa. Therefore, the effect of audio mediation depends on the presence of visual mediation. This result suggests that enjoyment does not depend on any single mediation, but is affected by the number of mediations added.

Comments from Experimental Subjects. Comments from users provided qualitative and anecdotal information about the success of the VE as a storytelling medium. Numerous users responded positively to the sound and look of the fire. In fact, many mentioned the warmth of the fire. The fire cast random shadows around the cave and many users enjoyed this flickering fire light. The use of spatialised 3D sound was also very successful.

While some people felt that listening to a story was too passive for VR, there was much positive feedback about the storytelling experience in general. For example, the following comment:

> ...the story and the environment reminded me of stories that I was told when I was growing up by my elders.

5   Conclusions and Future Work

This paper has presented a large-scale study that explored the effects of audio and visual mediation on user presence, story involvement and enjoyment in a VE. This was effected using an environment in which a San story was told.

The knowledge gained from this study has valuable potential in the area of virtual storytelling. The importance of sound for enhancing user presence was highlighted, even though its effects are subtle. Its absence is often more noticeable than its presence. We also re-established the result that increasing visual mediation does not significantly increase presence[4]. However, visual mediation does increase involvement in the story. This makes it a powerful tool for increasing accessibility of the story. Appropriate visual mediation draws attention to the narrative, thus making listening a less passive and more interesting experience. Thus, it is particularly valuable in virtual storytelling. The effect of visual and audio mediations together shows that increasing the number of mediations in the VE increases enjoyment, but that the type of mediation is not necessarily important.

An further indication of the success of our VE as a storytelling medium comes from user comments. Several users commented that they were able to connect with the VE experience on a personal level. This result should be tested more rigorously in future work. Additional possibilities for future work include increasing the characterization of agents. This would allow the user to identify more with them. Avatar representations for users could also be included, in order to facilitate more embodiment and allow the users to feel more active in the VE.

References

1. Anstey, J., Pape, D., Sandin, D.: Building a VR Narrative. In: Proceedings of SPIE Vol. 3957 Stereoscopic Displays and Virtual Reality Systems VII. 2000, San Jose, California. Available: "http://www.evl.uic.edu/pape/papers/narrative.spie00/spie00.pdf".
2. Brooks, K.M.: Do story agents use rocking chairs? In: ACM Multimedia 96, 1996, pages 317-328.
3. Clarke, A., Mitchell, G.: Film and the Development of Interactive Narrative. In: Balet, O., Subsol, G., Torguet, P. (Eds.): Virtual Storytelling: Using Virtual Reality Technologies for Storytelling. Springer-Verlag, Berlin, 2001, pages 81-89.
4. Dinh, H.Q., Walker, N., Hodges, L.: Evaluating the importance of multi-sensory input on memory and the sense of presence in virtual environments. In: Proceedings of the IEEE Virtual Reality 1999 Conference, March 1999, pages 222-228.
5. Genesis3D Games Engine: Online document, "http://www.gen3d.de/indexh.html". Accessed: 10 April 2002.
6. Igroup: Survey on experiences in virtual worlds. Online HTML document, 4 May 2000, "http://www.igroup.org/". Accessed: May 2002.
7. Jackson, C., Lalioti, V.: Virtual Cultural Identities. Online HTML document, "citeseer.nj.nec.com/338118.html". Accessed May 2002.
8. Johnson, A., Leigh, J., Carter, B., Sosnoski, J., Jones, S.: Virtual Harlem. In: IEEE Computer Graphics and Applications 22(5), 2002, pages 61-67.
9. Lombard, M., Ditton, T.: At the heart of it all: The concept of presence. Journal of Computer-Mediated Communication, 3(2), 1997.

10. Murphy, D., Pitt, I.: Spatial Sound Enhancing Virtual Story Telling. In: Balet, O., Subsol, G., Torguet, P. (Eds.): Virtual Storytelling: Using Virtual Reality Technologies for Storytelling. Springer-Verlag, Berlin, 2001, pages 20-29.

11. Nunez, D., Blake, E.H.: Cognitive Presence As A Unified Concept Of Virtual Reality Effectiveness. In: AMC Afrigraph 2001: 1st International Conference on Computer Graphics, Virtual Reality and Visualization in Africa, 2001, pages 115-118.

12. Pausch, R., Snoddy, J., Taylor, R., Watson, S., Haseltine, E.: Disney's Aladdin: first steps toward storytelling in virtual reality. In: SIGGRAPH '96, 1996, pages 193-203.

13. Roussou, M.: The interplay between form, story and history: The use of narrative in cultural and educational VR. In: Balet, O., Subsol, G., Torguet, P. (Eds.): Virtual Storytelling: Using Virtual Reality Technologies for Storytelling. Springer-Verlag, Berlin, 2001, pages 181-190.

14. Schubert, T.W., Friedmann, F., Regenbrecht, H.T.: Decomposing the sense of presence: Factor analytic insights. Presented at the 2nd International Workshop on Presence, University of Essex, April 1999.

15. Schuemie, M.J., van der Straaten, P., Krijn, M., van der Mast, C.: Research on presence in virtual reality: A survey. In: CyberPsychology Behaviour, 4(2), 2001, pages 183-201.

16. Smith, A., Malherbe, C., Guenther, M., Berens, P.: The bushmen of southern Africa: A foraging society in transition. David Philip Publishers, Claremont, South Africa, 2000.

17. Szilas, N.: Interactive drama on computer: beyond linear narrative. In: Narrative Intelligence: Papers from the 1999 Fall Symposium, AAAI Press, 1999, pages 150-156.

18. Witmer, B.G., Singer, M.J.: Measuring presence in virtual environments: A presence questionnaire. In: Presence, 7(3), June 1998, pages 225-240.

Context Design and Cinematic Mediation in *Cuthbert Hall* Virtual Environment

Stanislav Roudavski and François Penz

Digital Studios for Research in Design, Visualisation and Communication,
University of Cambridge, Department of Architecture,
1 Bene't Place, Lensfield Road, Cambridge CB2 1EL, UK
stanislav.roudavski@cumis.cam.ac.uk

Abstract. This poster briefly describes the motivations behind the architectural decisions taken in the design of *Cuthbert Hall* virtual college and gives an example that demonstrates how cinematic mediation techniques can contribute towards dramatized interpretation of the environment.

1 Design Decisions

This poster outlines practical decisions that were taken in the design of *Cuthbert Hall* navigable interactive real-time 3D virtual environment (RT 3D VE). The environment under consideration was built as one part of the *Haven* research project that investigates how VEs can be made more meaningful, dramatic and expressive. Architecture, event-structure and mediation were designed together with the balance between interactive richness and authorial control in mind.

The spatial-structure design relates to the real-world architecture. This makes the users utilize their knowledge of places and gives the authors the capability to relate to this knowledge in order to suggest cultural, historical and functional dynamics of VEs with complex relationships and motivations. The impression of internal coherence encourages the users to explore the VE and make meaningful inferences from the unique dramatic events they encounter.

The design of *Cuthbert Hall* borrows from the layout of traditional Cambridge/ Oxford colleges that were originally built as monasteries. The buildings are arranged around an enclosed courtyard with controlled access. The contrast and rhythm of building-masses and openings around the courtyard helps orientation, separates the environment into distinct regions and provides visual interest. The main gate is the only point of entry. It serves as a clear threshold between inside and outside, the college and the city. To reinforce the compositional weight of the courtyard, the environment is arranged in a circular pattern. This pattern is apparent in all parts of the environment and the users are always (even if not consciously) oriented to its geometric and symbolic centre. Throughout the VE, the visual depth is emphasized using back-, middle- and fore-ground visual layers that are formed by colonnades, galleries, elevated paths or rows of trees. Such layers support multiple planes of movement and action as well as sophisticated camera-blocking. Distances, openings and obstacles are arranged to regulate the rhythm of movement.

O. Balet et al. (Eds.): ICVS 2003, LNCS 2897, pp. 112–115, 2003.
© Springer-Verlag Berlin Heidelberg 2003

The VE is divided into several **regions.** Each region has a distinct spatial and architectural character and a contrasting or complimentary relationship to the other regions. Their identity is designed to be as recognizable and memorable as possible. These identities are further emphasized by mediation techniques. The architectural elements of each region are arranged into spatial structures that provide direction to gaze and movement, set scale and perspective and create foci of attention. The objects are subdivided in order to avoid large planar polygonal surfaces and achieve the effect of sculpted form that is easily articulated by light. To help orientation and tie the layout with meaningful relationships, archetypal **landmarks** (*Gate, Dining Hall Steeple, Living Quarters Tower, Chapel*) with distinctive shapes, functions and histories (delivered through dramatic events) are strategically placed in the environment so that a unique visual combination of them is always available to the visitor. The environment is subdivided and held together by a system of **edges.** For example, low parapets and ditches separate the square from the college and guide the user towards the gate while a row of city-houses, the river and the garden fence confine movement and redirect the visual access. To ease navigation and provide visual interest, **paths** are built to create asymmetries along and across their primary directions.

The VE is presented via continuous cinematic mediation: no explicit interface-layer exists. The mediation layer is organized in a three-part Spatial Mediation Framework [1] that features *User Driven*, *Author Defined* and *Spatially Organized* constellations. The poster presents one example, the *Novice/Welcome* pre-scripted place-event sequence.

2   Example: *Novice/Welcome* Sequence

This sequence begins in the street, not far away from the college gate. The curved street has two distinct sides: the city and the college. This is apparent in the layout and suggests inequality. The street is connected to the gate by a prolonged square that invites visitors to come in, provides views towards the gate from the street and from the gate to the terraced houses of the city. The entrance to the college is dominant in the field of view of an approaching visitor and the vista behind shows the contrast between the city and college architectures. The square creates a stage for the events to happen and be observed, participate in or witness. The two corners at the connection of the square to the street have different articulation. On one side, a high tower indicates a junction. On another, a gallery warps around the corner providing views towards the square and creating multiple visual planes that reinforce the perspective and direct the gaze and the traffic towards the gate.

A two-part event-sequence is associated with the entrance to the college. The events momentarily disrupt the interactive flow in order to signify and dramatize the moment of arrival.

This sequence serves to signify the transition from outside to inside by articulating the socially significant zones around the entrance and associating the Gate with a memorable event and the porter-character. The boundary of the enclosure is identified, the identity of the user is queried in front of the entrance, the right of entry is granted and the user is converted from a stranger to a visitor. A spatial event acquires prominence in the user's mental image and contributes towards the general dark and mysterious atmosphere.

Fig. 1. *Novice* Event. (Row 1): The user approaches the *Gate* and triggers the cinematic prescripted place-event. The loud sounds of the street become subdued. The camera enters first: a counter-shot directs the user's attention to the street behind demonstrating the contrast. (Row 2): The porter appears. The framing of the shots is tight to retain suspense and delay the exposition of the identity of the approaching non-player character or show the insides of the college. (Row 3): The camera shows the reaction of the user avatar as the porter curtly enquires about the reasons for the user's late arrival. Cinematic mediation reveals that the gate is guarded and the entry can only be granted to certain people. The college behind adheres to the rules the newcomers are expected to comply with. (Row 4): The camera shows how the porter retires and with a counter-shot prepares the user to the return of interactive control.

3   Conclusion

The *Cuthbert Hall* VE, developed (with Michael Nitsche, supported by Funatics and Renderware) as a part of the *Haven* practice-based research project, implements mediation devices designed in conjunction with spatial context. The presented example demonstrates how context design and cinematic mediation can inform and guide the user, increase narrative potential, dramatize and assign meaning.

Fig. 2. *Welcome* Event. (Row 1): The user, feeling startled and somewhat unwelcome, moves further in when the second part of the sequence is triggered on the boundary of the inner courtyard. (Row 2): The camera moves up providing an establishing shot of the college and contrasting the lonely figure of the visitor to the vast dark and empty courtyard. The event ends and the user can resume free exploration.

References

1. Nitsche, M., Roudavski, S., Penz, F., Thomas, M.: Drama and Context in Real-Time Virtual Environments: Use of Pre-Scripted Events as a Part of an Interactive Spatial Mediation Framework. In: S.Goebel, N.Braun, U.Spierling, J.Dechau, H.Diener (eds.) TIDSE '03 Technologies for Interactive Digital Storytelling and Entertainment,: Fraunhofer IRB Verlag,, Stuttgart (2003) 296-310

Group Interaction
and VR Storytelling in Museums

Raúl Cid

Barco Simulation Products
Noordlaan 5, B-8520 Kuurne, Belgium
Raul.Cid@Barco.com

Abstract. This paper summarizes the design rationale of the Magic-ICE Table[1] as an example of a VR system that promotes group interaction and open-ended interactivity in informal learning settings.

1 A View of Informal Education

Informal education in museums could be seen as narrative, human encounter, and unpredicted action. As a narrative endeavor, informal education does not only include the museums storytelling activity but also the stories that visitors construct, and the tension between the authority of the museum and the role of an inquisitive audience [1], [2]. As human encounter, informal education focuses on the responsibility assumed by museum visitors towards one another. Visitors not only relate to the exhibition, but also to other human beings. In some cases, the exhibit may propitiate not only proximity in space, or kinship, but also proximity to the extent that one visitor becomes subject [3] to another. As unpredicted action, informal education strives to preserve the novelty within every visitor. Action means in this context to take an initiative and put something in motion. The fact that museum visitors are capable of action means that one should expect from them the unexpected [4]. How to encourage action and cope with the improbable depends on the type of museum. In some cases, a well-designed and well-staffed VR system may help meet this challenge.

This view of informal education advocates group interaction and open-ended interactivity as desirable conditions for a valuable museum experience. Group interaction is understood here as the processes of human exchange and unpredicted action described, not as the type of interaction that takes place, for example, in a multi-player computer game; and by open-ended interactivity I mean the type of system process and system-user interaction that favor problem solving and design activities, whose results are not fixed a priori by the system.

---

[1] The Magic ICE Table is a prototype development carried out by Barco N. V. in Kortrijk, Belgium, Alterface Computer Systems in Louvain La Neuve, Belgium, and Industrion, Museum of Technology in Kerdrade, The Netherlands, under the auspices of the Barco Innovation Partner Program. The author acknowledges the contributions of all people involved, particularly fruitul discussions with Gene Bertrand, Xavier Marichal and Alok Nandi.

O. Balet et al. (Eds.): ICVS 2003, LNCS 2897, pp. 116–119, 2003.
© Springer-Verlag Berlin Heidelberg 2003

2 The VR Layer

Inspired in the previous considerations, this section describes the different layers of a museum exhibit, making special reference to the VR layer. As we shall see all layers would contribute to make the VR layer possible. In this way, the description would come across as an integral set of principles applicable to exhibit design in general.

(1) The object layer is the main narrative thread of the exhibition; it generally consists of an icon representative of the central theme, plus a gallery of related objects located in peripheral displays. The medien.welten exhibition recently inaugurated at the Tech nisches Museum Wien in Austria[2], for example, deals with information technology in times of change and presents the historic development of two major processes: storage and transmission of information. The curator used artifacts representative of the two historic processes to create two parallel galleries —one on each side of the exhibit space, and made them converge into a central display showing that with the advent of the digital era the two processes merged into one. This is a good example of common procedures chosen by curators to arrange the object layer in an exhibition space. The idea is that a high-level reading of the message be possible at this point.

(2) The synthetic layer takes visitors through artistic imagery appealing mainly to the senses and to the emotions. In the artistic installation Smoke and Mirrors located in the Reuben H. Fleet Museum in San Diego, USA, the artist[3] created an electronic collage of imagery about cigarette smoking, using vintage advertisement images as well as related hospital imagery. The visitor faces the audiovisual collage traveling electronically through a maze of mirrors, and grasping subconsciously the emotional charge of the message. The synthetic layer is useful on a second reading of the message.

(3) The analytic layer allows visitors to think about the problems at hand using an individualized pace and style. A typical implementation of this layer is through touch screen computers or push-button interactive stations that allow users to grab information, acquire certain skills, understand processes or simply think about a controversy or an event. Museums, particularly interactive museums, are full of such devices. This layer allows visitors to deconstruct the story in its basic elements, juggle around with them and understand the logic of the processes involved.

(4) The VR layer immerses visitors in collective problem solving promoting horizontal exchange and negotiation of meanings and solutions. This is the layer in which the VR system is located and can be pictured as a small stadium accommodating 20 to 30 people participating at different levels. At the core of this layer, visitors would live through the excitement, human sharing, flow and focus that occur in a real stadium. Additionally, visitors would have full command in creating the objects and the dynamics that shape the stadium arena. So in the end, visitors would not only have listened to the museum stories but have also created and performed their own scripts. This layer is central to the exhibit design and there are few museums currently experimenting with it.

---

[2] Cf. www.medien.welten.at for a visual description of this exhibit or contact Otmar Moritsch, Curator at the Technisches Museum Wien.

[3] Cf. http://www-crca.ucsd.edu/ sheldon/sm/index.html for a description of this installation by its creator Sheldon Brown.

(5) And finally, the reflective layer that creates the necessary context for introspection, sharing and, possibly, further action and return visit.

All layers help build the story through different visitor channels. Rather than seeing the layers apart from each other as most museums do, I propose to see them always together integrated in a Museum Experience Cycle (MEC). In this sense, the VR layer would be part of a concerted effort to build a narrative. The success of the VR layer depends on the visitors integral use of all layers.

The main problems in the VR layer have to do with the dynamics that takes place in the VR arena. How to insure that the museums narrative would come across, and how to direct the visitors activity towards useful results. If we take a purely interactive game-like route, we will leave the museums narration practically out of the picture since traditional games present the world through the eyes of the players, privileging continuity of time, space and action [5]. If, on the contrary, we think of a more filmic approach in which we are allowed to use all the resources available for the mise en scene, shots, editing and the like, we would be giving a strong voice to the museums narration, but leave the visitors in a passive role. One possible solution consists of (1) using large, multiple screens and (2) separating the group of visitors in different tiers. Large, multiple screens, besides providing immersion, allow the traditional player point of view at the same time than cuts in time, space and action. Separating visitors in tiers, on the other hand, opens the possibility of having different participant roles that can be assigned to different screens. These considerations gave origin to the Magic-ICE table system.

3   The Magic-ICE Table System

The system consists of (a) a display structure, (b) a theater-like layout, (c) a control room, (d) an interactive system, and (e) story contents. The display system includes a conical screen plus 3 projectors capable of displaying a seamless picture with geometry distortion to fit the curved screen, and a projection table using one additional projector and a mirror. The theater-like layout features a seat arrangement for 20 people, plus a scenario to accommodate in addition 6 to 10 people around the table. The computer control room is located behind the seats and is spacious enough to accommodate a PC cluster rack, a desk, several monitors, as well as a control system for the show. The interactive system includes a real-time engine plus a set of wireless wands for the public to participate, and a series of objects on the projection table. The contents consists of pre-rendered video streams plus a graphic database for real-time rendered contents. The full system fits well within a footprint of 150 m2, with a minimum height of 4.60 m.

Visitors come into this room in groups of twenty to thirty people after having experienced other layers through the Museum Experience Cycle. The system would have tracked through smart cards the whereabouts of each participant in the previous layers, the time spent in different stations and the reactions to the different issues introduced. Based on this information, the system would divide the public into (a) actors, (b) supporters, and (c) voters. People would engage in the activity directed by an animator who is part of the museum staff.

In the case of Industrion, the Science Museum at Kerkrade NL, the topic chosen was the historic importance of the River Maas in the development of the region. The message of the exhibition was twofold: (1) decisions made at the present time can affect future generations, and (2) nature and technology should be analyzed as a unit. The activity at the Magic-ICE table arena was only one step in the museum experience cycle of the exhibition.

The Magic-ICE table would project the natural landscape of the riverbed on its tabletop using a birds eye perspective. Laying on the tabletop there would be an assortment of objects representing different technologies aimed at the solution of human needs: factories, river dams, communities, water supply infrastructures, canal systems. The ICE table would react to the position and value of these objects by changing the projected landscape according to the expected effects of technology on nature. Moreover, at the push of a button, the ICE table would project in time the accumulated effects of a particular array of objects, and show the results graphically on the landscape. Each member of the group around the table would assume a role that opposes his/her personal position expressed throughout the exhibition. There would be six active roles: ecological, economical, political, social, technical, and industrial. The four other people at the table would have supporting roles: fact finder, time traveler, navigator and monitor.

Visitors sitting in the theater would have the role of voters in certain decisions, and would act as a cheering crowd as well. The front screen would be used for presentations in the beginning and in the end of the show; and, in the middle, the curved screen would become three screens showing images that contribute to the storytelling activity. One screen would display the story from the point of view of the museum showing the appropriate video streams at the right moment. Another screen would support the activities at the table using a game-like approach. And the third screen would be a general feedback screen showing mostly facts and data.

References

1. Roberts, L.: From Knowledge to Narrative. Smithsonian Institution Press, Washington (1997)
2. Laurel, B.: Computers as Theater. Addison Wesley, New York (1997)
3. Lévinas, E.: Éthique Et Infini. Librairie Arthème Fayard, Paris (1982)
4. Arendt, H.: The Human Condition. University of Chicago Press, Chicago (1958)
5. Clark, A. and Mitchell, G.: Film and the development of interactive narrative. In Balet. O., Subsol, G., Torguet, P. (eds): Virtual Story Telling. International Conference ICVS 2001. Springer-Verlag, Berlin Heilderberg New York (2001)

Beyond Human, Avatar as Multimedia Expression

Ron Broglio[1] and Stephen Guynup[2]

[1] School of Literature, Communication & Culture, Georgia Institute of Technology,
rbroglio@earthlink.net
[2] Department of Communications, Georgia State University,
jouslg@langate.gsu.edu

Abstract. The Avatar, the representation of the user in three-dimensional chat environments, serves as a visual identifier for the user and through gestures/ costumes acts as a means of expression for the user. The Avatar also serves as a point through which the user receives information and manipulates the environment. Abstracted into programming terminology, the Avatar is not a humanoid representation endowed with gestural expression, but a four dimensional point (3D & time) for data exchange. Accepting this abstraction of the Avatar opens the door to a world of simple, yet previously unthinkable, possibilities for expressive communication.

1 Limitations and Affordances

Viewing the Avatar as a four-dimensional point for data exchange and focusing on the needs of communication within a virtual space, we apply the limitations and affordances of screen-based, mouse-driven environments. In this context, the subtle and fluid realm of human expression translates very poorly into the sliding x, y values of a mouse and/or a combination of pressed keyboard keys. In fact, the mouse and keyboard are already overtaxed by taking on the interactive and navigational roles of hand and foot and within virtual space. This overtaxing suggests a need to move away from reality-based humanoid expression and to begin utilizing the affordances of the media. Users exist within a computer-generated space, a space in which, as Ivan Sutherland wrote in 1965, the rules of reality need not apply.

The multimedia presentation is the conventional method for delivering information to an assembled audience. Simple and direct, this process can be mapped onto the Avatar. The performer's/teacher's Avatar can communicate by morphing into a series of images, objects and environment. This permits great deal of information to be presented and appraised with minimal effort on behalf of the presenter/teacher and viewers. Although the production of a multimedia presentation can be very complex, its delivery requires only a series of mouse clicks. Our multimedia methodology builds from conventional computer presentations in the same way that conventional computer presentations build from older photographic slideshows. The new innovation is that we combine the projection screen with the presenters' Avatar. Also in step with real world precedents, the Avatar as multimedia expression methodology can be applied to online genres such as music, theatre, poetry, and perhaps most directly – distance learning.

O. Balet et al. (Eds.): ICVS 2003, LNCS 2897, pp. 120–123, 2003.
© Springer-Verlag Berlin Heidelberg 2003

Preliminary surveys of participants have been very positive. Because presentations to viewers can be as simple as a slide show, new viewers quickly adapt and accept the multimedia methodology. Educating the viewer to participate in more complex and unfamiliar situations is done progressively within an individual presentation or in subsequent presentations. Examining the success of viewer interaction, the following benefits of the Avatar as multimedia expression methodology emerge:

- Unwieldy interactive/navigational processes are broken into focused operations.
- Maximum utilization of screen real estate.
- Performer/Teacher controls environment through graphically dominant action.
- Performer/Teacher is intuitively responsible for new content appearing on screen.
- The above benefits provide a stable mechanism to guide the social dynamic.

2 Applications in Education and Music

Bespace (2003). A synchronous distance-learning project at Georgia Tech and Georgia State University, Bespace utilizes the Avatar as multimedia expression methodology to deliver an in depth, hour-long lecture educational lecture on factors and forces that influenced Charles Darwin. The project maintains the look and feel of realistic space. The desire was to promote the sense of an actual classroom, with fellow students and a live human teacher and then blend that sense with the immersive and interactive educational properties of virtual space. To allow the students to focus on learning, not the facilitation of learning, we route knowledge directly in front of them through the teacher's Avatar.

Fig. 1–4. Bespace, transformation of teacher into title http://bespace.lcc.gatech.edu

Fig. 5–8. Bespace, selected screen captures http://bespace.lcc.gatech.edu

Memory Plains Returning (2003). This musical performance project highlights the creative expanse of the multimedia expression methodology. A ghost-like audience is situated within three large abstract musical Avatars. Space itself is devoid of architecture; the only structures are the three performers. The collaborative movement, audio and morphing of the performers creates a uniquely dynamic environment that provides a beautiful, conceptually rich space that redefines the role of the body. In the blunt terms of popular culture, MTV has entered the Matrix.

Fig. 9–11. Screen Captures - Memory Plains Returning http://www.yamanakanash.net/

3   In the Larger Context

During the last decade, stories such as Waiting for Godot and Henry IV have been enacted online. With humanoid Avatars, these performances have sought to mirror real world performances. Even the Meet Factory's very creative Conversations with Angels (1996) still represents a "lateral" expansion of reality - that is to say, that if one had actors in costume, a stage set and a WWI Fokker Triplane they could perform the work. Pushing the boundaries is PlaceHolder (1994). It allowed the users to shape shift into "Critters" by touching animal totems. In contrast to our use of shape shifting, this process is for the benefit of the user and not applied to the user's ability of outward expression. The divide of inward and outward expression also separates us from Michael Heim's assertion of the Avatar as a "networked cursor" and the "mind of the human subject who is navigating information". While Heim's argument concerns data exchanges through the Avatar, the direction he stresses is inward, that the Avatar gathers information. The broader idea of data exchange to *and* from the Avatar is not covered. To interpret the concept of Avatar as multimedia expression, Janet Murray, looks not to virtual media, but to "Duck Amuck", a Warner Brothers cartoon. The cartoon pits a Bugs Bunny as animator against his animation, Daffy Duck. Daffy is constantly being redrawn in new and unsettling ways. His body morphs, dissolves and is distorted against him, The multimedia Avatar, like Daffy's body, utilitizes the affordances of virtual space for the purpose of telling a story.

Understanding why the multimedia presentation methodology may not be acceptable for many virtual narratives lies in Murray's statement that "Duck Amuck … emphasizes the border, celebrates the enchantment and tests the durability of the illusion." Most virtual stories immerse the user in a fantasy world and seek to maintain that illusion. The concept presented in this paper crosses the border and breaks this illusion. Users are forced to acknowledge that they exist in a computer-generated space when its affordances are "celebrated". Duck Amuck solves this problem by providing a metaphor in the construct of Bugs Bunny as animator and provides the viewer a model for understanding the story. This leaves us with two choices: to provide the viewer with a suitable metaphor –such as the character is an animator, genie, alien; or to look to genres that allow the multimedia nature of virtual space to be accepted as real - education, music, poetry and generic chat spaces.

The goal is to empower human interaction, not replace or mirror it. The process is simply one of adapting the fundamentals of human expression into a new medium, into a computer-generated environment. The choice of Charles Darwin in the education prototype was no accident. The evolution of the human form in a computer-generated environment is now beginning. The rules of natural selection have become digital.

References

1. Carlson, K., & Guynup, S. (2000). Avatar as Content Delivery Platform. Future Generation Computer Systems, 65-71.
2. Heim, M. Mots Pluriels. (2001, October).
   http://www.arts.uwa.edu.au/MotsPluriels/MP.html
3. Murray, J. (1997). Hamlet on the Holodeck. Cambridge: The MIT Press.
4. Nash, A. Memory Plains Returning. (2003, August).
   http://www.yamanakanash.net/3dmusic/mpr_live/artist_report/report_index.html
5. Salomon, Gavriel "Technology and Pedagogy: Why Don't We See the Promised Revolution?", Educational Technology Mar-Apr 02, 71-75
6. Shotsberger, Paul G. "The Human Touch: Synchronous Communication in Web-Based Learning" Educational Technology Jan-Feb 00, 53-56
7. Strickland, L. B., & Tow, R. (1994, May). Placeholder: Landscape and Narrative in Virtual Environments. Computer Graphics, 28(2), 118-126.
8. Sutherland, I. E. (1965). The Ultimate Display. New York: Proceedings of IFIPS Congress. (Vol. 2, pp. 506-508)
9. Winn, William and Jackson, Randy "Fourteen Propositions About Educational Uses of Virtual Reality", Educational Technology July-Aug 99, 5-1

Virtual Characters

Building Virtual Actors Who Can Really Act

Ken Perlin

NYU Media Research Lab., Department of Computer Science, New York University
719 Broadway, 12ᵗʰ Floor, New York, NY 10003
perlin@nyu.edu

Abstract. When we think of "acting" in computer games, we tend to use a lower standard than the way we think of acting in live action films or theatre. Why is acting in computer games so bad? This is an important question because we will only be able to develop compute games into a more psychologically mature narrative medium when we can imbue them with actors that audiences can believe in. In this paper we present an approach to virtual actors in games that we believe will make it easier for audiences to willingly suspend their disbelief.

1 Introduction

The field of computer graphics has through the years gradually emerged from something with a rigid machine-like aesthetic, driven by technical limitations, to one with a more fluid and flexible aesthetic. For example, the visual look of early computer graphics appeared highly machine-like, reflecting the technology's original roots in Computer Aided Design.

Today a similar situation pertains to how characters move in real-time graphics applications, such as computer games. Character motion generally consists of canned movements, which have been either key-frame animated, or else motion-captured from human performance.

A deficiency of these approaches is that to an audience it is very obvious when a character is using canned movements, since the same exact movements will appear again and again. The result is a loss of the "willing suspension of disbelief" that would allow an audience to easily pretend that an actor is experiencing a given inner psychological state.

We describe an alternate procedural approach to real-time virtual actor movement which proceeds "from the inside out." In our approach, actor movement and posture is always informed by an inner psychological state. Rather than being animated by canned movements, the actor always appears to be psychologically present; all movements convey the actor's continually varying mixture of moods and goals.

2 History

In the early days of computer graphics, even the visual look of things seemed highly artificial. For example, TRON created a strong sense of an immersive visual world. Yet because of technology limitations, everything in the world of TRON looked cold and machine-like.

O. Balet et al. (Eds.): ICVS 2003, LNCS 2897, pp. 127–134, 2003.
© Springer-Verlag Berlin Heidelberg 2003

In other word, technical limitations drove the aesthetics of the content. Shortly after the release of TRON, the author introduced the ideas of procedural noise and the use of a procedural shading language [1]. This approach allowed programmer/designers to write simple programs, now called "shaders," which would run at each visible point of a computer graphic object. Below we can see several different procedural shaders applied to different portions of a sphere.

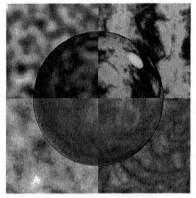

This approach allowed designers to incorporate the sort of controlled randomness we associate with natural surfaces and materials, as in the marble vase below.

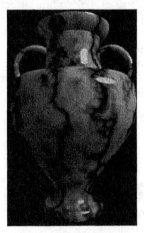

Similarly, it is possible to create a "texture" of intentional movement. Since the late 1980's we have been exploring this approach to human movement that conveys personality. Before describing this work, it is important to examine the question of *agency*.

2.1 Where Is the Agency?

A central question in dealing with interactive characters is the question of where *agency* is situated. In other words, who has the power to decide what happens next? Is this decision made by the character in the narrative, or by the observer of the narrative? In a more traditional linear story form, such as a novel or cinematic film, the observer has little or no power to change the course of events. In a trivial sense, the reader of a novel can skip around or peek at the ending, and the viewer of a film can walk out or enter in the middle, but the audience really has not ability to effect the choices made by characters in the story, within the reality presented by that story.

The structure below represents this dichotomy:

An interesting example is given by Harry Potter and Lara Croft. Harry Potter in the book (and to a lesser extent in the film) is made to go through a number of internal psychological decisions. In contrast, the Electronic Arts game is focused on solving puzzles. In the game, the character of Harry Potter himself is really an extremely well rendered game token; the character himself is not making decisions; the player is. Consequently the player of the game does not deeply care about the character.

There is an interesting contrast with the development of the character of Lara Croft from the game Tomb Raider. When Tomb Raider was just a game, Lara Croft herself was really just a game token. The user made all the decisions (run, jump, shoot). There was a backing story to the game, explaining who Lara Croft was *supposed* to be, but that strong-willed character was not what the player of the came encountered.

Then the movie came out, and for the first time people could finally meet this intelligent and strong-willed character about whom they had only read. But in this incarnation, it was impossible for people to interact with Lara Croft. Once brought to life, she became fixed and immutable.

Who do we bridge this gap? How do we create a character about whom we care, and yet with whom we can interact in psychologically interesting ways? The key issue is believability. Note that this is not at all the same as realism. For example, the character of Bugs Bunny is quite believable, in the sense that we have a pretty good idea about his internal psychological makeup, his attitudes, what he would plausibly do when faced with a given new situation. Yet he is not at all realistic: were Bugs Bunny to walk in the door of your house, you would probably need to rethink your view of reality.

A key way to frame this issue is to ask what the character is doing when you are not there. For example, when we play Tomb Raider, we don't have a sense of what Lara Croft the game character would do while we are not playing. That is because we have not seen her make any choices; in the course of game play, we have made all the choices for her. Therefore we have not built a model in our heads of what she herself might do. We literally have no idea who she really is.

On the other hand, when we put down a Harry Potter book, we have a visceral sense of the continuing presence of Harry Potter, and his life at Hogwarts School. J.K. Rawling has given us a compelling illusion that her novel is merely a peek into a continuing world, in which many other adventures are happening just around the corner and slightly off the page. In some sense, we know who Harry Potter is.

The key difference, again, is that Lara Croft in the game Tomb Raider has no agency, where has Harry Potter in one of Rawling's novels has complete agency. So the creation of psychologically compelling interactive narrative must solve the following puzzle: How do we create characters who have *intermediate* agency? In other words, characters who can be somewhat responsible for their own actions, but about whom we can also be somewhat responsible?

A limited illusion of this is neatly conveyed by the characters in the game The SIMS, designed by Will Wright. The major limitation of the "actors" in The SIMS is that all of their movement consists of predesigned sequences of linear animation. For example, if a young mother in The SIMS is playing with her baby, and the player tells her to feed the baby, she will respond by putting down the baby, thereby ending the "playing with baby" animation. Then she will pick the baby up again to begin the "feeding baby" animation. While the larger story is indeed being conveyed, the movement itself is highly unbelievable. The player does not end up feeling as though the mother character has an inner life or sense of motivation. Instead, the mother character is positioned in the player's mind as a game token embodied as a moving doll figure, switching unthinkingly from one discrete state to another.

We have done a number of experiments in the last few years to create characters that can have a more layered set of behaviors. Let us go back to the notion of *procedural texture*, but apply it to human movement rather than to visual appearance. Intentional movements (walking, reaching, etc.) can be combined and layered with procedurally generated pseudo-random movements that signify continuing presence, such as weight shifting and blinking,

This was the basis for the Improv project at NYU [2]. Below are shown a few characters in that system.

The principles underlying the behavior of these characters were: Layered behavior Subsumption architecture Good "fuzzy" authoring language Controlled randomness.

Much of this work was turned into a line of commercial products by **Improv Technologies** for non-linear animation. They were designed to be complementary to the standard animation tools, such as Alias Maya, 3D Studio Max, etc.

Some more recent experiments conducted by the author include studies of interactive dance, of facial animation, and of embodied actors that interact with each other while conveying mood, intention and personality. In particular, one experiment concerned analyzing and synthesizing facial affect. The questions asked here were as follows: What are the simplest components that will convey effective and believable human facial affect? How are these components effectively combined to make a language? What would be the simplest such language that would still be effective?

We found that a small number of degrees of facial freedom could be combined to make a large emotive space of facial expressions. In a sense, simple expressions such as "mouth open", "eyes wide", "sneer", etc., can be thought of as notes on a kind of emotional instrument. More complex facial expressions are created by playing combinations of these notes together, to create chords, or even arpeggiated chords.

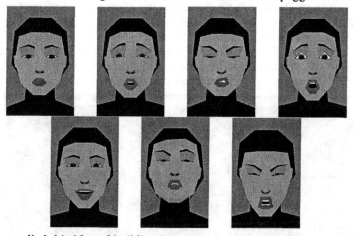

We also applied this idea of building "emotional chords" from simpler emotive components to the synthesis of fully embodied emotionally expressive humanoid actors. We followed the following basic principles to allow an embodied actor to convey personality. Rather than simply stringing together linear animations, we create *activity* components (which serve the same approximate function as "verbs"), as well as *affect* components (which serve the same approximate function as "adverbs"). The key to making this approach effective is to have a run-time architecture in which a simulated actor is always running. The movements and posture of the actor are continually adjusting to reflect changes in a maintained inner "mood state".

At a high level of abstraction, an actor performs the following tasks in succession in order to create each individual frame of the interactive animation: First the actor determines his global position and the direction he needs to be heading in the scene. This decision is generally made to conform with the general blocking of the scene, resulting from a negotiation between the actors in the scene and a director agent.

Then the actor figures out the approximate joint angles of the limbs his body should assume (elbow, shoulder, spine, etc), so as to convey the particular mood and action he is trying to convey. For example, various emotional signifiers can be conveyed by such postural attributes as shoulders thrust back, elbows kept out or in, back

curved or straight, head or hips tilted. At this stage, the actor also figures out an optimal weight shift between his two feet.

Next he determines where he should ideally place his "contact parts": those parts of
his body that need to be in contact with the world. Most of the time these are hands
and feet. Then he uses the above info to compute what all his joint angles should be.
This process will generally result in the proper bodily attitude, but will not place his
contact parts in the proper place.

Finally, he does a simple inverse kinematics computation for his contact parts, so
that hands, feet, etc., touch or grip the external objects that they need to contact. The
inverse kinematics needs to be the very last step because contact constraints are
"hard" constraints which must be maintained exactly.

The interesting part of the above is the process of maintaining bodily affect. This is
handled through a number of competing controller processes, each of which is jockey-
ing to try to maintain some constraint (shoulders back, spine twisted halfway, etc.).
These attitude signifiers continually shift in importance as the actor varies his mood
and focus of attention. Because these constraints are always in competition with each
other, at any moment in time they will settle into an optimal negotiated configuration
that reflects the actor's internal process at that moment.

Below is a sequence of images from a simple rendering of an interactive scene
played by two of these actors. Note how the body language of each actor shifts from
moment to moment, to convey what that actor is emotionally expressing.

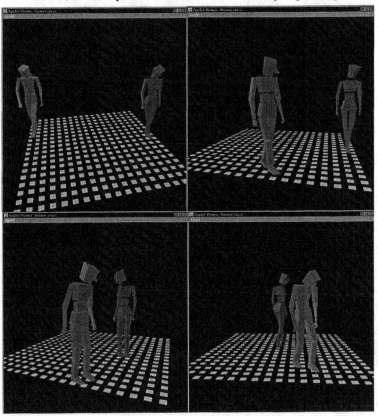

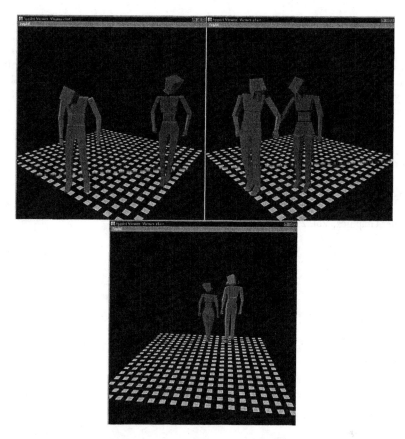

This style of actor can change the nature of how interactive narratives are structured. It becomes much more important to create to think of the actor's inner process when creating the narrative, then it would be in the typical computer games of today. Even simple operations such as reaching for an object or turning to look at another actor can become infused with meaning, since the actor is constantly making little adjustments in pose and body language to "sell" an interior emotion.

It becomes possible for the same action to convey such higher level ideas as being in love, encountering one's natural enemy, being in a sacred place, or even just having had a great breakfast.

One key to fully exploiting this approach for creating psychologically compelling interactive narratives will be to allow different kinds of authors to work in complementary layers. At the bottom layer is the enabling technology, which allows actors to convey believable personality and body language within a real-time game engine. Above this is the set of choices that defines a particular actor. The next layer up is the set of choices that defines a particular character.

We anticipate that there will be three distinct kinds of people who will be interacting with these actors. The first could be called professional actor builders. They will actually dig down and create the body language, particular pauses and hesitations, quirks of movement, that enable an actor to "sell" a character. Then there are power users, who do not go as deep as professional actor builders, but can develop new moves and routines, working in a higher abstraction layer. Finally, there will be most users, who will function as directors.

What comes next? We are currently getting the actor simulation to work within the *Unreal* engine. This will allow these actors to be used in Machinima movies. Ultimately, we would like to enable a genre that has some of the richness of The SIMS, but with much more expressivity and personality in its characters.

References

1. Perlin K., An Image Synthesizer, Computer Graphics; Vol. 19 No. 3. (1985)
2. Perlin K., Goldberg A., A System for Scripting Interactive Actors in Virtual Worlds, Computer Graphics; Vol. 29 No. 3.

The V-Man Project:
Toward Autonomous Virtual Characters

Eric Menou, Laurent Philippon, Stéphane Sanchez, Jérôme Duchon, and Olivier Balet

Virtual Reality Department, CS, Toulouse, France
Jerome.Duchon@c-s.fr

Abstract. There is no doubt that the seamless integration and simulation of highly realistic **autonomous virtual characters** within **3D real-time applications** are two important and challenging technological objectives for virtual storytelling. The V-Man project aims at developing a Virtual Character Authoring and Animation toolkit optimized for real-time applications. The V-Man system provides very innovative and promising features such as techniques for 3D scanning real people, character casting and dressing, character/object interaction with real-time physics, voice interaction as well as cutting-edge character animation algorithms including an advanced locomotion system, a path and task planning engine as well as adaptive generation of motions.

1 The V-Man Project

The V-Man project is a 3 year long European Commission funded Research & Technology Development project developed by a consortium of six partners[1] with the ambition to create an intuitive authoring and animation toolkit allowing non animation specialists to create, animate, control and interact, in real-time, with 3D virtual characters. These autonomous characters are intended for use in interactive systems such as games and virtual reality applications.

The V-Man system comes as an easy-to-use cross-platform Software Developer Kit including authoring tools and software modules that bring together state-of-the-art video game, research and industrial 3D technologies allowing realistic modelling and simulation of body motion.

In the remainder of this paper, we will introduce the different tools available in the V-Man system for acquiring, preparing and optimizing the required data (i.e. bodies, motions, etc.). Then, we will describe the main components of the V-Man SDK.

---

[1] CS (F), University of Glasgow (UK), MathEngine (UK), Sail Labs (A), CSTB (F), HD Thames (UK).

O. Balet et al. (Eds.): ICVS 2003, LNCS 2897, pp. 135–145, 2003.
© Springer-Verlag Berlin Heidelberg 2003

2 The Authoring Workflow

The V-Man authoring workflow can be entered at any level depending on the requirements of the application. An entire process would consist in scanning, skinning
and texturing body meshes and garments, modelling facial expressions, capturing
specific motions, defining high-level interactions, setting-up the characters' behaviour, and integrating the results into a virtual environment.

The different stages of the V-Man authoring workflow are presented in the following figure [Figure 1].

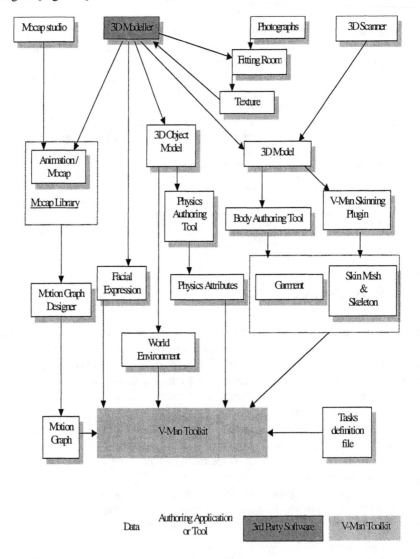

Fig. 1. The V-Man Authoring Workflow.

A typical use of the entire workflow can be divided up into the steps presented hereafter.

2.1 Body and Garment Geometry Design

Both body and garment geometries can be automatically acquired with a **3D scanner**. The method uses *stereo matching* to produce accurate 3D static photo-realistic models of real humans. The garment meshes are obtained by capturing a same individual in a specific position with and without clothing [19]. The V-Man system uses a reference mesh, modelled by a graphics designer, and makes it conform with the data measured on the real body [17]. Thus, the user can control the accuracy of the resulting mesh by adding more vertices, where precision is needed, in the reference mesh. It is also possible to import body and garment models that have been created with a third-party 3D modelling tool.

The **V-Man Fitting Room tool** [Figure 2] offers very intuitive means to texture body or garment models from **photographs** of real models. The user provides a flattened out mesh of the generic mesh and a set of photos that will be used as texture maps. Then he/she sets landmarks on the photos corresponding to predefined landmarks on the flattened out mesh. Finally, a warping procedure generates the corresponding texture maps that can be applied on the 3D mesh. A detailed description of this innovative technique can be found in [19].

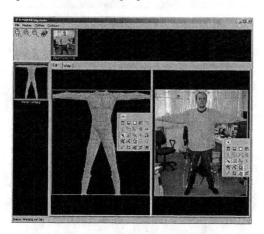

Fig. 2. The V-Man Fitting Room Tool.

2.2 Skin Mesh and Garment Setup

Once the 3D model of the body has been created, textured and dressed, it has to be attached to a skeleton. Both the skin and the garment models must be correlated by defining the influence weights of each bone for the surrounding vertices. The user can choose either to model the skeleton and paint the weights using the **V-Man Body**

Authoring Tool [Figure 3], or to use the 3DS Max **V-Man Skinning plug-in** [Figure 4] to let the system automatically compute this data.

While the former solution requires time and skill to achieve convincing results, the latter is fully automatic. However it also requires additional data that is, a set of 3D scanned postures of the model to compute the associated weights.

Another possibility is to use the Body Authoring tool to refine the data automatically computed by the 3DS Max Skinning plug-in. At the end of this process, a **Weighted Mesh File** is created to be exploited by the V-Man Character Animation module.

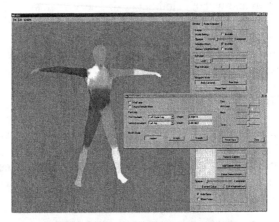

Fig. 3. The V-Man Body Authoring Tool.

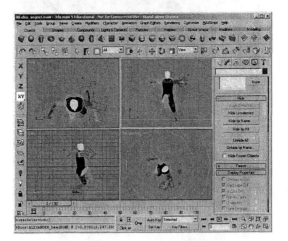

Fig. 4. The V-Man Skinning plug-in.

2.3 Definition of Dynamic Properties

The V-Man system uses an optional dynamics simulation toolkit (ex: Karma from Mathengine or Havok 2) to enhance the realism of the virtual character's interaction within the story world. Physical attributes are not only defined for the virtual humans but also for any of the props of the story, thus allowing the physically realistic animation of the characters and the objects they interact with. Therefore, the **V-Man Physics Authoring Tool** [Figure 5] is used to define physical properties such as the mass, the friction, the type of mechanical joints, etc.

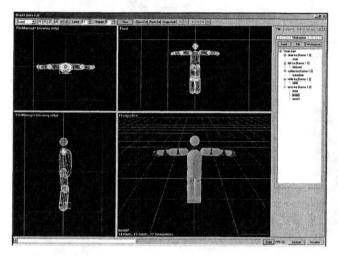

Fig. 5. The V-Man Physics Authoring Tool.

2.4 Motion Acquisition and Setup

V-Man comes with a comprehensive and extensible library of the most common movements. The user can choose to either create new motions by hand (using a 3D animation tool) or to use *motion captures* (mocaps). All the motions provided with the V-Man system have been acquired via a motion capture system, Ascension's **MotionStar,** one of the most popular tracking system using electromagnetic sensors. One important feature of our system is that new motions do not need to be acquired or modelled for a specific skeleton. Indeed, the V-Man Animation System will retarget [6] them automatically if needed.

Several motions of the library can be organized in the form of a **Motion Graph** [9] using the **Motion Graph Authoring Tool** [Figure 6]. This tool automatically calculates the most optimal transitions between the different motions loaded by the user. Then, the user can graphically create a graph defining the possible transition from one movement to another. Such a graph is required by the Animation System when a *Graph Behaviour* is assigned to a character.

3 The V-Man Toolkit

This chapter describes the main modules of the V-Man SDK which is divided into several C++ modules that can be used together or independently.

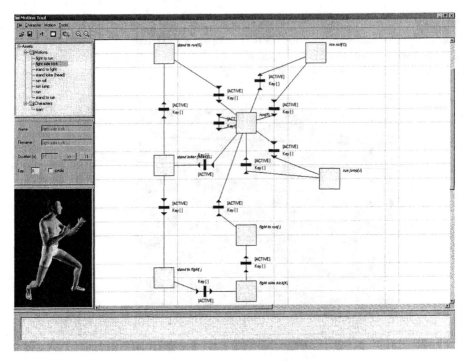

Fig. 6. The Motion Graph Authoring Tool.

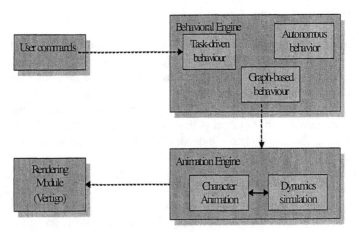

Fig. 7. The V-Man Toolkit modules.

3.1   Behavioural Module

The user can choose to assign a particular type of behaviour to a character in order to control it with high-level commands (ex: "go there", "have a seat"). That way, the **Behavioural module** drives the **Animation Module** and lets the user concentrate on the main aspects of the scenario rather than tuning the animation precisely. Three types of behaviour are provided with the V-Man system, but the user can extend the system by developing his own if needed.

- The **Task-driven behaviour** module uses a set of predetermined actions to control the virtual character. An action is the combination of a verb and a set of parameters, such as "Take the yellow ball on the red chair". All the actions are described in an XML file. They are created by hierarchically building up existing actions. Only basic actions have to be implemented into the V-Man system. A simple action can also be created from a mocap of the motion library. Then, higher level actions are defined using the V-Man scripting language.

- The **Graph-based behaviour** module exploits the Motion Graphs presented in section 2.4. This behaviour will typically be used for real-time applications where the user can control the avatar. A motion graph is composed of *action nodes* (related to mocaps) and *transitions*, a transition being defined as the duration between the current and the next action. The system keeps track of the current action node and identifies the actions that can be performed from there depending on the context (ex: physical constraints, environment). When the user provides a new order, the Task Behaviour module computes the shortest path (in terms of time) in the motion graph to reach the corresponding action node. This phase is achieved using a standard Dijkstra's algorithm. As a result, intermediate motions (ex: "wake-up" -> "stand-up"), between the current action node (ex: "sleeping" node) and the node corresponding to the action to perform (ex: "Jump!"), are passed to the Animation System.

- The **Autonomous behaviour** module is best suited for applications populated with autonomous agents. With such a behaviour, a virtual character will take decisions depending on its needs (hunger, thirst, etc.), its desires and goals (such as reaching a particular object or evacuating a building) and its environment. At the top of the system, a classifier [7] triggers high-level actions that are implemented as layered sub-actions combining several methods: scripts, finite state machines, expert systems and classifiers [12].

3.2 Character Animation Module

The **Animation System** is the core of the V-Man system. It is the only part of the toolkit that can not be disabled. It can be used independently or driven by one of the behavioural modules. Given a set of motions and keyframes and their timing, this module combines several distinct and well-established techniques to produce credible motions with seamless transitions.

Motion Synthesis: Actions can be played from one or several motion captures (mocaps). The *retargeting* module [6] [8] adapts, in real-time, a motion provided for the skeleton of a given morphology to that of a virtual actor of a different morphology, subject to some kinematic constraints. The system thus prevents foot skating, a common occurrence when a motion is applied to a different skeleton. The system first detects zero-crossing of the second derivative of the position curves for specific hot-spots on the character (e.g. location of the feet). Then, it uses an inverse kinematics solver to warp the motion at these frames thus enforcing the constraints detected in the original motion.

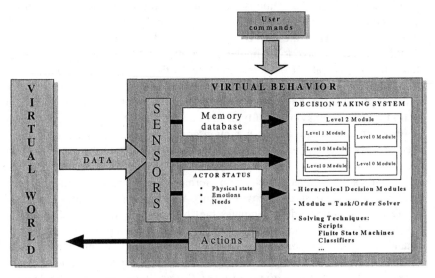

Fig. 8. The Autonomous Behavioural system.

Layered animation allows different animations to be applied to different parts of the body. For example, the user can choose to playback a walk motion on the lower part of the body together with a set of more expressive movements (e.g. phoning, scratching, ..) on the upper body.

Inverse kinematics [21] [22] can be used to produce procedural moves according to the character's environment or specific design poses.

Locomotion: The locomotion along a path, essential to most scenarios, requires particular attention in order to produce realistic movements. The V-Man system generates credible path animations [2] [16] by using a totally innovative layered approach. A first algorithm distributes the footsteps of the motion along a given, or autonomously defined, path. A specific algorithm is used, when the path follows stairs, to ensure that there is exactly one foot per stair.

A reference motion (e.g. walk motion) is then analysed to detect the constraints of its original footsteps (position of the steps and timing of the left and right support phases) and edited with several algorithms (offsetting, IK, ...) according to the generated footstep constraints to produce the *path animation*.

Motion Editing: A set of dedicated *editing algorithms* [3] [4] allows the user to warp an existing motion in order to enforce new geometric constraints. Thus, a pre-recorded motion, such as sitting on a specific chair, can be automatically adapted and used to sit on any chair used in the story. Thanks to the definition of hotspots on the objects and on the character itself, any character can interact with any object of the scene if this interaction has already been designed for a character and an object of the same type.

Non-linear Edition: The *non-linear editor* (NLE) module generates seamless transitions between those different motions thanks to automatic positioning in time and space of two consecutive motions.

This module computes the closest frames (in terms of position of the end effectors) between two consecutive motions to detect the optimal transition. As in [9], this is not done locally but on a time window in order to take into account the temporal aspects of the motions (speed). The feet constraints on the incoming and outcoming motions are computed so that the user may add the right motion depending on the current support foot (left, right, or both) of the character. Moreover, the system can adjust the position of the added motion in such a way as to keep the support foot in place during the whole transition period. The system generates the transition using an ease-in/ease-out blending algorithm and the optional use of inverse kinematics.

Finally, *time warping* can be used to slow down or speed up existing motions or entire parts of the sequence.

The combination of all these algorithms allows a wide range of new realistic animation sequences to be created without requiring additional mocaps.

3.3 Rendering Module

The V-Man rendering system is generic and cross-platform. It is available for a wide range of graphics libraries, from pure OpenGL to SGI's Performer or CS' Vertigo.

Fig. 9. A storytelling application based on the V-Man system.

4 Conclusion

V-Man is a comprehensive and high-performance system integrating and combining the most recent animation techniques to produce high quality real-time character animations. It comes with several tools for intuitively acquiring and creating dressed characters, movements and behaviours and an easy to use C++ toolkit.

The system, currently in beta release, is now undergoing an evaluation phase until April 2004. The final release will be available by fall 2004. The first application results are extremely promising. Indeed, V-Man is already successfully used in several projects such as the *VISTA Project*, aiming at developing a storyboarding application using Virtual Reality technologies, or by the CSTB[2] for visualizing building evacuation simulations.

The V-Man system will be a very valuable tool for any creator interested in populating his/her virtual stories with autonomous and interactive virtual actors.

More information is available at http://vr.c-s.fr/vman/

References

1. B. M. Blumberg, "Old Tricks, New Dogs: Ethology and Interactive Creatures.", Media Laboratory. Cambridge, MA, MIT. 1996
2. S. Chung & J. K. Hahn, "Animation of human walking in virtual environments", Computer Animation'99, pages 4–15, May 1999.
3. K.-J. Choi, S.-H. Park & H.-S. Ko, "Processing motion capture data to achieve positional accuracy", Graphical models and image processing: GMIP, 61(5):260–273, 1999.
4. M. Gleicher, "Comparing constraint-based motion editing methods.", Graphical models, 63(2):107–134, 2001.
5. M. Gleicher, "Animation from Observation: Motion Capture and Modtion Editing", Computer Graphics. 33(4), 51-55. November, 1999.
6. M. Gleicher, "Retargetting Motion to New Characters", proceedings of SIGGRAPH, 1998
7. J. H. Holland, "Escaping brittleness: the possibilities of general-purpose learning algorithms applied to parallel rule-based systems. In R. S." Michalski, J. G. Carbonnell & T. M. Mitchell (Eds.), Machine learning, an artificial intelligence approach. *Volume II.* Los Altos, California: Morgan Kaufmann., 1986
8. A. Iglesias & F. Luengo, "Behavioral Animation of Virtual Agents", Computer Graphics and Artificial Intelligence 2003, Limoges, France, May 14-15, 2003
9. L. Kovar, M. Gleicher & F. Pighin, "Motion graphs", Proceedings of SIGGRAPH '02, 2002.
10. M. Kallmann, J.S. Monzani, A. Caicedo & D. Thalmann, "ACE: A Platform for the Real time simulation of Virtual Human Agents", In Eurographics Workshop on Animation and Simulation 2000, Interlaken, Switzerland. August 21-22, 2000.
11. Y. Koga, K. Kondo, J. Kuffner & J.C. Latombe, "Planning Motions with Intentions", Proceedings of SIGGRAPH, 1994

---

[2] The French organization for scientific and technical research in buildings.

12. H. Luga, C. Panatier, O. Balet, P. Torguet & Y. Duthen, "Collective Behaviour and Adaptive Interaction on a Distributed Virtual Reality System", Proceedings of ROMAN'98, IEEE International Workshop on Robot and Human Communication, 1998.

13. P. Maes, "How to Do the Right Thing", Connection Science, 1989. 1(3): p. 291-323

14. E. Menou, O. Balet & J.P. Jessel, "Global Vs Local Processing for Editing Virtual Character's paths", Proceedings of VRIC 2003, Laval, 2003

15. S.R. Musse, M, Kallmann & D.Thalmann, "Level of Autonomy for Virtual Human Agents", Proc. ECAL '99, Lausanne, Switzerland, pp.345-349.

16. F. Multon, L. France, M.-P. Cani-Gascuel & G. Debunne, "Computer animation of human walking: a survey", The Journal of Visualization and Computer Animation, 10(1):39–54, 1999.

17. J.-C. Nebel, "Soft Tissue Modelling from 3D Scanned Data", Deformable Avatars, Kluwer, pp. 85-97, 2001

18. K. Perlin K. & A. Goldberg, "Improv: A System for Scripting Interactive Actors in Virtual Worlds", Proceedings of the ACM Computer Graphics, SIGGRAPH 96

19. A. Sibiryakov, J. Xiangyang & J.C. Nebel, "A New Automated Workflow for 3D Character Creation Based on 3D Scanned Data", proceedings of ICVS'03, Toulouse, 2003

20. S. Saxon & A. Barry, "XCS and the Monk's Problem", Second International Workshop on Learning Classifier Systems (IWLCS-99), Orlando, FL, USA, July 13, 1999.

21. D. Tolani, A. Goswami & N. Badler. "Real-time inverse kinematics techniques for anthropomorphic limbs", Graphical Models, pages 353–388, 2000.

22. C. Welman. "Inverse kinematics and geometric constraints for articulated figure manipulation", Master's thesis, Simon Fraser University, 1993.

Tell Me That Bit Again...
Bringing Interactivity to a Virtual Storyteller

André Silva[1], Guilherme Raimundo[1], and Ana Paiva[1]

IST and INESC-ID, Rua Alves Redol 9, 1000 Lisboa, Portugal
{andre.silva,guilherme.raimundo,ana.paiva}@gaips.inesc.pt

Abstract. Stories and storytelling are a constant presence in our lives since very early childhood. Who does not remember a story narrated by a good storyteller? However, real human storytellers do not always tell the story the same way. They observe their "audience" and adapt the way they are telling the story to better respond to their reactions.

This paper focuses on how to bring interactivity to a virtual storyteller by allowing users to influence the story. The storyteller is a synthetic 3D granddad that uses voice, gestures and facial expressions to convey the story content to be told. The character's behaviour and the way the story is narrated, is influenced by the user's input. Such input is done by a tangible interface (a kind of mail box) where children put the cards they want in order to influence what will happen in the story being told. A preliminary usability test was made with sixteen children, with ages between nine and ten years old. The results showed that the way interactivity is introduced was quite successful.

1 Introduction

We are all storytellers. Stories and storytelling are a constant presence in our lives since very early childhood. Children like to be told a story, over and over again, every time enjoining the situations, the sounds, the events and the worlds portrayed in the story. But, it is not only the story that matters.

The storyteller, himself, plays a fundamental role in children's stories, dragging them into the story, keeping their attention and freeing their imagination. In fact, a storyteller can turn a story into a good or a bad one. The use of the voice, facial expressions, and the appropriate gestures, are basic ingredients for transforming the content of a simple story into the most fascinating narrative we have ever heard. But this need for a storyteller to be expressive, to balance the words and the tone, to use gestures appropriately, poses major research challenges if one aims at building a "synthetic" storyteller. However, recent developments of embodied agents such as [3], [2], [7] and [9] among others, have shown amazing advances, which allows us to consider the technical challenges for building a virtual storyteller can in fact be overcome and achieve, under limited circumstance, a believable storyteller.

In fact, in [11] a simple virtual storyteller was already presented. Our ultimate goal is for the virtual storyteller to be able to tell the content of a story in a natural way, expressing the proper emotional state as the story progresses and capturing the user's attention in the same way a human storyteller would.

O. Balet et al. (Eds.): ICVS 2003, LNCS 2897, pp. 146–154, 2003.
© Springer-Verlag Berlin Heidelberg 2003

But, storytelling is not only narrating a text in a compelling way. It also involves understanding the audience, reacting to it and even adapting the story and the way the story is told to the cues given by the audience.

In the work here presented, we will show how we have incorporated interactivity in a virtual storyteller, which will adapt certain aspects of the story being told to some "cues" the user/child will be providing during a storytelling session.

This paper is organised as follows. First we will describe the idea for the interactivity of the storyteller. Then we describe the character, the structure and contents of the stories embedded in knowledge of the character. Then we show how the user influences the stories being told, and draw some final conclusions.

2   The Idea

Real human storytellers do not always tell the story the same way. They observe their "audience" and adapt the way they are telling the story to better respond to their reactions. This means that the storyteller gets feedback from his audience and uses that feedback to shape the story the way he or she believes it should be told, at that particular moment. Using this idea our virtual storyteller must be interactive, adapting the story being told to the input he gets from the user. So, the storytelling process will follow a behaviour as shown in Figure 1.

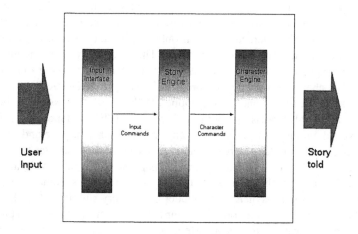

Fig. 1. System Behaviour

The user supplies the virtual storyteller with certain input, which can be done in several different ways, allowing the character to decide how the story should be told. For instance, the user may decide he wants to hear a more terrifying version of the story, supplying this simple wish to the virtual storyteller. The virtual storyteller is then responsible for choosing the course of the story that is most suitable for the user's input and for adapting his visible behaviour to the user's intentions. The Input Interface module is responsible for receiving and handling the input from the user, organizing it for future processing by the story engine. Also, since the input can be supplied at any time, it is also this module's responsibility to store it in a coherent way when the Story Engine module isn't ready to process it yet.

The Story Engine module contains the story itself, parsed from a story file. This module is responsible for parsing the story, organizing it and maintaining the necessary information to decide how to tell it, according to the input received from the Input Interface module. Note that here, a story is intended to be a non-linear story. Depending on the decision made by the Story Engine, different commands are sent to the Character Engine. The Character Engine is responsible for processing the bits of story that need to be told guaranteeing that the synthetic character performs the adequate actions, moves and gestures to convey the desired meeting. Moreover, the Story Engine tells the Character Engine how it should set the character's behaviour in order to maintain coherence with the direction that the story will take.

3   The Character

The storyteller is a synthetic 3D granddad that uses voice, gestures and facial expressions to convey the story content to be told. The character's behaviour and the way the story is narrated, is influenced by the user's input. For instance, the user may express that he or she would want the story to be told in a more scary way. Therefore, the character's emotions are affected by the user's choices. Consequently the virtual storyteller's visible behaviour (its facial expression, voice and gestures) is also influenced by the user's input. The character's verbal output is affected gradually, allowing for several levels of emotional change in the voice. This is done by changing the Text-to-Speech system's parameters (the Eloquent TTS system), adjusting them so they convey the emotion the character is trying to express. For instance, the character can be mildly sad or very sad. The same concept was applied to the facial expression of the virtual storyteller. The facial expression engine follows the MPEG-4 standard [8] in which the six universal emotions of joy, sadness, angriness, disgust, surprise and fear [4] are contemplated. According to the present emotional state of the character the emotional facial displays are blended together. This way it is possible to convey several emotions simultaneously having each contribute to the final output with a specified weight.

At the moment the lip-synch of the model is still very simple. When the voice is heard the facial engine generates random visemes (the visual equivalent of a phoneme). Due to this random nature the visual output you get is cartoon-like where the facial display doesn't match exactly the audio. However, due to a cartoon-like appearance of Papous, although quite simple, this approach, still widely used, leads to quite satisfactory results.

4   The Stories

A human author creates the story files for our synthetic character to narrate. The stories themselves are written using a specific interface and are represented in the story file in XML format. This story file is initially parsed and organized by the Story Engine module until it becomes ready to be narrated. Figure 2 depicts the story creation interface.

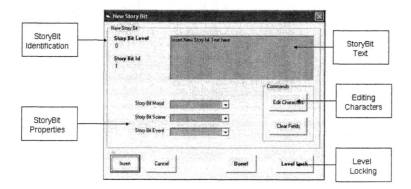

Fig. 2. Story Creation Interface

The story is created in levels. There can be as many levels as wanted. When the virtual storyteller progresses between different levels, he is progressing towards the story's end. In each level, there are multiple StoryBits (inspired by the notion of Beat [6]), each one with its different properties (each has a function according to Propp's [10] functions), characters and events. The author of the story defines not only the several StoryBits in each level but also as many levels as he sees fit, setting the different properties for each one of them separately. Each bit can be connected to many different bits in the next level. Thus, the author can make his story as flexible or as linear as he or she wants. Figure 3 depicts an example of a possible story structure, with several levels and various StoryBits for each level.

If the author wants a very flexible story, with lots of different ways the story can progress, s/he can choose to have many levels and several StoryBits for each level. If, on the contrary, the author of the story wants a linear narrative, all s/he has to do is to define only one StoryBit available for each progression level. Note that in the example shown above, the author has decided to create a single StoryBit in level 3, which means that all the story instances will have at least that particular stage in common. On the other hand, the story can have two different ways it can start, depending on the input that the user decides to provide before the story commences (see the next section for details).

Also, the author creates the Storybits in each level separately, which means that he cannot create Storybits from different levels at the same time. Thus, the author is encouraged to create each stage of the story individually, defining for that particular level, all the possibilities that may occur. When he is finished defining the level, he may lock it (see figure Figure 2) and proceed to the next level. This is done to facilitate the creation of non-linear stories which can become a very tiresome task (trying to maintain a clear idea on what happens in each parallel "story reality").

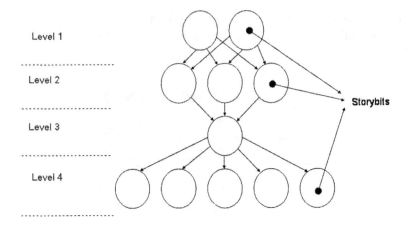

Fig. 3. Basic story structure

5   Interactivity

When the virtual storyteller progresses through the levels, it must choose which Story-Bit to narrate, according to the user's input. There are two underlying problems to solve here: (1) the first one is the user's input. What type of input can we get from the user? The second one is navigation. That is, given the user's input, how will the storyteller decide which bit to pick next, maintaining the coherence of the story?

5.1   User's Input

Concerning the first question, we decided to use a tangible interface that will get the user physically involved with the story. We investigated the use of several different types of input, such as voice or even SenToy [1]. However, due to the fact that we wanted to provide some "story meaning" to the input, and at the same time get the user physically involved, we decided to use the Influencing box [5], as we could associate "images" and meanings to the input. With the box, the user just needs to insert illusive cards (which are tagged with bar codes). The user may choose the most appropriate card for a particular situation (for example, choose a scary sign or a forest) which will then influence the whole story. Figure 4, depicts the use of the Influencing box as input for the system.

The user stands in front of the box, which allows him to insert the cards without much effort, while the character itself is projected onto a wall. Before the story commences, the user can insert cards too, and this input information will be used to decide how the story will start, a kind of setting up the scene (this "pre-story" input will only be considered by the system if the human author has decided to provide more than one way for the story to begin).

Inside the Influencing box, these cards are identified and their meaning is sent to the Input Interface module for processing (shown previously in Figure 1).

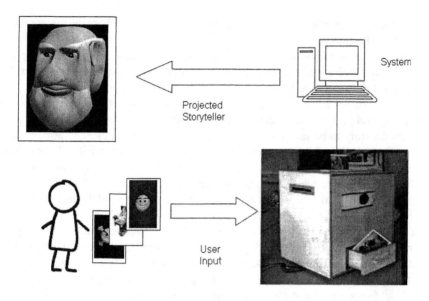

Fig. 4. Input using the Influence Box

There are four types of cards: Propp function card's; character cards; mood cards and scene cards. All the cards are available all the time, which provides a large diversity on the possible progressions in the story. The user can supply these cards at any time, and their meaning is stored by the system until it becomes ready to use that information, which means, when it becomes necessary to choose the next Storybit for narration.

5.2   Navigation through the Story

The input supplied by the user is used to guide the virtual storyteller, helping him decide which StoryBits to choose. Thus, according to the user's input, the storyteller decides which of the different StoryBits available at the current level he should choose to narrate.

Although the stories' are quite simple in terms of non-linearity, given the knowledge structure associated to each StoryBit, the process of navigating through StoryBits is quite rich and is based on heuristics that rely on the StoryBits properties (the emotion/mood of that bit, the characters, the scenario and the Propp function of the bit).

The decision made by the storyteller is based on a desirability factor that all StoryBits have. Naturally, this desirability factor is not a constant and depends not only on the input received at each moment as a card but also from the previously narrated StoryBits.

Thus, with each level transition, the virtual storyteller calculates the desirability factor for each available StoryBit and then decides which one to choose. The system calculates the desirability factor by trying to match as many available StoryBit properties as it can with the user's input (the chosen StoryBit is the one with the highest desirability factor). For instance, if the user wishes the story to be told in a happier way, then the virtual storyteller will try to accommodate his wish by choosing the appropriate StoryBits in the future.

The user inputs themselves are received and weighed, considering the time when they arrive and their type. This means that the most recent input has a bigger part in the decision that the storyteller has to face with each level transition.

For instance, let us assume the user decides that he wants the story to be told in a scarier way and provides the necessary input. He can then change his mind and decide he wants the story to be sadder. The user's most recent input is more important for the choice of which StoryBit to narrate and therefore, the next StoryBit will be coherent with his later choice, making the virtual storyteller tell the story in a sadder way.

However, there are two situations that may occur, with which the system has to be capable of dealing with: the lack of input provided by the user and the lack of adequacy between the user's wishes and the StoryBits available for narration.

If the user chooses not to provide input to the system, then the virtual storyteller assumes that the story is pleasing the user and, in the next level, the character searches for StoryBits as similar as possible to the ones he has already narrated. This way, if the user is enjoying the way the story is being told, the system maintains coherence throughout the rest of the story. This system behaviour is obviously consistent with a real human storyteller's actions.

When the user provides input that cannot be satisfied by the StoryBits available for narration, the system uses a similar approach. This means that, unable to suit the user's intentions, the system chooses the next input as if there had been no input from the user, i.e., choosing the next StoryBit according the one previously narrated. This approach seems reasonable, considering what a real human storyteller would do in this situation, and it yields quite satisfactory results.

6   Results and Final Comments

A preliminary usability test was made with sixteen children, with ages between nine and ten years old, in order to evaluate the text to speech engine, the facial model and facial expressions and the tangible interface when comparing to a classic menu. The test consisted of the narration of the story of Little Red Ridding Hood and a questionnaire that children answered after hearing and interacting with the virtual storyteller.

Based on the given answers we can draw the following initial conclusions:

- The application is of easy use
- The main obstacle to the understanding of the story is the quality of the text-to-speech
- The "looks" of the story teller were pleasing
- Sometimes, the facial expressions were not completely identified by the children
- The tangible interface was a success having 14 children chosen this one over the classic menu interface

The story teller is still at an early stage having several aspects that need to be improved. After our analysis we think that using another text-to-speech or human recorded voice provided by a professional actor will improve considerably the quality of the overall application. However this last solution poses some problems because we want to use a continuum of emotional state. Even if we consider discrete intervals, the number of recorded sets needed to achieve a smooth transition might not be feasible. Regarding the model we concluded that it needs to be more cartoon-like and that the facial expressions need to be more exaggerated.

Another aspect that should be improved is the story creation interface. Future work will include the facilitation of the interactive stories' creation. In fact, creating a non-linear interactive story with the current version of the system's Story Creation Interface is a tiresome and difficult task, although feasible. Trying to maintain a clear idea on all that is happening in all of the possible versions of the story is a complicated job for a human being, which should be left for the computer to handle.

Thus, including more information regarding the narrative context dependencies of all the possible versions of the story would allow the computer to become more effective in assisting the creation of the non-linear interactive stories.

The final version of the storyteller's body is still being improved, but the character's gestures and body expression will also be influenced by the emotional state of the character [12]. By connecting the input from the user with the utterance of the voice, the emotional state, facial and body expression in an interactive emotional storytelling system, we hope to deliver a pleasing and didactic experience to the user.

Acknowledgements

Thanks to Fernando Rebelo for the design of Papous. Thanks to the GAIPS team for their comments and criticisms during the development of this system. Thanks to Phoebe Sengers for allowing us to use the Influencing Machine.

The work on Papous was funded under the Sapiens Program- Fundacão para a Ciência e Tecnologia, project number POSI/SRI/41071/2001.

References

1. P. A., A. G., H. K., M. D., C. M., and M. C. Sentoy in fantasya: Designing an affective sympathetic interface to a computer game. *Personal and Ubiquitous Computing Journal (Ub Comp)*, (5-6), 2002.
2. J. Cassell, T. Bickmore, L. Campbell, H. Vilhjalmsson, and H. Yan. Conversation as a system framework: Designing embodied conversational agents. In e. a. J. Cassell, editor, *Embodied Conversational Agents*. MIT Press, Cambridge, MA, 1999.
3. J. Cassell. Nudge nudge wink wink: Elements of face-to-face conversation for embodied conversational agents. In J. C. et al., editor, *Embodied Conversational Agents*. MIT Press, Cambridge, MA, 1999.
4. P. Ekman. *Emotion in the Face*. New York, Cambridge University Press, 1982.
5. S. et al. The enigmatics of affect. In *Proceedings of Designing Interactive Systems-DIS'2002*. ACM Press, 2002.
6. M. Matheas and A. Stern. Towards integrating plot and character for interactive drama. In *Socially Intelligent Agents: Creating Relationships with Computers and Robots*. Kluwer, 2002.

7. T. Noma, L. Zhao, and N. Badler. Design of a virtual human presenter. *IEEE Computer Graphics and Applications*, 20(4):79–85, 2000.
8. I. Pandzic and F. R. (editors). *Mpeg-4 Facial Animation - The standard, Implementation and Applications*. John Wiley & Sons, 2002.
9. C. Pelachaud and I. Poggi. Subtleties of facial expressions in embodied agents. *Journal of Visualization and Computer Animation*, 2002.
10. V. Propp. *Morphology of the folktale*. Austin: University of Texas Press, 1968.
11. A. Silva, M. Vala, and P. A. Papous: The virtual storyteller. In *Intelligent Virtual Agents*. Springer, 2001.
12. M. Vala, M. Gomes, and A. Paiva. Affective bodies for affective interactions. In *Animating Expressive Characters for Social Interactions*. John Benjamins Publishing Company, 2003.

A New Automated Workflow for 3D Character Creation Based on 3D Scanned Data

Alexander Sibiryakov, Xiangyang Ju, and Jean-Christophe Nebel

University of Glasgow, Computing Science Department
17 Lilybank Gardens, G12 8QQ Glasgow United Kingdom
{sibiryaa,xju,jc}@dcs.gla.ac.uk

Abstract. In this paper we present a new workflow allowing the creation of 3D characters in an automated way that does not require the expertise of an animator. This workflow is based of the acquisition of real human data captured by 3D body scanners, which is them processed to generate firstly animatable body meshes, secondly skinned body meshes and finally textured 3D garments.

1   Introduction

From the dawn of human civilisation, story telling has been a key element of culture and education where human characters have been given a central role. Although story telling has been evolving beyond recognition with the advent of computer graphics and virtual reality, human figures still play a significant and irreplaceable part in narration. Creation and animation of these characters have been among the most difficult tasks encountered by animators. In particular the generation of animatable character meshes, which include modelling and skinning, is still a manual task requiring observation, skills and time and on which the success of the narrative depends on.

2   Creation of 3D Models of Humans from Real Data

On one hand a talented animator requires few weeks, if not months, to produce a convincing model of 3D human. On the other hand specific human models can be generated in hours by using any of the two main automatic or semi-automatic techniques: the deformation of generic 3D human models and 3D scanning. In the first case, a set of pictures [2,3] or a video sequence [1] is mapped on a generic 3D model, which is scaled and deformed in order to match the pictures. The main limitation is the similarity between the human model and the generated model depends on the viewpoint. The other way of generating automatically realistic humans is by using 3D scanners [6,7,12]. Models are more realistic, however they contain little semantic information, i.e. data comprises an unstructured list of 3D data points or mesh without any indication of what body component they represent.

O. Balet et al. (Eds.): ICVS 2003, LNCS 2897, pp. 155–158, 2003.
© Springer-Verlag Berlin Heidelberg 2003

The method we propose, detailed in [4], is a combination of the two previously described techniques: a generic 3D model is deformed in order to match 3D data. This is a two-step process: global mapping and local deformation. The global mapping registers and deforms the generic model to the scanned data based on global correspondences, in this case manually defined landmarks. The local deformation reshapes the globally deformed generic model to fit the scanned data by identifying corresponding closest surface points between them and warps the generic model surface in the direction of the closest surface (see Figure 1).

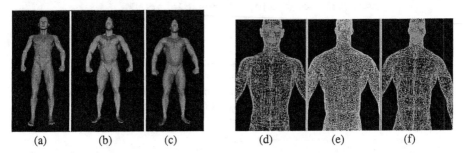

(a)   (b)   (c)   (d)   (e)   (f)

Fig. 1. Generic model (a), 3D imaged body data (b) final conformed result (c), generic mesh (d), 3D imaged body mesh (e) and final conformed mesh (f)

3   Character Skinning Based on Real Data

The animation of 3D characters with animation packages is based on a hierarchic rigid body defined by a skeleton, which is a supporting structure for polygonal meshes that represent the outer layer or skin of characters. In order to ensure smooth deformations of the skin around articulations, displacements of vertices must depend on the motion of the different bones of the neighbourhood. The process of associating vertices with weighted bones is called skinning and is an essential step of character animation. That task requires time and artistic skills, since skinning is performed iteratively until a visually acceptable compromise is reached. Our solution is based on a more rational approach: instead of experimentally trying to converge towards the best skinning compromise, we offer to automatically skin a model from a set of 3D scanned postures which are anatomically meaningful [5] (see Figure 2).

The skinning process itself is based on the analysis of the motions of points between these different postures. Using the set of 3D points, we start by tracing each point from the reference posture and we obtain the 3D deformation of each point (range flow). Then the positions of the centre of each limb can be calculated in all the 3D models of the sequence and finally we analyse the motion of each point in its own local coordinate system and assign to each point of the 3D model a set of weights associated to each bone (see Figure 3). The vertex weights are calculated as coefficients in linear equations defining the motion of the vertex in joint coordinate system. In this system two bones defining the joint are considered as axes of a coordinate system. Vertex weights are considered as coordinates of vertex in that system.

Fig. 2. Character scanned in different positions   **Fig. 3.** Weight distribution

In recent papers [12,13] the postures are used to improve the skinning by fitting the skin deformation parameters to postures. Our method uses the postures for direct calculation of skin vertex weights. It can be considered as an extension of SSD (Skeletal Space Deformation) approach, where the weights are not necessary normalized and they can change their values depending on orientation of the bones.

4   Textured 3D Garment Generation from Real Data

Three main strategies have been used for dressing 3D characters. Garments can be modelled and textured by an animator: this time consuming option is widely spread in particular in the game industry where there are only few characters with strong and distinctive features. A simple alternative is to map textures on body shape of naked characters, however that technique is only acceptable when characters are supposed to wear tightly fitted garments. Finally garments can be assembled: patterns are pulled together and seamed around the body. Then physically based algorithms calculate how garments drape when resting. This accurate and time-consuming technique (requiring seconds [8] or even minutes [10] depending on the required level of accuracy) is often part of a whole clothing package specialised in clothes simulation.

Among these strategies, only the third one is appealing since it provides an automated way of generating convincing 3D garments. However since we do not intend to animate clothes using a physically based animation engine and we do not have direct access to clothes pattern, that strategy does not impose itself as the best solution.

Instead we offer to use the following innovative technical solution: the generation of 3D garments is done by capturing a same individual in a specific position with and without clothing (see Figure 4). Generic garment meshes are conformed to scans of characters wearing garment to produce 3D clothes. Then body and garment meshes can be superposed to generate the 3D clothes models (see Figure 5).

Each 3D outfit is connected to a set of texture maps providing style and appearance. The process of texture generation is the following: using the given flatten mesh of a generic mesh and a set of photos which will be used as texture maps, users set landmarks on the photos corresponding to predefined landmarks on the flatten mesh. Then a warping procedure is operated so that the warped images can be mapped automatically on the 3D mesh (see Figure 5). Moreover areas where angles should be preserved during the warping phase – i.e. seams defining a pocket - can be specified.

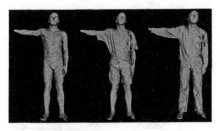

Fig. 4. Model scanned in different outfits

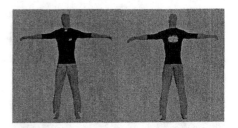

Fig. 5. Textured model

5   Conclusion

We presented an automated workflow for the creation of 3D characters based on scanned data. The creation process does not require expertise and skills of animators, since any computer literate person can generate of a new character in a couple of hours. This workflow is currently in use in the development of the intuitive authoring system allowing non-computer specialist to create, animate, control and interact with a new generation of 3D characters within the V-Man project [9].

References

1. N.D'Apuzzo, R.Plänkers, A.Gruen, P.Fua and D.Thalmann, Modeling Human Bodies from Video Sequences, Proc. Electronic Imaging, San Jose, California, January 1999.
2. V.Blanz and T.Vetter, A Morphable Model for the Synthesis of 3D Faces, SIGGRAPH'99 Conference Proceedings, pp 187-194, 1999
3. A.Hilton, D.Beresford, T.Gentils, R.Smith and W.Sun, Virtual People: Capturing human models to populate virtual worlds, CA'99 Conference, May 1999, Geneva, Switzerland
4. Xiangyang Ju and J. Paul Siebert, Individualising Human Animation Models, Proc. Eurographics 2001, Manchester, UK, 2001.
5. J.-C.Nebel and A.Sibiryakov, Range flow from stereo-temporal matching: application to skinning, IASTED Int. Conf. on Visualization, Imaging, and Image Processing, Spain, 2002.
6. R.Trieb, 3-D-Body Scanning for mass customized products - Solutions and Applications, Int. Conf. of Numerisation 3D - Scanning, 24-25 May 2000, Paris, France.
7. P.Siebert, S.Marshall, Human body 3D imaging by speckle texture projection photogrammetry, Sensor Review, 20 (3), pp 218-226, 2000.
8. T. Vasilev, Dressing Virtual People, SCI'2000 conference, Orlando, July 23-26, 2000
9. V-MAN project website: http://vr.c-s.fr/vman/
10. P.Volino, N.Magnenat-Thalmann, "Comparing Efficiency of Integration Methods for Cloth Animation", Proceedings of CGI'01, Hong-Kong, July 2001
11. S. Winsborough, An insight into the design, manufacture and practical use of a 3D-Body Scanning system, Int. Conf. of Numerisation 3D - Scanning, 24-25 May 2000, Paris, France.
12. B. Allen, B. Curless, Z. Popovic, Articulated body deformation from range scan data. SIGGRAPH'02 Conference Proceedings, pp. 612-619, 2002
13. A.Mohr, M.Gleicher, Building Efficient, Accurate Character Skins from Examples, SIGGRAPH'03 Conference Proceedings, pp 562-568, 2003

Using Motivation-Driven Continuous Planning to Control the Behaviour of Virtual Agents

Nikos Avradinis[1,2], Ruth Aylett[1], and Themis Panayiotopoulos[2]

[1] Centre for Virtual Environments, University of Salford, Salford, M5 4WT, UK
N.Avradinis@pgt.salford.ac.uk, R.S.Aylett@salford.ac.uk
[2] Knowledge Engineering Lab, Department of Informatics, University of Piraeus,
80 Karaoli & Dimitriou Street, 185 34, Greece
{avrad,themisp}@unipi.gr

Abstract. This paper discusses the use of intelligent planning as a control mechanism for agents situated in a virtual world. Virtual environments require a planning system that is flexible enough to handle situations impossible to predict before execution has started. In order to produce believable results, the planner should also be able to model and handle emotions. Working towards this direction, the authors propose a motivation-driven, continuous hierarchical planner as an appropriate paradigm.

1 Introduction

Intelligent planning has been widely applied in virtual storytelling environments as a means to provide a high-level reasoning mechanism that decides and generates agent behaviour. The step-by-step, action based nature of planning techniques make them particularly suitable for this purpose, as it is very close to the concept of story generation as the production of a chain of dependent actions. Several virtual agent systems using planning to control agent behaviour have been presented, like Interactive Storytelling [1], Mimesis [2], Façade [3] and Emile [4].

However, the majority of the work produced so far adopts the classic offline planning paradigm (first plan thoroughly, then act following the plan), based on the assumption that the world state remains unchanged throughout the whole planning and acting phase, while also the agent is supposed to have detailed knowledge of the world state as well as the effects of his actions [5,6].

Constantly changing environments, such as multi agent societies call for a more flexible solution, where the planning agent can adapt itself to changes in world state during execution. This means that the planning system should be able to monitor execution, drop goals or generate new ones according to changes that might occur, either due to its own actions or due to external factors.

In real world situations it is also often very difficult or infeasible to acquire complete information on the conditions holding at planning time. Moreover, sometimes planning goals or sub goals might only be partially completed, which, although not being exactly the desired outcome, can be acceptable under circumstances. The planning system should, therefore, demonstrate some form of tolerance both in terms of input information and possible results, thus being capable to reason even under uncer-

O. Balet et al. (Eds.): ICVS 2003, LNCS 2897, pp. 159–162, 2003.
© Springer-Verlag Berlin Heidelberg 2003

tain conditions. This could imply postponing execution of parts of the plan until all necessary data is collected, initiating execution expecting to collect more information in due course or even producing conditional plans which provide alternative solutions at specific key points.

Requirements such as the above have led the research community over the past few years to introduce the term "continuous" or "continual" [7,8] planning to define planning architectures that interleave planning, execution and monitoring in order to allow the plan to be revised if new conditions are detected. This special "flavour" of planning is necessary in dynamic applications like intelligent virtual environments, as has also been argued in [5]. In this paper we describe some preliminary work on the development of a continuous planning system able to handle emotions that will be used to control the behaviour of agents in a virtual storytelling environment.

2 Hierarchical, Motivation-Based Continuous Planning

In [4,9], Jonathan Gratch argues on the importance of emotions for any model of intelligence, and therefore, the necessity of a planning system that is aware of emotions and takes them into account in the decision-making process. Adopting this argument, we are working towards the direction of a continuous planning system aware of emotions, modelled using *motivations* [6,10]. Motivations can be defined as emotional, mental or physical states or long term, high-level drives that affect a situated agent's existing goals or generate new ones, and are themselves affected by the agent's own actions, other agents' actions or environmental conditions [11].

The concept of motivations is of key importance to our approach, as, apart from affecting the agent's decisions by causing different goals or actions to be selected, they can also act as a seed to generate new goals for the agent, or as a reason to drop goals previously selected. For example, let's consider the following scenario:

Jeremy settles down at his desk one evening to study for an examination. Finding himself a little too restless to concentrate, he decides to take a walk in the fresh air. His walk takes him past a nearby bookstore, where the sight of an enticing title draws him to look at a book. Just before getting in the bookstore, however, he meets his friend Kevin, who invites him to the pub next door for a beer. When he arrives at the pub, however, he finds that the noise gives him a headache, and decides to return home without having a beer, to continue with his main goal-studying for the exam. However, Jeremy now feels too sick to study and his first concern is to cure his headache, which involves taking some medicine and getting a good rest, thus postponing studying until the next morning.

This scenario features a constant change of goals and re-evaluation of priorities, mainly triggered by changes in the agent's motivations. Jeremy's decision to go for a walk could be triggered by an increase of the weight of the attribute *boredom*, caused by the failure of the durative action *study*. This would result in an increased priority for the *reduce_boredom* motivation. Jeremy's spotting the book supports the *reduce_boredom* motivation better than the action *take_a_walk* does, so he decides to buy the book. Before he executes that action, however, Kevin's introduction of the *have_a_beer* subplan changes the situation-the *have_a_beer* subplan decreases the *boredom* weight even more, so the action *go_to_pub* takes priority and is selected, causing the *buy_book* goal to be dropped.

Although this scenario is too abstract to be easily formalised into proper planning definitions, it clearly shows the effect motivations could have on the planning process and the selection of the agent's actions. Jeremy's has a fixed medium-term goal, which is to study for the exam, however, his short-term plan to achieve this goal is always changing, because of the changes in the priorities of motivations. Another interesting feature is the constant changes and turns in the plot. A classical, offline planner would not be able to cope with this scenario, as Kevin's appearance or Jeremy's spotting the book could not have been predicted before execution. This demonstrates the need for a continuous planning system that will operate in parallel with the execution system, receiving feedback from the virtual world in real time in order to be able to adjust and re-plan in real time.

One could have noticed our almost equivalent use of the terms "action", "goal" and "plan". This is because a concept like "have_a_beer" could be any of the three, depending on the level of abstraction. *Have_a_beer* could be a plan to achieve a goal like *feel_relaxed*, but it could in turn be a goal, when the agent is in the bar, or even a primitive action, when the agent finally has the beer served. An appropriate planning paradigm to support this reasoning over multiple levels of abstraction is Hierarchical Task Network planning [12]. HTN's hierarchical nature allows partial planning, avoiding plan failures when complete domain knowledge is not available, while backtracking to a previous level if a primitive method fails is relatively easy and replanning can be performed on a local level rather than requiring the generation of the whole plan from scratch.

The planning algorithm we are working on is based on two previous planners: MACTA-planner, a non-hierarchical continuous agent-based planner using motivations and SHOP, a non-continuous hierarchical generative planning system that has proven expressive and efficient enough to handle complex domains [12]. The planning strategy combines elements from both planners, aiming to combine SHOP's hierarchical nature with MACTA-planner's continuous operation and motivation support in order to be able to handle unpredictable scenarios like the described one.

3   Applying Continuous Planning in Virtual Storytelling

We aim to apply the proposed planning technique for the creation of an emergent narrative system that adopts a "reality show/soap opera" approach, using the planner as a mechanism to control the behaviour of non-human agents participating in the environment. Our final aim is an interactive system, where the user assumes the role of a main character, however, as a first step we opt for a character-based, non-interactive system where all agents will be non-human.

Instead of a specific high-level goal, persisting for the whole session, our character would have a trivial goal, like getting back home after work. On its way back home, the character will interact with other agents in the virtual world, who introduce new data to his set of knowledge and affect his motivations. These changes will have as an effect the introduction of new goals and the re-evaluation of the priority of old ones, resulting in a story emerging where there was only an abstract and trivial goal.

We wish to investigate the potential of the use of motivations as a source for new goals, where factors like hunger, tiredness, boredom, fear or pleasure will affect the agent's decisions and generate an unpredictable outcome, mainly dependent on the interactions of the character with the virtual environment and other agents. Although at first consideration the proposed approach does not guarantee an interesting plot, we suggest that motivations, especially time-dependent ones, like hunger or boredom, will create unexpected twists and turns in the plot, especially when combined with factors that introduce non-determinism, such as random placement of objects or characters in the environment. The fact that there are no fixed goals and even top-level goals can be dropped can also generate unexpected endings, like in the "Jeremy" scenario. However, we believe that the stories generated will be much more interesting when we introduce interactivity in the system, as a final aim. User actions, by nature non-deterministic, will strongly affect the decisions of non-human characters, resulting in truly unpredictable situations, and proving this way the need for a continuous emotional planning system to control agent behaviour.

This work has been partially funded by the University of Piraeus Research Centre

References

1. Cavazza, M., Charles, F., Mead, S.J.: Character-Based Interactive Storytelling. IEEE Intelligent Systems, 17(4) (2002), 17-24
2. Young, R.M.: An Overview of the Mimesis Architecture: Integrating intelligent narrative Control into an existing gaming environment. AAAI Spring Symposium on Artificial Intelligence and Interactive Entertainment, Stanford, CA, March 26-28 (2001)
3. Mateas, M., Stern. A.: Architecture, Authoral Idioms and Early Observations of the Interactive Drama Façade. Internal Report, Carnegie Mellon University, CMU-CS-02-198
4. Gratch, J.: Emile: Marshalling Passions in Training and Education. Proceedings of the 4th International Conference on Autonomous Agents, ACM Press, Barcelona, Spain, June 2000
5. Pollack, M., Horty, J.F.: There's more to life than making plans: Plan management in Dynamic, Multi-agent Environments. AI Magazine 20(4) (1999), 71-83
6. Aylett, R.S., Coddington, A.M., Petley, G.J.: Agent-based Continuous Planning, PLANSIG 2000, Milton Keynes, UK, December 14-15 (2000)
7. Myers, K.L.: Towards a Framework for Continuous Planning and Execution. AAAI'98 Fall Symp. Workshop on Distributed Continual Planning. Orlando, Florida, Oct. 23-25 (1998)
8. desJardins, M.E., Durfee, E.H., Ortiz, C.L. Jr., and Wolverton, M.J.: A survey of research in distributed, continual planning. AI Magazine, 20 (4) (1999), 13-22
9. Gratch, J.: Why you should buy an emotional planner. Agents' 99 Workshop on Emotion-based Agent Architectures, Seattle, USA, May 1 (1999)
10. Coddington, A.M.: A Continuous Planning Framework for Durative Actions. TIME '02, Manchester, UK, July 7-9 (2002)
11. Avradinis, N., Aylett, R.S.: Agents with no aims: Motivation-driven Continuous Planning. Intelligent Virtual Agents '03, Irsee, Germany, September 15-17 (2003)
12. Nau, D., Muñoz-Avila, H., Cao, Y., Lotem, A. and Mitchell, S.: Total-Order Planning with Partially Ordered Subtasks. IJCAI 2001, Seattle, USA, August 4-10 (2001)

Mixed Reality

The Art of Mixing Realities

Sally Jane Norman

Ecole Supérieure de l'Image, 134 rue de Bordeaux, 16000 Angoulême/
26 rue Jean Alexandre, 86000 Poitiers, France
norman@wanadoo.fr

Abstract. How we mix reality of our everyday environments with human-made conceptual or physical realities built for highly specific purposes, and how we articulate their respective boundaries and overlap, are crucial questions for many people, including and especially artists. Art testifies to our need to instantiate arenas of existence set apart from commonplace contingencies: by positing realities consecrated to spiritual and symbolic, as opposed to temporal and material endeavour, such arenas foster activities that are determinant for cultural development. Yet the very existence of these alternative realities depends on their specific, codified linkages to everyday reality. This paper explores some of the relationships which characterise the mixing of realities undertaken by artists using information technology (IT) tools. It is not focussed on storytelling per se, but deals with various kinds of hybrid environments which are being forged by contemporary artists, and which are likely to impact new storytelling worlds.

1 Introduction

Art practices and processes are dynamic, evolving activities that must constantly renegotiate their forms and formats to maximise their resonance within changing social environments. Artists are uniquely engaged in extending the limits of the collective imagination, reinvigorating our capacity to perceive and conceive, serving as poetic interpreters of existing and emerging realities. Our aptitude to view familiar realities under a new light, or to entertain visions of unprecedented realities, largely depends on how these visions are presented with respect to the everyday realities that serve as our references. In other words, our receptiveness to creative projections of reality is hinged on the way these projections relate to consensually acknowledged, common sense reality. How is their demarcation instated and upheld, and how permeable is it? Do these different kinds of reality operate as extremes of a single continuum or, rather, are they to be confronted as discrete, completely dissimilar entities?

Art-making essentially involves taking the stuff of (our experience of) the world, and framing it in sensible, perceptible form so that we can adopt a contemplative and/ or critical distance from it. This framing activity employs many kinds of more or less subtle rhetorical devices, devised to elucidate and heighten the beholder's experience of the creative artifact[1]. In painting and sculpture, for example, use of picture frames and pedestals over the centuries translates strategies to enhance the physical and so-

---

[1] For a series of essays on this question, cf. Duro, P. (ed.): The Rhetoric of the Frame. Essays on the Boundaries of the Artwork. Cambridge University Press, Cambridge USA (1996).

O. Balet et al. (Eds.): ICVS 2003, LNCS 2897, pp. 165–178, 2003.
© Springer-Verlag Berlin Heidelberg 2003

cial positioning of art works, thereby elevating that of their commissioners and collectors. Rhetorical devices that underpin performing arts include techniques to estrange modes of everyday speech (e.g. scansion or singing) and gesture (e.g. codified movements of classical dance or commedia dell'arte), together with techniques to transfigure the actual physical locus of dramatic action, via stage architecture and audience positioning, décors, lighting, etc[2].

Much recent creation has sought to embroil the boundaries between space- and time-based media, as evidenced by interdisciplinary endeavours of the past decades: installations, land art, space art, environments and site-specific works, performances, body art, happenings, interventionist art, live mixes of projected sound and image, etc. (a seemingly unclassifiable corpus of hybrids which may one day turn out to constitute a distinct art history category). While the earlier phases of this interdisciplinary activity drew heavily on video to provide real-time coverage of events occurring parallel to fictive or staged action, the subsequent introduction of internet chatlines, sound and images has opened up another set of possibilities for artists choosing to experiment in the domain of technologically mediated and distributed live action. Each new genre, and indeed each new creation, must in turn posit its rules and rhetoric for the proposed experience.

1.1   Negotiating/Implementing Effective Rhetoric

The power of estrangement and "artificialisation" exerted by rhetorical devices tends to vary and fluctuate over time, with the development of original forms by artists seeking to break with prevailing conventions, and to challenge or appeal to changing audience expectations. It is this constant, acute state of negotiation between creators and their publics that gives art its singular communicative edge and vitality as a social force.

New forms and formats redefine relationships between mundane and artistically framed worlds. Thus, for example, each of the countless manifestations of romantic and realist art, of heavily ornamental and austerely minimalist aesthetics encountered over the past centuries bears specific sets of codified relations to its social environment. These movements and genres may coexist and develop in parallel, just as they may succeed and supplant one another. For the purposes of the present paper, emphasis is not on the intrinsic features of such movements, but on the broader issue of how they might be linked to the reality within which they are entrenched and to which they historically belong.

1.2   Art-Making with and within Humachine[3] Reality

Apart from their exploitation of cutting edge IT tools of various kinds (this does not necessarily mean use of the most expensive computing equipment), a common trait of what are here called "mixed reality" art works is their creation of hybrid worlds an-

---

[2] For a brief overview of physical devices used in performing arts, see Benford, S., Norman, S-J, Bowers, J. et al: Pushing Mixed Reality Boundaries. erena, Esprit Project, Royal Institute of Technology (KTH), Stockholm, www.nada.kth.se/erena/pdf/D7b_1.pdf (1999).

[3] Author's contraction coined to denote the human-machine world.

chored in the muddy waters where increasingly technologically conditioned everyday experience encounters artistically mediated experience. These works contrast with research geared towards securing maximum autonomy and verisimilitude of computer constructs, as seen in virtual reality worlds where real-time rendering permanently refreshes attributes ranging from behavioural quirks to shadows, fleshing out vivaciously solid actors, and as seen in the growing use of vampire scanners to populate shared virtual environments with portraits provided on the fly – wittingly or unwittingly - by living specimens like you and me. Research of the latter kind tends to be driven by a demiurgic wish to generate independent virtual worlds able to run parallel to and vie with the tangible reality they so ingeniously simulate. Many papers at this conference present technical solutions invented to augment the performance of virtual realities as autonomous worlds.

Yet there remains another distinct area of investigation explored by artist developers focussed on the tenuous, constantly shifting dividing line between spontaneous percepts derived from our immediate environment, and percepts generated and mediated by IT tools and platforms. In response to the seventies concept of CAD, the nineties CAN acronym, coined by artists Knowbotic Research (KR+cF) to denote Computer-Aided Nature[4], exemplifies this swing in thinking, with its instatement of a single, inextricably humachine world, in place of supposedly separable, coexistent technological and natural worlds. In its investigation of technologically remodeled urban space, KR+cF emphasises this interweaving of digital and real space: "*It is our aim not to have the investigations of the urban take place in an independent, virtual space. Rather than submersion in a distinct, detached environment, we are trying consciously to enhance the oscillation between the fields of action of the real urban space, and those of the data space. (...) What we are interested in is not so much the border between electronic and non-electronic fields, but the overlapping areas in and between them which demand new forms of agency and work. (...)We are no longer so much concerned with the processing and handling of given data, but with strategies of dealing with imprecisions and uncertainty between experiential space and data space, between technology, perception, and action.*"[5]

Many artists are engaged in forging and highlighting experience arising from the fringes of the social and technical environment in which we have become irreversibly enmeshed, with its unholy mix of hard-, soft-, and wetware. Among the tools and platforms that challenge these artists, information technologies represent obvious strategic interest for conveying and sharing reflection on our fast-changing world. Harnessing these massively proliferating, normative systems to fire the collective imagination demands formidable creative cunning.

2 From Virtual to Augmented to Mixed Realities

After a juvenile technophoric period in the early nineties, when cyberspace was sometimes seen as a platonic realm of pure abstraction, and immersive virtual reality was

---

[4] For a Kr+Cf definition of CAN, cf. http://netbase.t0.or.at/~krcf/antarctica/dkit/chimera.html.
[5] Knowbotic Research: The Urban as Field of Action. In: TechnoMorphica.V2 Publications, Rotterdam (1997).

prone to quasi-mystical conjecture[6], research has increasingly dwelt on so-called integrated or augmented realities, where virtual displays coexist with and extend percepts offered by the real world.

Over the past decade, psycho physiologists, ergonomists, ethnographers and researchers from other fields grounded in "soft" human as opposed to "hard" (inhuman?) sciences, have been forming multidisciplinary groups engaged in the borderline area where computer generated worlds spill into the real world and vice versa. These groups have tackled a number of urgent pragmatic needs, including finer control of prostheses and human substitutes intervening in environments which may be hazardous (robots in nuclear plants, outer space, etc), or require superhuman gestural precision (laser surgery, molecular synthesis to develop new materials, etc).

All kinds of interfaces have been devised to optimally graft computer data onto ambient environments: translucent HMDs and half-silvered glasses, powerfully spatialised auditory systems, haptics devices adding computer-generated kinesthetic and proprioceptive pressure to hands-on experience, etc. The quest to reconcile different kinds of perceived realities has led to major effort being invested in the area of mixed reality boundaries. This is a term used by Nottingham University's Mixed Reality Lab (MRL), an interdisciplinary research unit that draws together computer scientists, engineers and psychologists, and that has long referred to "mixed reality" in an explicit and programmatic fashion[7].

Scientific research steadily generates conceptual and physical tools which accompany and condition the development of new visions, in accordance with preoccupations which often converge with those of artists, despite their generally being explored by very different methodologies. This convergence may make tools built for scientific exploration - which tend to heavily outweigh those available in the cultural sector - deeply interesting for artists. Access may occur when technology patrons wishing to redeem their public image act as cultural philanthropists, making powerful means available to the creative community. Artists may also gain access to enviable IT tools by bringing to high tech facilities specific skills and projects with clear potential to catalyse research. Such situations tend to favour the eclosion of mixed realities, since they institute energy intensive platforms mobilising acutely motivated, differentiated lines of scientific and artistic research. Points of convergence are concretely experienced in/ as a shared technological environment, while the distinctive perspectives of scientists and artists fuel provocative, uniquely productive points of divergence.

2.1 Diversified Research for Socially Meaningful Technologies

Parallel to the burgeoning practical applications afforded by finely layered and interconnected real and virtual worlds, there has been steadily growing awareness of

---

[6] For example, see the Cyberconf5 presentation (Madrid, 1996) by Mark Pesce, co-inventor and developer of Virtual Reality Modelling Language (VRML), inspired by Teilhard de Chardin's noosphere to propose "Worldsong", a real-time spatialised environment for literally giving voice to the newly connected global community:
http://www.telefonica.es/fat/epesce.html. For reflection on a number of early immersive virtual reality artworks, cf. Moser, M.A. and MacLeod, D. (ed.): Immersed in Technology. Art and Virtual Environments. MIT Press, Cambridge, Massachusetts (1996).

[7] For further information, see http://www.mrl.nott.ac.uk.

this sector's broader cultural potential, and reciprocally, of the potential value of actively involving diverse categories of cultural agents in its development. The uptake of technology can only be broadened if that technology addresses a broader user base, and extending the user base means elaborating strategies and models likely to attract new audiences.

As a corollary, experience and expectations with which new audiences can identify must be built into technology design, the more so when dealing with communications platforms with essential social repercussions, where complexities of human-human interaction have to be taken into account in order to manage the complexities of human-computer interaction.

Computer Supported Cooperative Work techniques (CSCW) have evolved spectacularly since the early nineties, thanks to interdisciplinary research. Social scientists showed up the shortcomings of excessively schematic social and behavioural models that were then (dis-)serving computer scientists developing communications platforms, and brought their own praxis to bear in the study of human interactions, notably analysing such subtle issues as proxemics, attention spans, hierarchised listening to multiple partners, etc. The resultant ethnomethodology studies have provided interdisciplinary groups with accessible, exploitable findings and models more apt to translate the complex dynamics and organisational traits which subtend social activities. This knowedge has immeasurably enriched and enlivened the design of shared virtual spaces, demonstrating the usefulness of diversifying research platforms in order to bolster technology development.

2.2 Artistic Visions to Multiply, De- and Re-focus Perspectives

A recent step in interdisciplinary IT research consists of soliciting artists to extend the spectrum of approaches to tools essentially built for communications purposes[8]. Teams and institutions highlighting art and technology research have sprung up all over the world, supported by market forces (e.g. Xerox Park, Sony CSL), national and public bodies (e.g. Zentrum für Kunst und Medientechnologie in Karlsruhe, Ars Electronica Centre in Linz), interstate authorities (e.g. European Commission R&D programmes) and, more and more often, mixed funding pools implicating diverse categories of sponsors (e.g. Hexagram in Montreal). Many SMIs, SMEs and informal associations clustered around increasingly affordable equipment have also made artistic input a pivotal part of their development strategies.

Alongside pragmatic task- and applications-driven contributions of technology designers and social scientists specialised in workplace organisation, artist contributions have sometimes potentiated IT research in unexpected ways. Artists have a knack of ingenuously and ingeniously querying widely accepted tenets which

---

[8] For a European panorama of new media-related cultural development, see Boyd, F., Brickwood, C., Broeckmann, A., Haskel, L., Kluitenberg, E., Stikker, M. (ed.): New Media Culture in Europe. Uitgeverij de Balie/ The Virtual Platform, Amsterdam (1999). For a recent trans-Atlantic equivalent, see the work authored by the Committee on Information Technology and Creativity: Beyond Productivity: Information Technology, Innovation, and Creativity. Computer Science and Telecommunications Board, National Academies Press (2003).

may turn out to be arbitrary when removed from their usual context, and a downright handicap to innovation. Consequently, artists may usefully counter a tendency rife amongst shortsighted IT manufacturers, which consists of the wholesale cutting and pasting onto virtual worlds, of simplistic "real-world" behavioural patterns, on the assumption that these purportedly generic patterns (which in fact correspond to specific, context-dependent behaviours) are perfectly transposable to nascent virtual environments (which likewise require in-depth appraisal of their specific contexts). Yet questions relating to user engagement and interactive involvement, crucial to the development of socially relevant IT platforms, can only be satisfactorily answered if the unique attributes and affordances of virtual worlds are analysed thoroughly and from multiple viewpoints. This is precisely where the mix of artistic pragmatics and symbolic vision may come in useful.

As proverbial go-betweens and forgers of novel perspectives through their often irreverent manipulation of materials and symbols, artists offer invaluable, albeit unruly input to the elaboration of new communications processes, which demand conceptual agility and audacity rarely encountered in the "just-in-time" industrial ethos. Moreover, aesthetic preoccupations with rhetoric and framing to instantiate realms of experience distinct from the everyday, make artists uniquely challenging contributors to technologies that promote and depend on mixed realities.

3   Poetics of Mixed Reality Boundaries: Case Studies

The following works play on the boundaries of mixed realities in different ways. All make use of the internet as part of their technical panoply. In its dovetailing of private and public spheres, the world wide web weaves a complex fabric of spaces and times, where the unique flavour of simultaneity and co-presence is often equalled by a taste of physical estrangement and unattainability. The internet allows a potentially infinite, widely distributed population to simultaneously access a given data set or "site" (Uniform Resource Locator). This shared virtual locus is endowed with increasingly enhanced interactive functionalities which let multiple connected users experience, exchange, and manipulate all kinds of digitally processable information (texts, images, sounds, etc.). Their resultant heightened sense of live(ly) joint activity contrasts sometimes poignantly with the extreme physical distances which may separate them. Many artistic experiments involving online creation deal with this issue of the shifting, indefinable addresses of virtual spaces, and with how to meaningfully link these spaces to definable physical correlates.

The first piece described below, which dates back to 1996, is an early milestone in the area of networked mixed reality artwork, and exemplifies attempts to link urban and data space by generating a collision between an overwhelmingly physical event, and a networked counterpart event.

The second piece uses the internet to provide citizens with new affordances in physical space, notably allowing them to re-appropriate a public meeting place often deprived of its primitive communal function. Unlike the preceding work, which was installed in several different urban settings, this site-specific piece derives essential meaning from anchorage in a targeted geographical, historical and political environment.

The third work, which dates back to 2001, exemplifies strategies to access powerful tools designed by and for the scientific community, in order to open up specific, highly contemporaneous avenues of exploration and to make the harvested materials available to the broader artistic community.

Finally, the last work, developed over the past three years, is an example of recent incursions of artists working with new technologies into the world of gaming, mobilising cutting edge R&D competence to reach a broad, highly diversified public.

Selected from the substantial repertory of mixed reality art that has marked the past decade, this spectrum pretends to be neither exhaustive nor exclusive, but to constitute an emblematic, hopefully useful array of mixed reality explorations. It should be pointed out that all the artists implicated in the case studies have developed significant bodies and ranges of works up- and downstream of these examples, chosen to spotlight particular, complementary lines of investigation.

3.1   Urban/Data Interweaving and Emergent Patterns: *Anonymous Muttering*, Knowbotic Research, Dutch Architecture Institute, Rotterdam, 1996[9]

Anonymous Muttering (AM), was a partly web-based, partly physically located work created by Knowbotic Research (KR+cF) during the 1996 edition of the Dutch Electronic Arts Festival (DEAF), Rotterdam. AM was designed to allow multi-user creation of sound and light events, experienced simultaneously by internauts via audio and graphics on a website, and by visitors to the physical installation, a skeletal cylindrical platform stationed high above water surrounding the Dutch Architecture Institute, accessed by climbing a vertical steel ladder. The truncated cylinder base measured about five meters across and eight meters in length; its hooped ribcage, which arched five meters above the platform base, was rigged with a set of powerful stroboscopic projectors and speakers. Sound sources consisted of live DJ input gleaned from various Rotterdam events scheduled during DEAF (this sampling of sound from realtime productions of professional mixers added a further layer of complexity to the edifice). Internaut engagement was ensured by a flexible mesh graphics interface, which could be tweaked with a standard input device to modify the available sound fabric. Visitors to the physical installation could similarly tweak and manipulate a pliable silicon membrane on the AM platform to produce audio modifications, as well as response from the stroboscopic lights. Perceptive experience offered by the platform environment was geared to overwhelm: violence of the stroboscopic projection system endowed gestures of visitors manipulating the silicon membrane interface with a strangely ritualistic quality. Thinness of the AM website, with its sparsely linear graphics and symbols, constituted an effectively rarefied counterpoint to the physical installation.

Like other KR+cF pieces, AM focussed on links between the real and digital networked environment, and on notions of interaction, group identity, and thought and behavioural patterns arising in shared digital and real worlds. The installation was built to intensify participant awareness of interaction with fellow humans, and with large masses of digital data as a (similarly) responsive, evolving force. As the name of the piece indicates, the (often strident) mutterings remained anonymous, since

---

[9] See http://www.khm.de/people/krcf/AM_rotterdam/long.html.

multiform, multi-user inputs to the system excluded readily traceable actions : *"The partial appearance of the event can no longer be ascribed either to the public space of a city or to the private terrain of an individualised data space. An Anonymous Muttering without beginning or end".*[10]

By proposing a mix of urban and networked spaces over a time-frame of several successive nights, *Anonymous Muttering* challenged issues of agency and identity in hybrid, collective systems where human, technological, and informational energies become an indissociable magma. The complexity of multiple interactions was made evident by the rendering of constantly permuted data as changes in light and sound, and as alterations in online graphics. Spaces and times anchored in networked ubiquity and omnipresence, and those proper to tangible, sensorial experience, were effectively engineered to ghost one another, their mapped and mappable features generating a curious echo, a kind of morphogenetic resonance. Although the work seemed to have a life of its own (which often felt closer to a tumultuous thunderstorm than to anonymous muttering), those who entered it were disconcertingly aware of the fact that they controlled – at least partially - its seemingly chaotic input and output. Individual identity and traceability – the hallmarks if not raison d'être of much interactive work - were eschewed, the hybrid, process-bound situation being contrived rather to heighten awareness of the collective patterns of nascent humachine behaviours.

Anonymous Muttering's emotional force resided in the spectator-interactors' experience of its ambivalent energy, at once alienating in its calculated, mechanical ferocity, and attractive in its apparent responsiveness. The realisation that it was futile to try and discern individual input in such a complex environment proved liberating rather than frustrating, prompting spectators to tune in to the patterns of light, sound, and graphics that eventually (inevitably) emerged. Eliciting a contemplative attitude from subjects plunged into a heavy metal, data-crunching environment built to dramatise the chaotic contours of humachine "dialogue", was precisely one of the more paradoxical goals and strong points of *Anonymous Muttering*.

3.2 Networking to Re-territorialise the Agora: *Vectorial Elevation*, Rafael Lozano-Hemmer, Zocalo Plaza, Mexico City, 1999–2000[11]

Rafael Lozano-Hemmer's site-specific works, which the artist dubs "relational architecture", exploit digital tools to highlight historical qualities of urban locations, providing contemporary re-readings of distinctive cityscape features, while using the internet to open these perspectives up to a planetary audience of spectators and interactors. His installations reach large publics, in both physical space (the Zocalo Plaza accommodates up to 230,000 people) and virtual networked space (the website drew 700,000 internauts during the actual event). *Vectorial Elevation* (VE) aimed to reterritorialise an agora often deprived of its essential origin as a popular meeting place, this function being regularly upstaged by political and military authorities. The

---

[10] Ibidem.
[11] See http://www.alzado.net/eintro.html; Lozano-Hemmer, R. (ed.): Vectorial Elevation. Relational Architecture No.4. Conaculta and Ediciones San Jorge, Mexico City (2000).

Zocalo Plaza occupies the ancient emplacement of Tenochtitlan, the Aztec capital destroyed by Cortés in the early sixteenth century. VE was commissioned to celebrate the turn of the twenty-first century on this same emplacement. At the same time, and significantly for this particular art work, numerous free access public terminals were deployed throughout Mexico to promote internet access to the dawning millenium.

The artist installed a battery of eighteen robotic xenon searchlights around the Plaza, linking these projectors to a computer simulation platform allowing beam positions to be programmed and adjusted. This simulator was accessed by internauts who used the model to design their own eight-second lighting sequence. When they clicked the "send" button in the simulator application, xyz coordinates of the searchlights in the virtual world were sent over TCP/IP to Mexico, where they were translated into real coordinates using a programme calibrated with Global Positioning System trackers. Emails acknowledging receipt of proposals, and announcing programmed launch times of the sequences, were issued so that persons who had submitted light designs could follow the live internet outcome, choosing between views offered by three webcams stationed over the square. They could also download and keep as souvenirs filmed images of their individual designs, together with the corresponding computer graphics models. Many local participants physically came to the square, to share their experience of the work and identify their own creative contributions among the motifs of the monumental, ephemeral fabric of light, woven at a planetary scale. As pointed out by artist and eye witness Daniel Canogar : "Viewing this project becomes especially exciting knowing that the shaping of every single configuration of the 18 searchlights corresponds to a different person somewhere in the world"[12].

The Zocalo Plaza was vigorously reappropriated during the twelve successive nights VE was scheduled, by Mexicans and by virtual visitors from eighty-nine other countries. The Plaza was overtaken by a mix of Amerindian souvenir hawkers (habitués who have haunted the Zocalo since Moctezuma's demise), loiterers, tourists, and informed seekers of a novel urban and cultural experiment. Public control of an extremely powerful light architecture with ominous historical connotations – including Albert Speer's infamous 1935 Nazi Congress hommage, and World War II anti-aircraft surveillance projectors – playfully dissolved these totalitarian and militarist overtones. The heavy heroics often associated with large-scale light shows gave way to a carnavalesque spirit of participation, an ingenuous sense of creative identification, and an irrepressible, genuinely popular sense of belonging. The connected citizen was here instated as a provider, a creative actor, breaking with habitual passive consumer status, as electronic and electrical energies converged to shed new light on a public place exceptionally dedicated to interaction. "Vectorial Elevation succeeds in giving visual form to the digital by extending the implosive world of the Internet into Mexico City's urban space (...) in crystallizing an otherwise invisible phenomenon: the electronic transmission of infinite computer data crossing the Internet." (Canogar)[13].

---

[12] Canogar, D.: Spectral Architectures. In Vectorial Elevation, op.cit., and available online at http://www.alzado.net/book.html.
[13] Ibidem.

The internet as the ultimate "u-topos" was thus used to reinforce the poignancy and social pregnancy of an extremely specific historical and geographical locus, as people from all over the planet thronged to a virtual forum in order to participate in a real, identifiable, intensely situated event. The sense of engagement by proxy (i.e. disengagement or disempowerment), which tends to characterise much sociopolitical activity in modern democracies, was upstaged by this unique opportunity to intervene recognisably and at an unimaginable scale, in an agora increasingly intolerant of spontaneous exuberance.

3.3 Mixing (with) Cosmic Signals: *Acoustic Space Lab*, Riga, 2001[14]

The Acoustic Space Lab was the spectacular launch event of the International Acoustic Space Research Programme, which aims "to develop a cross-disciplinary platform, to explore the social and creative potential of sound and acoustic environments, to formulate relations between data streams and radio waves, and to develop collaborative broadcasting and streaming strategies alongside socially dynamic communication."[15]

From 4th-12th August 2001, thirty media artists – sound artists, net and community radio activists - gathered in Irbene, western Latvia, at a 32m diameter radio telescope left by the Soviet Army after its 1993 withdrawal from the Baltic States, baptised "Little Star"[16]. Classified among the world's top ten high precision radio telescopes (0.5 mm accuracy), Little Star was used under the Soviet regime to detect planetary, stellar, and extragalactic radiation, for Very Long Baseline Interferometry, and – primarily – for surveillance purposes. Salvaged by the Ventspils International Radio Astronomy Center (VIRAC), a company founded by Latvian enthusiasts from various scientific institutes, the radio telescope was made sufficiently operational to interest RIXC/Re-Lab[17] artists led by Rasa Smite and Raitis Smits, who have a solid pioneering history in acoustics and radio streaming. Together with artist and project coordinator Derek Holzer, the RIXC obtained use of Little Star for a creative workshop and symposium conducted in cooperation with VIRAC scientists.

With technical guidance from Dmitry Bezrukov (VIRAC), three working groups were set up : the "acoustic group" explored expressive possibilities of the actual dish, a rich sound source by virtue of its sheer dimensions and movements (the parabola represents an 800m2 surface area, for a 600 ton mass poised on a 25m concrete tower). The group rigged microphones at the dish's primary and secondary foci, picking up eerie rustling of the Latvian forest, bird cries, and wind noise. They also recorded sounds generated by the telescope's groaning mechanics as it tilted and panned. The "surveillance" group, headed by Marko Peljhan's Makrolab contingent,

---

[14] See http://acoustic.space.re-lab.net/history.html.

[15] Ibidem.

[16] In addition to information from the Acoustic Space Lab website (cf. supra), this account draws on a description by Mukul, available at http://www.ambienttv.net/2001/asl/wire.html, and an email report sent by Nina Czegledy to the Syndicate mailing list (Acoustic Space Report, 11-08-2001). The author of the present article followed live streaming throughout the Acoustic Space Lab event.

[17] RIXC : Riga Center of New Media Culture, http://rixc.lv.

resuscitated the dish's darker past as a spying device, switching the feed horn's 11 GHz primary focus over to 1.5 GHz to eavesdrop on communications satellites, notably INMARSAT systems serving analogue mobile phone services, ship-to-shore communications, air traffic control signals, and various data packet transmissions. The third "radio astronomy" group followed the dish's more orthodox vocation as a planetary observation device, processing the harvested data to produce 2- and 3-D renderings, line graphs, and control data for audio applications.

A profusion of images testified to these same activities: stills and footage of the actual telescope and its "visions", and of the lab's overall activity, were contributed to the multimedia resource used for streaming. After four days and nights amassing this material, the group migrated to Riga to ensure a marathon six-hour web cast, with remote participation from several organisations including Kunstradio in Vienna (which issued daily bulletins on the lab throughout its duration). Internauts tuned in to an unforgettable encounter of recognisably human-scale and vertiginously extraterrestrial realities, via adroitly manipulated image and sound sequences. Among the leitmotivs that patterned the web cast, shots of the telescope's scaffolding produced a visual field which oscillated between an abstract, constructivist grid and an eminently identifiable, very material construction that soon felt like "home". Among the sound leitmotivs, the voice of a Tamil sailor reporting his maritime position as a series of digital coordinates, captured by INMARSAT snooping, and looped for its incantatory qualities, haunted the event like an archaic techno-tabla sequence.

Audio, video and web archives have been made available for artists wishing to tap into and reinterpret this vast resource. For Rasa Smite and Raitis Smits, curators of the ongoing compilation, signals conveyed by radio waves constitute an immensely rich, generally invisible fabric from which to forge new artistic experiences, likely to resonate more acutely with phenomena and energies of our times. "In the seemingly chaotic "noise" originating from info streams, nature and the observations of the universe, certain structures, rhythms, and cycles exist. By processes of filtering, emphasizing and amplifying these rhythms of the electromagnetic waves and data structures, artists and musicians are remodelling the con-texture of acoustic space."[18]

3.4   Mixed Reality Manhunt:
Can You See Me Now?, Blast Theory, Various European Cities, 2001–2003[19]

Blast Theory, a London-based artists' group which has developed interactive performances, installations, and diverse mixed reality projects for over a decade, has collaborated with MRL (Nottingham University) since the mid-nineties[20]. After an innovative project entitled *Desert Rain*, hailed by artistic and technology development communities alike, Blast Theory's latest collaboration with MRL is based on a mixed

---

[18] Smite, R., Smits, R.: http://kunstradio.at/PROJECTS/CURATED_BY/RR/mainframe.html

[19] See http://www.blasttheory.co.uk/cysmn/

[20] Regarding MRL's collaboration with Blast Theory, see the interview with Professor Steve Benford, the lab's principle investigator, at
http://www.bbc.co.uk/shootinglive/shootringlive1/blasttheory/mrl.shtml

reality chase, where players in urban space pursue internauts on the loose in a virtual representation of the same city (the game area measures 300m x 300m). *Can You See Me Now?* (CYSMN) is probably no more indebted to chase-based board games like *Scotland Yard* (where players track Mister X through London) than to films like *Tron*, because CYSMN is precisely positioned at the boundary between the real world and the game screen.

Coloured icons individualise real and online players. The latter use keyboard arrows for mobility, while two or three runners, each equipped with a handheld computer connected to a GPS receiver, monitor their virtual competitors, who in turn track the physical players on the website. In addition to being able to visualise all players on their handheld scanners, a walkie talkie audio stream allows the runners to develop joint tactics, and to link back to home base for strategic advice. In a true spirit of fair play, this audio is also available for internauts seeking loopholes to shake off their pursuers. The runners win the game when they "catch" the virtual players (within a 5m radius): the win is announced and the exact spot tagged by photographing the physical location. This documentary proof is uploaded to the website so that online players can see where they were actually sighted, and discover physical attributes of the fateful spot previously experienced in abstract map form.

Whereas many art works address the totalitarian threat of today's tightly interrelated surveillance systems, portraying satellite-relayed networks as the oppressors of physical freedom and mobility, Blast Theory creates a flipside to the problem, by building a game where physical players pursue and triumph over internauts : the sweat of trickster urban guerillas triumphs over the laborious manoeuvres of their armchair assailants. The city map, with its schematic grey-scale codes to designate variably penetrable spaces, initially appears a somewhat meagre reference for virtual players competing with runners immersed in tangible, physically charged urban space, but repeated gaming allows internauts to navigate with increasing ease between abstract and real space, developing their competitive prowess. Yet the runners' learning curve is also rising constantly, as they learn the ropes of their physical world (cities hosting the project include Sheffield, Rotterdam, Oldenburg, and Linz).

While *Desert Rain* implemented rhetorical and temporal features inspired by the arcade game world, CYSMN encroaches on the blurred medium of so-called reality games[21]. The work complies with many basic principles of online gaming, its screen facade effectively triggering a sense of identification via cursory graphics and icons. There is a sense of challenge involved in learning one's way around the abstract urban map, in memorising dead ends and thoroughfares to prolong onscreen life. This classic ingredient of outlasting one's rival - a key feature of games ranging from chess to arcade racing - is contaminated in CYSMN by seepage of real-world matter and noise into the usually discrete screen world. The audio channel conveys the physical runners' efforts with disturbing intensity: the sound of their panting sprints across con-

---

[21] In these often clandestine games, commands and information are relayed via communications networks to players who can be constantly tracked via their TCP-IP and cell phone coordinates, so that data issued by the game controller gradually and surreptitiously infiltrates everyday experience. The sometimes intoxicating fascination exerted by such activities – as in many role-playing games – is largely due to their willful dissolution of the barriers between make-believe and real-life experience.

crete, grass, and bitumen surfaces (not to mention mud and puddles) is charged with meaning for the pursued internauts, who remain oddly dependent on their rival's muscular exertion and senses to guide them through the detached online representation.

The players' sense of engagement remains curiously torn between awareness of the reality gap that separates their two species, and the realisation – woeful for the virtual losers, joyful for the physical winners - that the game is designed precisely to allow this gap to be jumped. Despite – and because of - its ostensible simplicity, *Can You See Me Now?* creates an edgy tension between physical and screen realities, a tension oddly spiked with adrenalin of the very game culture it travesties.

4 Conclusions

Integrating multiple registers of reality is nothing new for artists. On the contrary, it has been an essential part of their work for thousands of years. The art of mixing realities requires masterful orchestration of the codes and rhetoric governing the various realities welded to form art works: for the articulation of multiple, hybrid spaces to be effective, these codes have to be clearly thought through. This does not mean that they have to be pedantically explained – an excessively didactic approach may overkill, particularly where the layperson's intuitive ability to use symbolic reasoning is underestimated (a danger in much IT development which shies away from more implicit, complex meanings in favour of simplistic, often vapid stances). It DOES mean that components of a mixed reality world, whether grounded in pragmatic reasoning or in symbolic language, have to be well analysed and their interactions thoroughly codified at the conception and implementation levels.

The works presented above embark on mixing realities in keeping with very different techniques and goals, in order to open up new fields for artistic exploration. All four works use the recognisable rhetorics of quite specific experiential registers to build realities imbued with a certain coherence and cohesion, but mix and outstrip these same rhetorics and registers to reveal unexpectedly new terrain.

Anonymous Muttering's strobe-pulsed disco environment aptly conveys the sense of chaos and emergent patterns sought by Knowbotic Research. Behaviours that have become conventional in the interactive arts – tweaking a graphics interface and manipulating a fetishist artifact – are implemented in an environment where their usually gratifying cause-and-effect traceability is inoperative. Yet recognising the futility of one-to-one interactive gestures is here a step towards a deeper apprehension of the complexity of humachine interactions.

Vectorial Elevation instates all the ambivalent, fascinating, often alienating ingredients of a triumphal political celebration – big lights, big broadcast –, then brazenly places the anonymous citizen at the center of the system. The fact that the entire event is designed to grant momentary, inconceivable empowerment to usually passive individuals – however limited their sphere of action - gives an odd twist to the rhetoric of spectacle that generally subtends festivities in large public places.

The *Acoustic Space Lab* builds a unique artistic resource from information streams produced by astronomical and terrestrial radiowave surveillance. The lab's indissociable missions (data harvesting, interdisciplinary exchange, webcasting events) are all pervaded, conditioned, and amplified by networking, in its technical and social guises. Like Russian avant-garde visionaries of the early twentieth century, the RIXC-based group is creating new kinds of artistic material likely to have unimaginable cultural resonance for decades to come.

Can You See Me Now? pushes tracking technologies to construct a game reality/ reality game that adheres to the basic rules subtending several kinds of play (board games, arcade and online games, street gang games), thereby appealing to a wide audience without sacrificing its creative, critical edge. Stereotyped ideologies of agency cannot account for the strange form of interdependence that links online and physical players, nor for the fact that, despite an intoxicating urgency of gaming, the win-or-lose question ultimately proves irrelevant.

As artists working with information technologies, the makers of these works strongly vindicate their concern with the hazy areas of confusion, incredulity, and ambiguity, and their unique mission as creative disruptors and dispellers of "idées reçues". Their works thus contrast radically with cultural products geared towards demystifying and popularising IT, by promoting clear-cut accessibility and reassuring levels of understanding. The generally market-driven approach that subtends the latter products is diametrically opposed to artists' often contentious, disturbingly equivocal apprehension of the complex, contradictory facets of our fast evolving technosphere. Yet the latter social stance is at least as important as well-meant didactic positions, if humans are to grasp the deeper significance of today's and tomorrow's mixed reality worlds, and if they are to actively espouse and challenge the new forms of hybrid intelligence they are engendering. The artistic endeavours presented here prepare fertile terrain for audacious forms of storytelling, keyed to today's and tomorrow's realities.

References

1. Duro, P. (ed.): The Rhetoric of the Frame. Essays on the Boundaries of the Artwork, Cambridge University Press, Cambridge USA (1996)
2. Moser, M.A. and MacLeod, D. (ed.): Immersed in Technology. Art and Virtual Environments, MIT Press, Cambridge, Massachusetts (1996)
3. Benford, S., Norman, S-J, Bowers, J. et al : *Pushing Mixed Reality Boundaries*. erena, Esprit Project, Royal Institute of Technology (KTH), Stockholm, www.nada.kth.se/erena/pdf/D7b_1.pdf (1999)
4. Walldius, A.: Patterns of Recollection. The Documentary Meets Digital Media. Aura Förlag, Stockholm (2001)
5. Manovich, L.: The Language of New Media. MIT Press, Cambridge, Massachusetts (2001)

Note: all websites accessed by the author on September 2nd 2003.

"Just Talking about Art" – Creating Virtual Storytelling Experiences in Mixed Reality

Ulrike Spierling[1] and Ido Iurgel[2]

[1] FH Erfurt, University of Applied Sciences, Schlüterstr. 1, Erfurt, Germany
spierling@fh-erfurt.de
[2] ZGDV e.V., Department of Digital Storytelling, Fraunhoferstr. 5, Darmstadt, Germany
ido.iurgel@zgdv.de

Abstract. This paper reports on interdisciplinary findings and first results of the ongoing EU-funded R&D project "art-E-fact". Within the project, a generic platform for building a particular genre of Mixed Reality interactive storytelling experiences is under development. It enables artists to script interactive dialogues for multiple virtual characters and a human participant, as well as to freely design any interaction devices and modalities. The interactive play "Just talking about art" will be illustrated as an example. With an edutainment motivation, it introduces virtual characters positioned next to real art pieces in an exhibition. These characters discuss art, while prompting visitors for their opinions and questions. They also provide entertainment by enacting personal conflicts. The content and design issues of the play will be shown as one representative example of what can be built with the art-E-fact platform. The main technical components for the direction of interactive dialogues are explained, and authoring issues are pointed out.

1 Introduction

1.1 Motivation

Storytelling is a communication means and an expressive art form, which has been employed since the beginnings of humankind. It appears in any medium that was ever invented, assuming unique forms and producing new genres. The term Mixed Reality refers to a continuum between the perception of virtual information and that of the real world. Virtual reality and Mixed Reality, together with virtual autonomous characters that react to user interaction, now have an impact on what future story genres will look like. One of the major prerequisites for future successful interactive storytelling applications in Mixed Reality is the availability of generation platforms, providing artists access to the creation of the content, as well as to the creation of an overall experience for their users. This includes the design of physical interaction devices, bridging the gap between participants and the virtual world within a specially designed installation, as well as of interactive dialogues.

However, there are still numerous obstacles preventing artists and designers from accessing the actual tools for the creation, even from finding methods for experimentation with Mixed Reality and Virtual Storytelling [1]. According to C. Crawford [2] and A. Stern [3], a really interactive storytelling artwork has "to talk", "to think" and

O. Balet et al. (Eds.): ICVS 2003, LNCS 2897, pp. 179–188, 2003.
© Springer-Verlag Berlin Heidelberg 2003

"to listen" to the audience. With this in mind, in our framework, the major artistic design issues that have to be addressed for creation are:

- CHARACTER DESIGN: Characters constitute the main means of communicating the content within our interactive dialogue scenarios. Their design includes modelling in 3D and parameterization for autonomous behaviour and media integration (the artwork "talks" to the user);
- INTERACTION DESIGN: For Mixed Reality, this means the artistic creation of physical and multimodal interaction devices, which are relevant to the particular story and can be integrated smoothly into the abstract representation of story events (the artwork "listens" to the user);
- STORY DESIGN: The story design encompasses the definition of an overall story structure, writing of interactive dialogues and definition of contexts, and providing a coherent story arc presentation while giving the audience the possibility of experiencing agency (the artwork "thinks" while planning and processing).

1.2 Generic Platform for New Interactive Storytelling Genre

The EU-funded project art-E-fact (EU IST-2001-37924) [4] is currently developing a generic platform for interactive storytelling in Mixed Reality. The project is related to art in the dual sense that the tools shall be used by artists to create installations with Mixed Reality elements that, again, present artwork, e.g. in a museum context. The framework of experimental tools includes interactive storytelling dialogue structuring means, as well as an abstract device manager, for handling different forms of user input.

Art presentation encounters the hermeneutical fact of contingent, historically and culturally anchored perspectives, and the access to art presupposes dialogue with a concrete person, rather than solely the gathering of information. This unique set of prerequisites was already taken into account in the definition process of art-E-fact - by the introduction of a discussion group of personality-rich virtual characters, each representing a different perspective and alternative access to art. The characters speak with each other and with the user, thereby giving a "face" to opinions and points of view and allowing for identification with or for distancing of the user. This is inspired by the philosophical explorations in Plato's "Symposium" [5] [6], where drama, pronounced personalities and sophisticated educational dialogues are combined, and which can also include "half-truths" – generally aimed at a specific audience.

Thus, the framework envisages a particular genre of interactive storytelling: the interactive conversation of exhibition visitors with virtual characters about various viewpoints of art interpretation. The technical platform, however, is geared to be generic in order to allow all sorts of interactive discussion on any topic (e.g. in a car sales application) based upon that specific discussion scheme.

1.3 Integration of Artistic Approaches and Platform Mechanics

Artists as authors of the described interactive dialogue situations are addressed as the primary users of the generic platform. With the help of the system's authoring interfaces, they create experiences for participants of interactive scenarios. These participants, for example, visitors of an exhibition, are indeed the end users of resulting storytelling applications. The intention of the platform is to place as much design decision authority as possible into the hands of the artists, which, in turn, also makes them responsible for the end user experience. During the design process, they face all three aspects ("talk", "think", "listen"), each with its own design requirements (e.g. rule/game design, dialogue writing, visual design and UI design).

The project aims for integration of the artistic requirements into the platform. However, since the intended type of application is new, the typical open-ended creative issues and requirements are also explored and revised in parallel during the project.

In section 3, we give a description of the major design issues faced by artists. This section also shows exemplary details of a first designed story, focussing on interactive dialogues. Section 4 explains the technical issues associated with the conversation, which are addressed by the platform.

2   Related Work

Within the art-E-fact storytelling genre, the interaction goal of several virtual characters is to guide the audience through interesting predefined conversations while simultaneously prompting the individual members for interaction.

In interactive storytelling research, the character-based and the plot-based approach exist in diametric opposition. With our interactive conversations, we want to achieve a middle ground. A similar endeavour is present in M. Mateas' and A. Stern's "Façade" [7]. Mateas and Stern have developed the arguably first and only working interactive storytelling application with natural language conversation, but without educational purposes, or a mandatory set of scenes to present basic facts. In contrast, we want to enable the transfer of a certain degree of knowledge according to goals, and further, we intend to avoid the authoring obstacles and plot maintenance difficulties present in their approach. Our solution relies on a hierarchical and modular control approach (see section 4).

Further, other systems of interactive storytelling are currently being developed without emphasis on conversation.

As for expressive conversational characters, Bickmore and Cassell [8] have developed embodied conversational agents with complex gesture capabilities, but with little emphasis on storytelling. Presentation by character groups was first developed by André et al. [9], with a focus on the generation of conversations based on database information, with little interaction, without storytelling elements and without the emphasis on multi-faceted themes. Rickel et al. [10] developed a complex simulation environment for military training with storytelling elements; also, with limited interaction.

3   Design Issues and Story Example

The platform is especially designed for building a particular genre of interactive storytelling. However, within the genre, creators shall have real design choices. For example, the resulting interactive conversational play can be flexible in the sense that ample, the resulting interactive conversational play can be flexible in the sense that it can take place in a museum setting, employing all Mixed Reality interface possibilities, or in an individual session on a desktop computer delivered via CD–ROM or the Internet, while maximizing the natural language conversation. Conceiving the content for the Mixed Reality setting proved to be a challenging integration task. In the following paragraphs, typical design issues for educational storytelling in Virtual Reality or Mixed Reality are pointed out by means of an example.

3.1   Project Briefing

Our example is an edutainment application - the interactive play "Just talking about art". The objective is to provide knowledge in an entertaining way. People shall become interested in the presented art of the Renaissance through the introduction of personal stories concerning the topic. However, silliness is to be avoided: the focus is to be on the knowledge.

Two (or more) pictures from the Florentine Renaissance (15th century) are shown in an exhibition. They each depict a Madonna-and-child scene and serve as private meditation pictures. During the early Renaissance, painting techniques evolved from the schematic medieval style with golden background and tempera to fully developed oil painting techniques, the "sfumato" effects of the Leonardo art school.

The aspects of knowledge that visitors shall take away from this experience include painting techniques, pigment details, including their symbolic values, art historical movements within the Renaissance, and discussions of art appreciation, encompassing both modern interpretations and the emotional and historical contexts of the Renaissance.

The setting is a realistically sized Mixed Reality installation, including replicas of real artwork, interfaces for visitors and a projection of three virtual ghost characters having discussions with the visitor about the artwork, each representing a different viewpoint and different knowledge aspects.

3.2   Finding the Right Story Content and Structure for an Installation

The more or less "open" interaction scenario is a general source for design problems surrounding real time interactive storytelling, involving elaborate Mixed Reality technology in a public space setting. Therefore, the duration of dialogues will become a major issue in the design process.

A character-based interactive story has to fulfil the following requirements, thereby confronting the storyteller with open design issues:

- **Duration:** All content can only be transported through the dialogues of the characters. Visitors can only spend a limited amount of time at the exhibit.
- **Hook:** Visitors shall be captivated within the first few moments by something that makes them stay and be interested in the details of the main objective of the story. The main design question here is how much fiction is appropriate.
- **Agency:** It is also important that visitors perceive themselves as active participants with a direct influence on the dialogue itself within the first few moments. This has to be communicated immediately, by the interface or by the dialogue.

- **Characters:** Characters with complex interpersonal relationships interest people. However, it takes a great deal of time to relay these issues through dialogue alone. Design question: How much detailed personification and drama is appropriate, in terms of not putting the knowledge transfer in jeopardy?
- **Dramatic arcs:** There should be a satisfying story resolution to each visitor's individual experience. Visitors are either made to line up for a scheduled beginning, middle and end of a three-act story, or they are free to join in at several stages of an ongoing discussion designed for that purpose. (see Fig. 1)
- **Usability:** Interaction shall be possible with text-based input, as well as through actions. This evolves the usability issues of affordance and transparency. The application has to show the interaction possibilities for every situation.

The acceptance of the overall piece is dependent on all of these and even more aspects. The success of any storytelling educational VR/MR application will depend on a successful integration of these artistic issues with the mechanics that the runtime platform can provide. The platform for interactive dialogues shall be able to let artists define characters with personality, choose a story model to decide on possible dramatic arcs, and define interactions that are integrated within the written dialogue.

3.3 Story Example

In this chapter, one of several possible examples is illustrated very briefly.

- **Story scenario:** The story follows the briefing in 3.1.
- **Characters**: The three characters are ghosts living in the museum; they represent three different mental attitudes towards the pictures shown.
  - **Maria, the iconographer:** Daughter of Prof. Jo, learned how to analyze pigment layers in a monastery. Appreciation of art based on its emotional and symbolic value. Attraction and friendship with Fritz, because she is lonely.
  - **Prof. Jo, the art historian:** Experienced art historian, knowledgeable about Renaissance, different techniques of painting and artistic styles over the centuries. Art appreciation requires profound knowledge about historical issues.
  - **Fritz, the icon dealer:** Young man, makes a living by painting icons of "Madonna with Child" themes and selling them to tourists. Knowledge about painting techniques. Art appreciation is a matter of creating artwork oneself.
  - **Personal Dilemmas:** Maria is lonely and likes Fritz, but sees a conflict with her Christianity, and is afraid of being used. Prof. Jo cares for Maria, and also for his career. He is afraid of Maria becoming too religious with her nun teachers. Fritz wants Maria as a friend and mate and also needs her help. He tries not to annoy Prof. Jo, but wishes to defend his more simplistic, hands-on attitude towards art.
- **Hook:** Fritz wants to copy the meditation pictures in order to sell them to private clients. He wants Maria to organize the original pigments from her research studio and help him with the techniques. Prof. Jo tries to interfere.
- **Interaction:** We will assume two modes of interaction, "dialogue mode" with a focus on text conversation with the group of characters, and "action mode", where visitors can take along tracked physical props.

- **Dialogue Mode:** Type text with keyboard, or choose from among predefined switches.
- **Action Mode:** Choose one prop at a time to make friends with one of the characters and explore their in-depth knowledge. Candle: Maria talks about religious symbolism. History Book: Prof. Jo explains Renaissance topics. Brush: Fritz demonstrates how to draw and paint the different techniques.
- **Interactive story structure:** The story structure follows the scheme in Fig. 1. The circle points out that there is no mandatory entrance into the conversation, but several hook points within the dialogue. The circle is a map of scenes within themes. Along the outline of the circle, pure knowledge of the three characters is located in the map. In the middle of the circle, personal issues and general topics can be used to navigate the dialogue between the themes, and to help out with the problem of mistakable or ambiguous visitor input.

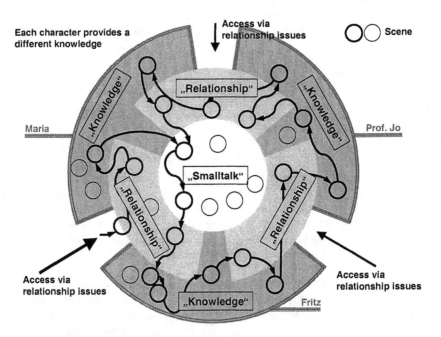

Fig. 1. Knowledge theme map as a conceptual planning device for authors

3.4 Story Design Summary

The main objective of the piece is knowledge transfer. Personal facts about the characters are only introduced briefly to serve as a catalyst for the thematic issues. The circular story model ensures several possible beginnings and suggestions for endings. It contains the possibility of a linear walkthrough of every thematic detail, as well as of using the interpersonal dialogues and smalltalk as a kind of lubricant for the interactive conversation with the visitor.

4   The Technical Platform for Art-E-Fact

The three design issues mentioned above: character design, interaction design, and story design, correspond to three technological aspects that are integrated and made accessible within art-E-fact: a system for autonomous characters, the Character Engine, an interaction framework, the Dialogue Engine, and the interactive story generation module, the Narration Engine. These three design and software levels correspond to three levels of adaptation for possible user interaction. Every engine is used to cope with the principal challenge of interactive storytelling, the coherent and suspenseful combination of interaction and narration. The Character Engines contribute to coherence maintenance with their improvisational and emotional capabilities, the Dialogue Engine with immediate responses, constrained by the current scene description, and the Narration Engine with the adaptation of the story line to interaction results. With this system, we seek a balance between free interaction, educational presentation, character believability, and narration.

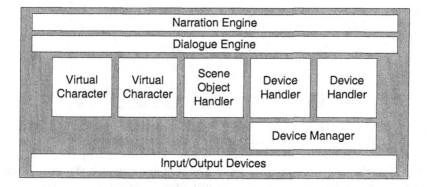

Fig. 2. Architecture Overview

4.1   Character Engines – The Personality Level

Currently, the characters are not autonomous to choose *what* to say, but rather *how* they say it, concerning their non-verbal, expressive behaviour. Emotional and social models of the characters determine corresponding context parameters. The emotion and expression rules of the characters include improvisational capabilities, i.e. they are able to adapt the emotion to what they shall say. E.g. a virtual character that is in a friendly mood will make a sad expression if it disagrees with the visitor, but a sad character might become angry.

4.2   Dialogue Engine – The Interaction Level

This engine handles interaction within the discourse of a single scene, whereas "interaction" comprises keyboard-based dialogues, but also action input from devices. It determines what the characters shall speak and do in response to input, and what shall

happen in the environment. For example, visitor input can result in a continuing dialogue, in a change of themes, or smalltalk to overcome ambiguous situations. Normally, at the end of a scene, a set of context parameters will have been set. Besides a
choice of themes, the context parameters include the basic emotions and a model of
social relationships, e.g. whether a certain character is a "friend" of the visitor. These
parameters influence the choice of the next scene by the narration engine.

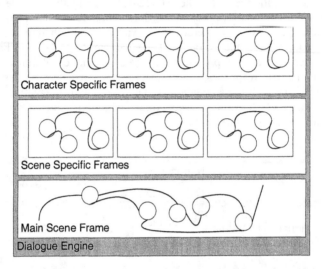

Fig. 3: In order to obtain the appropriate response to an event, the Dialogue Engine applies a
collection of thematic frames that was determined by the Narration Engine

The Dialogue Engine combines a finite state machine approach that uses thematic
frames (see Fig. 3) with pattern matching capabilities. The overall interaction is based
on conversational turns between the characters and the audience.

Authoring of the interaction includes the design of props (see examples in chapter
3.3), as well as the configuration of the interaction framework. Dialogue writers first
conceive whole scenes containing not only single spoken sentences, but actual dialogues with several turns, including possible user turns (see Fig. 4). Each scene has a
location on the thematic map (compare Fig. 1) and a preferred order of occurrence.

4.3 Narration Engine – The Story Level

The Narration Engine centrally controls the narrative development, ensuring a coherent plot. It works with an associated story model that enables the distinction of act-
like story morphemes, which we call "scenes". A scene is a short, interactive sequence
of directions to the virtual characters, to the virtual environment and to the devices.
With the help of the scene pool, an adapted story line can be mapped out at run-time,
according to user preferences, interaction history and time constraints. The output of
the Narration Engine consists of directions and constraints for the Dialogue Manager.

The Narration Engine is available either as a finite state machine for simple stories,
or as a story grammar that is implemented in Prolog. The first approach is easier to

change and to author, the second is more flexible and better if time constraints must be satisfied.

4.4 Integration with Software Components

The VR-viewer AVALON [11] is responsible for the graphical output, i.e., the rendering, but also for the presentation of sound, movies, and pictures. We are using a speech synthesis by AT&T.

Their emotional and improvisational models are hand-coded in JESS, a Java expert system [12]. We develop the animation software for the virtual characters, which relies basically on the real time selection and adaptation of predefined animations, meta-described with the help of our own AnimML format. The input to the virtual characters' animation module obeys an adapted RRL [13]; the overall description of scenes follows our independent SceneML format. The Dialogue Engine integrates an adapted A.L.I.C.E chatbot [14].

A current prototype already allows for interaction between characters and a user in front of a desktop. (see Fig. 4). Conversations are currently conducted without the Mixed Reality devices.

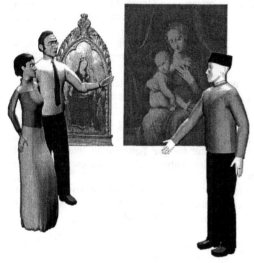

Example of interactive script:

MARIA: Oh Fritz, you know, my father worries about art forgery.

FRITZ: What the heck - I only want to create more of these, for people who love meditation.

MARIA: But the pigments they used had a symbolic value -- therefore, only the original facsimiles can praise the Lord appropriately!

FRITZ: Hey, guess why I want to use original pigments?!! I want to do it the best way possible!

MARIA: I don't know. <towards_visitor> My dear, what do you think? Is what Fritz wants to do art forgery?

EXPECTED FROM VISITOR:
<opinion or question or nothing>

Fig. 4. Conversation group of the current demonstrator, and example dialogue

5   Conclusion and Future Work

We presented a new concept of an interactive storytelling application, including a Mixed Reality interaction framework to be used in exhibition-style installations, enabling complex conversations between several characters and the user. In a collaborative effort between artists and developers, first artistic user requirements and design recommendations have been drawn from partial prototypes. Future work within the scope of the project includes the integration of the conversational prototype with the MR installation.

While enabling an ever increasing number of multimodal and conversational opportunities through technology, the complexity of the interface for interactive storytelling in VR/MR also increases. Based on the design issues stated thus far, we see the identification of usability design rules for the development of VR storytelling as a major future research issue.

References

1. Spierling, U., Grasbon, D., Braun, N., Iurgel, I.: Setting the Scene: Playing Digital Director in Interactive Storytelling and Creation. In: Computers & Graphics (2002) 26, 31-44
2. Crawford, C.: Understanding Interactivity. http://www.erasmatazz.com/book.html (2000) 5-12
3. Stern, A.: Deeper conversations with interactive art, or why artists must program. In: Convergence: The Journal of Research into New Media Technologies (2001) No. 1
4. www.art-e-fact.org
5. Plato. Symposium. Translated by Christopher Gill. Cambridge (1980)
6. Iurgel, I.: Emotional Interaction in a Hybrid Conversation Group. In: International Workshop on Lifelike Animated Agents, August 19, 2002. In conjunction with PRICAI (2002) Tokyo
7. Mateas, M., Stern, A.: Integrating Plot, Character and Natural Language Processing in the Interactive Drama Façade. In: Proceedings of TIDSE 2003, Darmstadt, March 24-26 (2003) 139-151
8. Bickmore, T., Cassell, J.: 'How about this weather?' - Social Dialogue with Embodied Conversational Agents. In: Proceedings of the AAAI Fall Symposium on Socially Intelligent Agents, North Falmouth, MA, (2000)
9. André, E., Klesen, M., Gebhard, P., Allen S., Rist, Th.: Exploiting Models of Personality and Emotions to Control the Behavior of Animated Interface Agents. In: Jeff Rickel (eds.), Proceedings of the workshop on "Achieving Human-Like Behavior in Interactive Animated Agents", in conjunction with the Fourth International Conference on Autonomous Agents, pp. 3-7, Barcelona, June (2000)
10. Rickel, J., Gratch, J., Marsella, S., Swartout, W.: Steve Goes to Bosnia: Towards a New Generation of Virtual Humans for Interactive Experiences. In: AAAI Spring Symposium on Artificial Intelligence and Interactive Entertainment, Stanford University, CA, March (2001)
11. www.igd.fhg.de/~avalon
12. herzberg.ca.sandia.gov/jess
13. www.ai.univie.ac.at/NECA/RRL
14. www.alicebot.org

Users Acting in Mixed Reality Interactive Storytelling

Marc Cavazza[1], Olivier Martin[2], Fred Charles[1],
Steven J. Mead[1], and Xavier Marichal[3]

[1] School of Computing and Mathematics, University of Teesside,
Borough Road, Middlesbrough, TS1 3BA, United Kingdom
{m.o.cavazza,f.charles,steven.j.mead}@tees.ac.uk
[2] Laboratoire de Télécommunications et Télédétection,
Université catholique de Louvain, 2 place du Levant,
1348 Louvain-la-Neuve, Belgium
martin@tele.ucl.ac.be
[3] Alterface, 10 Avenue Alexander Fleming, 1348 Louvain-la-Neuve, Belgium
xavier.marichal@alterface.com

> *"Do you expect me to talk?*
> *Oh no, Mr. Bond. I expect you to die!"*
> Bond and Auric Goldfinger – from "Goldfinger"

Abstract. Entertainment systems promise to be a significant application for Mixed Reality. Recently, a growing number of Mixed Reality applications have included interaction with synthetic characters and storytelling. However, AI-based Interactive Storytelling techniques have not yet been explored in the context of Mixed Reality. In this paper, we describe a first experiment in the adaptation of an Interactive Storytelling technique to a Mixed Reality system. After a description of the real time image processing techniques that support the creation of a hybrid environment, we introduce the storytelling technique and the specificities of user interaction in the Mixed Reality context. We illustrate these experiments by discussing examples obtained from the system.

1 Rationale

While research in Interactive Storytelling techniques has developed in a spectacular fashion over the past years, there is still no uniform view on the modes of user involvement in an interactive narrative. Two main paradigms have emerged: in the "Holodeck™" approach [10], the user is immersed in a virtual environment acting from within the story; in "Interactive TV" approaches, the user is an active spectator influencing the story from a totally external, "God-mode" perspective [2]. In this paper, we report research investigating yet another paradigm for interactive storytelling, in which the user is immersed in the story but also features as a character in its visual presentation. In this Mixed-Reality Interactive Storytelling approach, the user video image is captured in real time and inserted into a virtual world populated by autonomous synthetic actors with which he interacts. The user in turn watches the composite world projected on a large screen, following a "magic mirror" metaphor.

In the next sections, we describe the system's architecture and the techniques used in its implementation. After a brief introduction to the example scenario, we discuss the specific modes of interaction and user involvement that are associated with Mixed Reality Interactive Storytelling.

O. Balet et al. (Eds.): ICVS 2003, LNCS 2897, pp. 189–197, 2003.
© Springer-Verlag Berlin Heidelberg 2003

The storytelling scenario supporting our experiments is based on a James Bond adventure, in which the user is actually playing the role of the villain (the "Professor"). James Bond stories have salient narrative properties that make them good candidates for interactive storytelling experiments: for the same reason, they have been used as a supporting example in the foundational work of Roland Barthes in contemporary narratology [1]. Besides, their strong reliance on narrative stereotypes facilitates narrative control and the understanding of the role that the user is allowed to play. The basic storyline represents the early encounter between Bond and the villain (let us call him the Professor). The objective of Bond is to acquire some essential information, which he can find by searching the Professor's office, obtained from the Professor's assistant or even, under certain conditions, (deception or threat) by the Professor himself. The actions of the user (acting as the Professor) are going to interfere with Bond's plan, altering the unfolding of the plot.

The interactive storytelling engine is based on our previous work in character-based interactive storytelling [2]. The narrative drive is provided by the actions of the main virtual character (in this case, the Bond character) that are selected in real-time using a plan-based formalisation of his role in a given scene. The planning technique used is Hierarchical Task Planning, essentially for its representational capabilities [7]. We describe in section 3 how this technique has been adapted to the requirements of Mixed Reality Interactive Storytelling.

2   The Mixed Reality Architecture

Our Mixed Reality system is based on a "magic mirror" paradigm derived from the *Transfiction* approach [4], in which the user's image is captured in real time by a video camera, extracted from his/her background and mixed with a 3D graphic model of a virtual stage including the synthetic characters taking part in the story. The resulting image is projected on a large screen facing the user, who sees his own image embedded in the virtual stage with the synthetic actors (Figure 1).

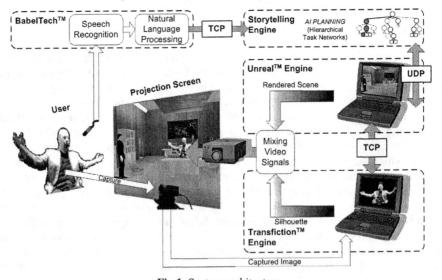

Fig 1. System architecture.

The graphic component of the Mixed Reality world is based on a game engine, Unreal Tournament 2003™. This engine not only performs graphic rendering and character animation but, most importantly, contains a sophisticated development environment to define interactions with objects and characters' behaviours [9]. In addition, it supports the integration of external software, e.g. through socket-based communication.

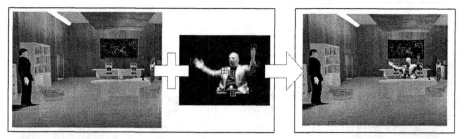

Fig 2. Constructing the Mixed Reality environment.

The mixed environment (Figure 2) is constructed through real-time image processing, using the *Transfiction* engine [6]. A single (monoscopic) 2D camera facing the user analyses his image in real-time by segmenting the user's contours. The objective behind segmentation is twofold: it is intended to extract the image silhouette of the user in order to be able to inject it into the virtual setting on the projection screen (without recurring to chroma-keying). Simultaneously, the extracted body silhouette undergoes some analysis in order to be able to recognise and track the behaviour of the user (position, attitude and gestures) and to influence the interactive narrative accordingly. The video image acquired from the camera is passed to a detection module, which performs segmentation in real time and outputs the segmented video image of the user together with the recognition of specific points which enable further processing, such as gesture recognition. The present detection module uses a 4×4 Hadamard determinant of the Walsh function and calculates the transform on elements of 4×4 pixels. As a result, it can segment and relatively precisely detect the boundary of objects and also offers some robustness to luminance variations. Figure 3 shows the overview of the change detection process with Walsh-Hadamard transform. First, the module calculates the Walsh-Hadamard transform of the background image. Afterwards, the module compares the values of the Walsh-Hadamard transform of both the current and the background images. When the rate of change is higher than a threshold that has been initially set, this module sets the area as foreground. As segmentation results can be corrupted in presence of shadows (which can be problematic due to variable indoor lighting conditions), we have used invariant techniques [8] to remove such shadows.

In this first prototype, the two system components operate by sharing a normalised system of co-ordinates. This is obtained from a calibration stage prior to running the system[1]. The shared co-ordinates system makes possible to position the user in the

---

[1] The first prototype does not deal with occlusion in Mixed Reality, which is also set at calibration time. We are currently developing an occlusion management system, which uses depth information provided by the *Transfiction* engine.

virtual image, but most importantly to determine the relations between the real user and the virtual environment. This is achieved by mapping the 2D bounding box produced by the *Transfiction* engine, which defines the contour of the segmented user character, to a 3D bounding cylinder in the Unreal Tournament 2003[TM] environment, which represents the position of the user in the virtual world (Figure 4) and, relying on the basic mechanisms of the engine, automatically generates low-level graphical events such as collisions and object interaction.

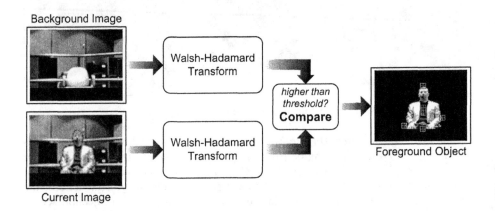

Fig. 3. Extracting the user's image from his background.

Fig 4. The 3D bounding cylinder determines physical interactions in the Unreal Tournament 2003[TM] engine.

The two sub-systems communicate via TCP sockets: the image processing module, working on a separate computer sends at regular intervals to the graphic engine two different types of messages, containing updates on the user's position as well as any recognised gestures. The recognised gesture is transmitted as a code for the gesture (plus, when applicable, e.g. for pointing gestures, a 2D vector indicating the direction of pointing). However, the contextual interpretation of the gesture is carried out within the storytelling system.

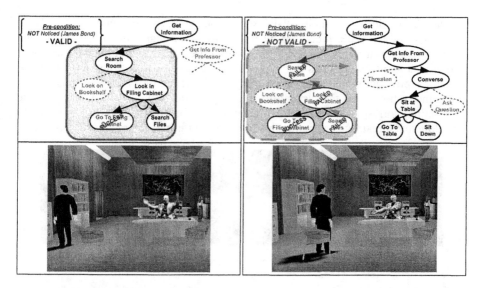

Fig. 5. An Example of User Intervention. The greetings of the user's character force a change of plans in the main character.

To illustrate briefly this implementation of interactive storytelling, we can consider the partial example presented on Figure 5. At this early stage of the plot, Bond has entered the Professor's office and has started searching for documents in the filing cabinet, thinking the room was empty. When the user greets him (with an expressive greeting gesture, as part of his acting), Bond becomes aware of the Professor's presence and has to direct himself towards him, abandoning his current actions. From that situation, there are many possible instances of his plan (hence the story) depending on the subsequent user's actions, as well as other characters coming into play.

3 User Intervention

In this context, where the user is allocated a role but is left free of his interventions, the specific actions he will take will determine the further evolutions of the plot. In contrast with Holodeck™-like approaches [10], the main character (Bond) is actually a synthetic actor rather than the user, and the storyline is driven by its role. This ensures a spontaneous drive for the story while setting the base for an implicit narrative control. The fact that the user visually takes part in the story presentation obviously affects the modes of user intervention: these will have to take the form of traditional interaction between characters. In other words, the user will have to act. As a consequence, the mechanisms of his normal acting should serve as a basis for interaction.

This fundamental aspects shapes the whole interaction, in particular it determines a specific kind of multi-modal interaction, composed of a spoken utterance and a gesture or body attitude. The latter, being part of the acting actually constitutes a semiotic gesture whose content is complementary but similar in nature to that of the linguistic input [3].

The recognition of a multi-modal speech act comprises an utterance analysed through a body gesture, processed by the *Transfiction* engine described above, and speech recognition. Body gestures from the user are recognised through a rule-based system that identifies gestures from a gesture library, using data from image segmentation that provides in real time the position of user's extremities. One essential aspect of the interaction is that the system is tracking symbolic gestures, which, as part of the user acting, correspond to narrative functions, such as greetings, threatening (or responding to a threat, such as putting his hands up), offering, calling, dismissing, etc.

Fig. 6. Examples of ambiguous gestures.

The gesture recognition process verifies whether first a body gesture has been recognised, then any speech input can provide additional information for the interpretation of the recognised gesture. In our system, speech input is used to help disambiguate gestures, compared to other multimodal approaches, where the gesture is used to disambiguate the speech. Figure 6 illustrates a few potentially ambiguous body gestures. The correct interpretation of user gestures will be provided by the joint analysis of the user utterance and his gesture.

The speech recognition component is based on the Ear SDK system from BabelTech™, which is an off-the-shelf system including a development environment for developing the lexicon. One advantage is that it can provide a robust recognition of the most relevant topics in context, without imposing constraints on the user (like the use of a specific phraseology) [5]. Finally, after speech and gesture have been combined to produce a multimodal intervention, extra information may be required from the current state of the virtual world, i.e. physical information such as location of objects and characters in relation to the user, etc.

Interactive storytelling has focussed its formalisation efforts on narrative control [11]. It has done so using the representations and theories of narratology. Yet, little has been said about the user's interventions themselves. While they should obviously be captured by the more generic representations of story or plot, there is still a need to devise specific representations for units of intervention.

This formalisation is actually a pre-requisite to successfully map the multi-modal input corresponding to the user acting to the narrative representations driving story generation. In particular, an appropriate mapping should be able to compensate, at least in part, for the limited performance of multi-modal parsing, especially when it comes to speech recognition. The basis for this formalisation is to consider the narrative structure of the terminal actions in the virtual character's HTNs. In previous work [2], we took essentially a planning view to the mapping of user intervention, especially for spoken interaction. This consisted in comparing the semantic content of a user intervention (i.e. a spoken utterance) with the post-conditions of some task-related operator. For instance, if the user provides through spoken interaction the information that a virtual actor is trying to acquire ("the files are on the desk"), this would solve its current goal.

In the current context, we should consider the narrative structure of terminal actions, which formalises explicitly roles for the user and a character. In other words, many terminal actions, such as enquiring about information, have a binary structure with an explicit slot for the user's response. This leads to a redefinition of the character's control strategy in its role application. To account for the fact that user interaction remains optional, all binary nodes (involving a possible user input) should be tested first before attempting a self-contained action from Bond.

One fundamental mechanism by which user actions can be interpreted with a robustness, which exceeds the expected performance of multi-modal parsing, is through the classification of that input using the highest-level categories compatible with interpretation. This approach capitalises on fundamental properties of narrative functions in the specific story genre we are dealing with. If we consider a scene between Bond and the Professor, the majority of narrative functions would develop around a central dimension, which is the agonistic/antagonistic relation.

If we assume that the final product of multi-modal interpretation can be formalised as a speech act, then we can bias the classification of such speech acts towards those high-level semantic dimensions that can be interpreted in narrative terms. The idea is to be able to classify the speech act content in terms of it being agonistic or antagonistic. Each terminal action will in turn have a narrative interpretation in terms of the user's attitude, which will determine further actions by the virtual Bond character (equivalent to success/failure of a terminal action).

There is indeed a fairly good mapping between speech acts in the narrative context and narrative functions, to the point that they could almost be considered equivalent. Examples of such phenomenon include: denial ("never heard of that, Mr Bond"), defiance ("shoot me and you'll never find out, Mr Bond"), threat ("choose your next witticism carefully ..."), etc.

The problem is that this mapping is only apparent at a pragmatic level and, within a purely bottom-up approach, could only be uncovered through a sophisticated linguistic analysis, which is beyond reach of current speech understanding technology. One possible approach is to consider that the set of potential/relevant narrative functions is determined by the active context (i.e., Bond questioning the Professor). And that it is the conjunction of the context and a dimensional feature (i.e. agonistic/antagonistic) that define narrative functions.

For instance, if at any stage Bond is questioning the Professor for information, this very action actually determines a finite set of potential narrative functions: denial, defiance, co-operation, bargaining, etc. Each of these functions can be approximated as the conjunction of the questioning action and a high-level semantic dimension (such as /un-cooperative/, /aggressive/, etc.). The multi-modal analysis can thus be simplified by focussing on the recognition of these semantic dimensions, whose detection be based, as a heuristic, on the identification of surface patterns in the user's utterances, such as ["you'll never"], ["you" ... "joking"], ["how would I"].

We illustrate the above aspects within the narrative context where Bond is questioning the Professor in Figure 7. Because of the set of potential narrative functions defined by Bond's current action (i.e. questioning the Professor), a test must be first carried out on the compatibility of the user's action (in this case that the Professor gives away the information) and only after can the character's action be attempted. It should be noted that this does not add any constraints on the user's actions than the one expected, which will impact on the character's plan at another level. In other words, this representation departs from a strict character-based approach to incorporate some form of plot representation, in order to accommodate for the higher level of user involvement.

In the example presented in Figure 7, the joint processing of the gestures and speech leads to interpreting the open arms gesture of the Professor and the identified surface pattern of his utterance *["you" … "joking"]* as an /un-cooperative/ semantic dimension. Finally, the conjunction of this defined semantic dimension and the current narrative context provide sufficient information to approximate the *denial* narrative function.

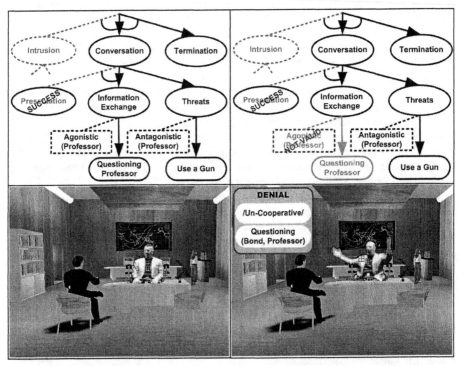

Fig. 7. An Example of Multi-Modal Interaction. Left: Bond is questioning the Professor for information. Right: the Professor replies *"You must be joking, Mr Bond!"* with a corresponding body gesture, denoting a defiance. The multi-modal speech act is interpreted as a *denial*.

4   Conclusions

We have described a first implementation of Mixed Reality Interactive Storytelling, which sets new perspectives on the user's involvement as an actor, which at the same time is also the spectator of the scene within which he is playing. Participating in such narratives potentially only requires that the user is instructed about the baseline story and possible actions, but does not (and should not) require knowledge of Bond's detailed plans and actions, or detailed instructions on his own character's sequence of actions. This work is still at an early stage, and further experiments are mandatory. Our current efforts are dedicated to the integration of robust speech recognition through multi keyword spotting, in order to support natural interaction throughout the narrative.

Acknowledgements

Olivier Martin is funded through a FIRST Europe Fellowship provided by the Walloon Region.

References

1. R. Barthes, Introduction à l'Analyse Structurale des Récits (in French). Communications, 8, pp.1-27, 1966.
2. M. Cavazza, F. Charles, and S.J. Mead, Character-based Interactive Storytelling, IEEE Intelligent Systems, special issue on AI in Interactive Entertainment, pp. 17-24, 2002.
3. M. Cavazza, F. Charles, and S.J. Mead, Under The Influence: Using Natural Language in Interactive Storytelling, 1ˢᵗ International Workshop on Entertainment Computing, IFIP Conference Proceedings, 240, Kluwer, pp. 3-11, 2002.
4. X. Marichal, and T. Umeda, "Real-Time Segmentation of Video Objects for Mixed-Reality Interactive Applications", Proceedings of the "SPIE's Visual Communications and Image Processing" (VCIP 2003) International Conference, Lugano, Switzerland, 2003.
5. S.J. Mead, M. Cavazza, and F. Charles, "Influential Words: Natural Language in Interactive Storytelling", 10th International Conference on Human-Conputer Interaction, Crete, Greece, 2003, Vol 2., pp.741-745.
6. A. Nandi, and X. Marichal, "Senses of Spaces through Transfiction", pp. 439-446 in "Entertainment Computing: Technologies and Applications" (Proceedings of the International Workshop on Entertainment Computing, IWEC 2002).
7. D. Nau, Y. Cao, A. Lotem, and H. Muñoz-Avila, "SHOP: Simple hierarchical ordered planner", Proceedings of the Sixteenth International Joint Conference on Artificial Intelligence, Stockholm, AAAI Press, 1999, pp. 968-973.
8. E. Salvador, A. Cavallaro, and T. Ebrahimi, "Shadow identification and classification using invariant color models", IEEE International Conference on Acoustics, Speech, and Signal Processing (ICASSP 2001), Salt Lake City (USA), 2001.
9. Special issue on "Game engines in scientific research", Communications of the ACM, 45:1, January 2002.
10. W. Swartout, R. Hill, J. Gratch, W.L. Johnson, C. Kyriakakis, C. LaBore, R. Lindheim, S. Marsella, D. Miraglia, B. Moore, J. Morie, J. Rickel, M. Thiebaux, L. Tuch, R. Whitney, and J. Douglas, "Toward the Holodeck: Integrating Graphics, Sound, Character and Story", in Proceedings of the Autonomous Agents 2001 Conference, 2001.
11. R. Michael Young and Mark Riedl, "Towards an Architecture for Intelligent Control of Narrative in Interactive Virtual Worlds", in Proceedings of the International Conference on Intelligent User Interfaces, January, 2003.

Is Seeing Touching?
Mixed Reality Interaction and Involvement Modalities

Alok Nandi and Xavier Marichal

Alterface, 10 avenue Alexander Fleming,
1348 Louvain-la-Neuve, Belgium
{nandi,marichal}@alterface.com

Abstract. The present paper elaborates on applications of a mixed-reality system, named Transfiction, designed for leisure and entertainment. It aims at identifying and characterising properties of the system in terms of design, development and usage. More specifically, this paper examines the assertion that the 'simple' blurring between touching and seeing allows users to be involved in the narration and helps them to interact with the system. After positioning this approach with respect to other approaches in Mixed-Reality, impacts in terms of technology and design are dealt with. This assertion is supported by empirical experiments commented in the perspective of enriching the potentialities of virtual storytelling.

1 Introduction

Within installations based on the Transfiction system, one common interaction modality appears to be the act of 'touching something'. The users feel as if they were touching something but in fact they only move their arms, legs and/or bodies in specific ways in order to interact with the reference points suggested on the screen. They are guided by the position of the image of their body on the screen. The present paper describes the process of designing mixed-reality stories in which users are involved and get out with the physical experience of 'having been through space, obstacles...', while looking at the added-value of such a paradigm for storytelling.

In section 2, the paper starts positioning the Transfiction system with respect to the concept of Mixed Reality. In this framework, the question of touching virtual objects is raised and one can then clearly introduce the approach chosen by Transfiction: namely to simulate touching only through visual interaction. Section 3 investigates the blurry frontier between touching and seeing from both technical and design points of view. Various considerations about ways to achieve touching through seeing are presented. Section 4 introduces results from various installations in order to illustrate cases of effective or non-effective blur between touching and seeing experiences. Finally, the conclusion attempts to define how and when the implementation of touching through seeing can be used as an efficient tool for storytelling.

O. Balet et al. (Eds.): ICVS 2003, LNCS 2897, pp. 198–207, 2003.
© Springer-Verlag Berlin Heidelberg 2003

2 Positioning

In order to clearly formulate the question of the possibility to simulate touching by seeing, the present section first familiarizes the reader with the Transfiction system that is used in the presented experiments of section 4, and how it relates to other Mixed-Reality or Virtual Reality systems.

2.1 Transfiction System

The Transfiction [1] system ensures that users/players are immersed into artificial and visual settings: as shown on figure 1, users see their own image on the screen and have to react according to certain stimuli, scripted in a scenario. The system reacts to body movements and gestures. Gloves, helmets or any physical sensors are not needed. Participation and involvement modalities were investigated under 'natural attitudes' for the users, through segmentation [2], body tracking [3] and gesture recognition algorithms.

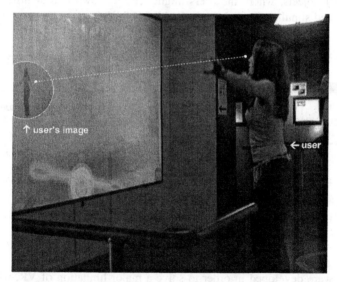

Fig. 1. Typical usage of the Transfiction system where the user sees herself/himself on the screen like within a magic mirror and can interact/navigate/investigate through body gesture

Transfiction uses the 'magic mirror' metaphor that has been initially explored by researchers/artists like Myron Krueger [4] or in set-ups where users see a virtually reproduced part of themselves such as N.I.C.E. [5], MIT's ALIVE [6] and ATR's Interactive Virtual Environment [7]. All these systems allow immersion in virtual spaces as well as interaction among human users and artificial environments and/or characters in front of a large screen. However, Transfiction is unique because of its combination of real-time immersion in any environment (no blue screen is needed) with multi-layered media asset management (from background to avatars). Moreover, the Transfiction system is now specifically oriented towards a design which allows several users to share entertaining moments, with games and/or stories.

2.2 Mixed-Reality Context

The Transfiction system positions itself within the Reality-Virtuality continuum introduced by Drascic and Milgram [8] in their definition of Mixed Reality (MR): "Real world objects can be displayed by simply scanning, transmitting and reproducing image data, as is the case with ordinary video displays, without the need for the display system to "know" anything about the objects. [...] On the other hand, *virtual* images can be produced only if the computer display system that generates the images has a model of the objects being drawn. [As illustrated in Figure 2,] Mixed Reality refers to the class of all displays in which there is some combination of a real environment and Virtual Reality. [...] *Augmented Virtuality* (AV) displays are those in which a virtual environment is enhanced, or augmented, through some addition of real world images or sensations. These additions could take the form of directly viewed (DV) objects, where the users might see their own bodies instead of computer-generated simulations, as is typical with VR." With respect to these definitions, Transfiction is clearly an AV system.

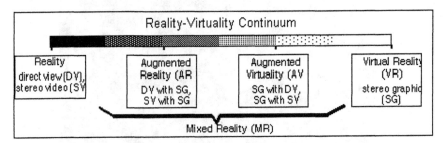

Fig. 2. Simplified representation of the Reality-Virtuality Continuum, showing how real and virtual worlds can be combined in various proportions, according to the demands of different tasks

Milgram and Drasic further argue that *"Augmented Virtual Tools* are an example of AV that were developed in order to solve a major limitation of VR, which is the absence of the sense of *touch.* In this system, real objects are fitted with special sensors and are used as the physical components of input devices for a VR system." They thereafter emphasize the need to localize objects that one can grasp/touch and they therefore recommend the use of stereoscopic displays "to facilitate accurate perception of three dimensional scenes, by providing a potentially powerful binocular cue to supplement whatever monoscopic cues are already present in the scene. However, because the human visual system is very robust and is able to work with only partial data, it is simple to create some sensation of depth. The difficulty lies in the creation of an *accurate* sense of depth. For example, a 2D display of the Necker cube is typically perceived as a regular cube rather than as a flat collection of line segments, despite the absence of any depth cues. However, the lack of depth information in this case results in uncertainty about the orientation of the cube."

Fig. 3. The Necker cube

2.3 Approach

In its current state of development, Transfiction uses only 2D visual scenes and 2D objects projected on a large screen, without any 3D display. For ease of installation and in order to provide the general public with an easy-to-learn system, it was decided not to use specific force-feedback devices. Therefore, the design challenge is to overcome the need of the human eye to look for an accurate visual space and to involve users by enforcing action and interaction. Our working assumption relies on the intuition that, contrary to the above quotations by Drascic and Milgram, the sense of 'touch' can be provided only by 'seeing', without headsets and stereoscopic displays. Only visual artefacts and sound effects are available as feedback effects to the users. The remaining part of the present paper explores some constraints that such a choice has imposed in terms of technology and design, and then introduces usage situations.

3 Touching = Seeing?

Willing to provide users with a sense of touching virtual objects only by seeing them requires a combination of technical capabilities along with a proper design of the audio-visual ambiances. Both these aspects are here presented independently although they are highly inter-dependent.

3.1 Technical Point of View

For Transfiction users, the most intuitive way to touch a virtual object on the screen is to move their own image so that some part of their body is superposed upon the object. In terms of graphical analysis, it just means 'collision detection': the object is touched if there is any overlap between its shape and the silhouette of the users. However, according to the type of objects, one does not expect to touch it with any part of the body. It is therefore important to enable more flexibility with the 'touching' rule: some objects can only be 'touched' with the hands, others with the feet, some only with the head. It therefore requires the system to be able to detect and track such body parts [3].

For users to know they have successfully touched something, feedback is needed: audio cues as well as visual effects are needed in order to emphasize the impact of user actions, as a reaction to it. The illusion of touching is reinforced by applying some rules of physics related a.o. to gravity of or with respect to virtual objects. The impression/perception of physical laws is simulated so that, at a distance, the touched object reacts as it would in daily life: a ball jumps and falls with successive hops; a kit flies if virtual wind is present...

These three technical capabilities – touching with specific body parts, receiving direct feedback about it and physical law simulation – can then be used by the design/perceptual approach in order to provide users with a seamless experience.

3.2   Design and Perceptual Point of View

The Transfiction set-up allows media combination and manipulation with a high degree of flexibility. Hence, there is a need to articulate the media assets to ensure that it is meaningful. The user experience spans over a certain time and a 'narrative' pattern can be applied to the usage experience. However, the focus here is on the interaction modalities where the simulated feedback is physical in order to reinforce the illusion of immersion. Then, the user has the feeling that there is no more interface, as suggested by Dove [9]:

"An interface has a recipe for the suspension of disbelief embedded in its operations that is similar to the recipes for the suspension of disbelief present in genre fiction. These codes are what we are willing to accept or believe to enter the world of a story. If interface design and genre fiction codes mutually support the vision of a story, an immersive world opens up. [...] The interface is the osmotic membrane – the means by which we fuse with the virtual space."

This notion of fusion is to be related to the notion of involvement. The engagement is physical hence emotional as it triggers the user for immediate, vigorous action in order to remain within the perceived rules of actions allowed in that universe. The "osmotic membrane" allows the fusion between the virtual and the actual spaces, and one way to make this fusion tangible is by working on the 'blurriness' between touching and seeing. While the fusion takes place at the global user experience level, the blurriness between touching and seeing happens at the level of gestual interactions and resulting perception

To validate our assumption, we have adapted some heuristics in order to design our interactive systems. Heuristics are principles, identified by experts, which can provide an understanding of the rules with which a system is designed and built. Although Jakob Nielsen's heuristics [10] were identified for regular software (WIMP paradigms and desktop screen), we have chosen to apply them to the Transfiction system: they need to be further worked and adapted for rich-media Mixed Realities applications. This approach allows the identification of heuristics in a (multimodal) interaction context, which aims at greater expressive power, naturalness and portability.

Heuristic 1: Visibility of System Status
In the Transfiction system, the user receives visual feedback through her/his own image and from changes of visual information in the environment and/or changes in

the behavior of the artificial objects. Such changes occur according to a scenario. Audio cues equally help draw people's attention while, in certain scenarios, a time limit bar indicates how much time the user still has to interact with the system. All these signals give the user precious feedback in real-time.

Heuristic 2: Match between the System and the Real World

In order to remain familiar to the user, the correlation happens at the level of navigation (i.e. body language interaction: move right or left, jump) and circulation metaphors. As implied by Transfiction, one looks at his/her image transported into fictional spaces. Hence, the matching remains focused on the movement coherency and credibility. This heuristic relates to the core task of designing a believable space (one that the user can understand/believe). This coherency is not only important in terms of visual ambiances but also in terms of the behaviors and movements of the characters and objects inhabiting the virtual world: they have to obey some physical laws.

Heuristic 3: User Control and Freedom

There should be in the system as much freedom as it is the case in the story or game intention. An 'undo' function is not needed in a story or game: in other words, the notion of going reverse in time is specific for regular softwares but not for narrative or entertainment applications. Freedom used for WIMP devices do not bear a narrative component, while here the user is caught into a temporal sequence and cannot have full freedom otherwise it will go out of the diegetic space. This heuristic allows one to keep guidelines on the movements and gestures allowed or not, wanted or not and to develop the scenario accordingly.

Heuristic 4: Consistency and Standards

Within a diegetic universe, each visual and audio element must remain coherent vis-à-vis the others. The standards are given by the nature of the fictional universe itself and the media components. 2D objects should be limited to 2D environments, except if the scenario guidelines build on multiple aesthetics, related to characters typification or universe specificity. The visual, narrative and interactive conventions have to be respected at all the levels of design and development so that the usage remains coherent: if a user hits on a flying object in a certain way and accordingly he gets a visual and audio feedback, this should remain similar at any event where the user hits a similar object.

Heuristic 5: Error Prevention

The range of possible actions the player can follow are set up in the rules of the game. One design constraint is that, due to the limited range of possible gestures and movements, there is a need for self-explanotary hints of what is allowed or not, with a rapid feedback, i. e. with visual or audio animation. This heuristic relates to the one before and has implications on the coherence at the scenario level. Experiments have shown that there is a need to generate a rapid visual or audio feedback when someone does a gesture or a movement which is not allowed by the system. There is a specific case where the system has also to be preventive: when a user does not move or touch an object, it needs to be highlighted visually.

Heuristic 6: Recognition Rather than Recall

The Transfiction system, in its design approach, assumes that the average user should interact with the universe in a rather natural way. Hence, intuition is a key factor for the user to get hold of the system and play with it. Recognition of movements of objects and situations should allow/reinforce the development of a fast learning curve for the system. A series of different scenarios and cases show that there is a need to make possible actions foreseeable. The user has a tendency to 'touch' something if it is dynamic and visually appealing (moving, changing shape).

Heuristic 7: Flexibility and Efficiency of Use

This heuristic helps one to make sure that both inexperienced and experienced users can optimally use the application. One part of the flexibility of use can be taken by the system (hence a complexity in engineering it) but the other part is left to the agility of the user. Several usage cases have shown that there is an inhibition on the part of adult participants in moving into space while children get hold very quickly and efficiently of the interaction modalities. Scenarios can therefore propose different levels of reactions according to the height at which an object is touched: the scenario is adaptive and an adult will have to act at a different speed than a child, simply according to the height of touching.

Heuristic 8: Aesthetic and Minimalist Design

This heuristic seems not relevant so far as the design is to be coherent with the scenario and has to ensure the feeling of immersion. The entertainment factor has more weight than the information factor in the applications of the Transfiction system.

Heuristic 9: Help users Recognize, Diagnose, and Recover from Errors

Per se, there is no error in the application that can never stop or crash. The user can behave freely, but only some of her/his actions or gestures will make the scenario evolve, in one direction or another. Consequently, the system has to provide enough visual and audio clues so that the user can navigate and reach a goal, related to a game or a story. This is particularly true for objects that are touchable with respect to objects that are not.

Heuristic 10: Help and Documentation

As part of the scenario in a Transfiction system, a specific help functionality is automatically activated when a user does not perform according to the scenario expectations. For example, if someone does not move at all while the scenario expects a displacement, then the help module pops up and suggests the user should move, using an iconographic language.

Overall, one can conclude that these heuristics are of interest for the interface aspects between the user and the system. They partly guide the storytelling or the game-

gameplay of the scenario. Specifically, the five first heuristics are of interest with respect to the 'touching is seeing' working assumption in terms of interaction design. Visibility, matching, coherency, consistency are to be taken into account so that the user 'touches what she/he sees'. The usage experience is meaningful and there is an impact through image and sound manipulation. One can say that the Transfiction approach is helpful in enlarging the narrative enveloppe by providing new emotions combining both physical interactions and cognitive projections in a fictional space.

This freedom in the spatio-temporal articulation allows a 'mise-en-scène' through multiplicity, juxtaposition, simultaneity, contiguity, as space is seen in a bergsonian way [11].

4 Results

In this paper, two specific cases are briefly evoked as they illustrate some specific implementations. The Transfiction platform has been used to design installations in a science museum (*Pass*, Frameries, Belgium) and in an entertainment park (*Mini-Europe*, Brussels, Belgium) where two different applications based on the Transfiction system are running in real-time all day long for several months.

Fig. 4. Scenes of the PASS installation

The first installation at *Pass* is part of a global theme (The Desire to Learn) and illustrates different modalities of learning or acquiring knowledge. In this set-up, the visitor has to catch sliding circles on the screen but his/her body randomly turns around, hence modifying her/his horizontal frame of reference. This cognitive displacement results in implicitely requestioning how to touch the moving objects: for instance when the user's image is presented upside down, the left and right moves are reversed. In terms of touching, the user gets a concrete experience of the importance of the position of his/her body while touching something which is moving. The impact of the installation is based on the collision of the body image and the movement of artificial objects.

The second case is part of the *EuropEmotion* installation where the set-up allows two simultaneous players to explore some European themes in a metaphorical way.

One scene shows flying coins from different European countries and the players have to hit them so that they get into a 'fire'. When all the coins are in that fire, they are transformed into a Euro coin. The aim of this scene is to show that European currencies have been transformed into one unified unit: the Euro. The players have the control on this 'transformation' by doing it themselves: they have to touch coins in a special way in order to direct their moves and to get them dive into the central fireplace. The coins have physical properties (gravity and bounce) and when people hit them, they move like soccer balls. Hence, users get fun by trying to touch them with their head or their feet, as if if they were playing football.

Fig. 5. Scenes of the EuropEmotion installation: Euro coins

The mise-en-scène for the installations has to provide a balance between the richness of visual setting and the type of interactions possible for the user. One observation is that the user gets highly involved if the interaction mechanics (to move, to jump, to throw) are based on rules not too far from expected real-life behaviour of objects. Rules based on non real-life paradigms are more difficult to be conveyed to the user and therefore cause trouble for her/him to interact with the system.

5 Conclusion

The claim that we can create 'touching simulation only through visualization' is giving believable results for the user if the narrative design contains physical rules not too far from real-life.

Such an approach with the Transfiction system brings something specific to virtual storytelling in terms of user experience, feelings and emotions, which are not possible nor with classical media (paper, cinema) nor with cumbersome VR devices where movements are somehow physically limited.

References

1. Nandi, A., Marichal, X.: Transfiction. Chapter 2 in Eskelinen, M., Koskimaa, M. (Eds): CyberText Yearbook 2000. Publications of the Research Centre for Contemporary Culture 68 (2001) 13-33
2. Marichal, X,, Umeda, T.: Real Time Segmentation of Video Objects for Mixed-Reality Interactive Applications. In proceedings of the SPIE's Visual Communications and Image Processing (VCIP 2003) International Conference, Lugano, Switzerland, July 2003.
3. Douxchamps, D., Marichal, X., Umeda, T., Correa Hernandez, P., Marquès, F.: Automatic Body Analysis for Mixed Reality Applications. In proceedings of the 4th European Workshop on Image Analysis for Multimedia Interactive Services (WIAMIS 2003), April 2003, London, 423-426
4. Krueger, M.: Artificial Reality II. Addison-Wesley (1990)
5. Roussos, M., Johnson, A., Leigh, J., Vasilakis, C., Barnes, C., Moher, T.: NICE: Combining Constructionism, Narrative, and Collaboration in a Virtual Learning Environment. Computer Graphics, 31(3), August 1997, 62-63
6. Maes, P., Darrell, T., Blumberg, B., Pentland, A.: The ALIVE system: Wireless, full-body interaction with autonomous agents. Multimedia Systems, 5(2), March 1997, 105-112
7. Kim, N., Woo, W., Tadenuma, M.: Photo-realisatic Interactive Virtual Environment Generation using Multiviews Cameras. In proceedings of SPIE's Visual Communication and Image Processing conference 2001 (VCIP 2001), vol. 4310, January 2001
8. Drascic, D., Milgram, P.: Perceptual Issues in Augmented Reality. In Bolas, M.T., Fisher, S.S., Merritt, J.O. (eds): SPIE Volume 2653 - Stereoscopic Displays and Virtual Reality Systems III, San Jose, California, USA, January - February 1996, 123-134.
9. Dove, T.: The Space Between: Telepresence, Re-animation and the Re-casting of the Invisible. In Rieser, M., Zapp, A. (eds): New Screen Media: Cinema, Art, Narrative. London: British Film Institute (2002)
10. Nielsen, J.: Heuristic evaluation. In Nielsen, J., Mark, R.L. (eds): Usability Inspection Methods, New York: John Wiley & Sons (1994)
11. Bergson, H.: Matter and Memory. Paul, N.M., Palmer, W.S. (trads) Zone Books, New York (1988)

Applications

Using Virtual Reality for "New Clowns"

Martin Hachet and Pascal Guitton

LaBRI (Université Bordeaux 1, ENSEIRB, CNRS) – INRIA
351 Cours de la Libération, 33405 Talence, France
[hachet,guitton]@labri.fr
http://www.labri.fr, http://www.hemicyclia.labri.fr

Abstract. This paper describes an experimental performance where theater clowns make a show using Virtual Reality (VR) technologies. The classical theater scenery is replaced by a large-scale screen on which 3D models are displayed in real-time, allowing the clowns and the audience to be immersed in highly interactive virtual environments (VEs). We put on a scenario where the clowns and the audience travel over a city and explore a mysterious planet. We describe the software and hardware solutions that we use for the generation of the VE and for the interaction with them. Using VR for new clowns allows the audience to feel new experiences. It gives the theater a new field of investigation. Last but not least, it allows VR to be closer to the people.

1   Introduction

We are investigating the use of Virtual Reality (VR) for theater clowns. This work is based on the similarity of two approaches by two different groups: a theater company, the *Théâtre du chapeau* [6], and our VR research group at the computer science laboratory of Bordeaux University.

On the one hand, the theater often aims to carry the audience in various periods and/or locations to provide perceptions of stories. Technically, one can notice that, during the shows, general lights are switched off and the scene is strongly illuminated in order to increase the *immersion* of the audience. The theater group we are working with creates performances where clowns continuously communicate with the audience and integrate the audience reactions in their interventions. Therefore, two performances of the same show may be very different according to the audience *interaction*.

On the other hand, our research activities concern VR. We develop algorithms and software applications for the generation of Virtual Environments (VEs). We use a large-display VR environment to increase the *immersion* of the users in the generated VEs. Finally, we develop devices and techniques to allow *interaction*, giving the users the possibility to perform basic tasks like navigation, control, or manipulation of the virtual objects.

The similarity of these two approaches led us to the creation of an experimental performance. The classical static theater scenery is replaced by a VE displayed on a huge screen, as shown in Fig. 1. The clowns and the audience are able to interact with this 3D computer-generated environment in real-time. By means of novel interfaces, they can navigate inside the 3D scenes or they can manipulate 3D objects. Hence, this new

O. Balet et al. (Eds.): ICVS 2003, LNCS 2897, pp. 211–219, 2003.
© Springer-Verlag Berlin Heidelberg 2003

Fig. 1. Two real clowns in front of a virtual scenery.

media allows an inexhaustible source of creation for the interactive theater. The limited classical sceneries do not restrict the stories anymore. Now, the actors and the audience are able to interact with a virtual environment, giving the theater a new dimension.

VR applications can produce many innovations in our everyday life. But, before the apparition of these new applications, it is necessary to show VR in other contexts than classical "serious" ones to break the science-fiction feeling, which is generally linked to VR technologies. An experiment mixing Theater and new technologies allows us to extract VR technologies from scientific and technical domains. It allows to make evolve these technologies, too.

We present in section 2 some existing work about the use of VR in the art area. In section 3, we specify the terms virtual reality and theater clowns. An experimental scenario is presented in section 4. The technical solutions that we use are described in section 5. We discuss the results of the experimental performance in section 6. Finally, in section 7 we conclude and give directions to future work.

2 Previous Works

As far as we know, live performances using VR for interactive scenery are not so common.

The Institute for the Exploration of Virtual Realities [2] used to be a pioneer for a decade. They have created several shows where scenic elements are computer-generated in real-time and operated by backstage technicians. For example, their last performance (The magic flute) uses different kind of projection systems. The main image (36 feet x 13 feet) is displayed on two large screens in the center of the stage by means of two rear-projectors. Moving images are produced by means of two spot-style projectors and six mobile screens.

In the Worcester Polytechnic Institute [8], some shows mixing VR and theatre have been performed for several years.

In the Virtual Reality Applications Center at Iowa State University [7], the Dance Driving project aims to build a multidisciplinary experience mixing dance, sound, and computer-generated elements. The actors wear wireless sensors to interact in an immersive environment.

Finally, a collaboration between a French research lab (IRIT) and a puppet company (Animacao) has led to shows where virtual puppets are animated in real-time by the actors [5].

3   Virtual Reality and "New Clowns"

3.1   Virtual Reality

The term virtual reality is often discussed, and there is no unique definition. We will consider that virtual reality aims to immerse users in a virtual environment. A virtual environment is a 3D model with which it is possible to interact in real-time. The immersion refers to the feeling of being somewhere else than in the real environment.

Virtual reality has been associated to Head-Mounted Displays (HMD) for a long time. Equipped with head-tracking systems, HMD allow to immerse a user in a VE. Generally, the user is able to interact with the VE by means of gloves and a set of sensors.

For a decade, from the concept of the CAVE [1], large-display VR environments have appeared. These systems allow several users to be immersed in VEs while being co-located. Large displays are used in the companies for several applications: virtual prototyping, project review, scientific visualization, and so on. We wanted to benefit from the power of these new equipments for more artistic applications, in particular in the field of theater.

3.2   "New Clowns"

"New Clowns" are not circus clowns. New clowns (or theater clowns) are simple and sincere characters living present moments. With lot of benevolence, but without complaisance, they express what they feel. Consequently, theater clowns shows are based for a lot on improvisation. Until now, the real environment provides the source of improvisation. For example a sneezing, a camera flash, or a child cry will cause an immediate reaction of the clowns.

By replacing the static sceneries by 3D real-time computer-generated worlds, the source of improvisation is extended by the virtual environment. The modification of the VE has an impact on the feeling of the clowns, and consequently, on what they express to the audience.

4   Experimental Scenario

We investigated the possibilities for the clown and the audience in a large-display VR environment by writing a short experimental scenario. In particular, we stress on a highly interactive scenario. At the moment, this scenario splits up into two main sections: the navigation in a city and the exploration of a planet. This scenario led to a demo experiment in which about twenty participants, including two clowns, are traveling inside virtual environments. We will see in the next section the technical solutions we choose for this experiment.

The clowns come in the room. They meet the audience and decide to transform the place in a spaceship. The screen becomes the windshield. The lights are switching off, the motors are becoming noisier and noisier, the spaceship is accelerating to the light velocity...

The spaceship arrives to the surroundings of a city. According to the audience requests, the clowns travel inside the city to explore it. The members of the audience are invited to drive themselves the spaceship. The audience progressively recognizes the city of Bordeaux, but without any inhabitants. The question is "where are the inhabitants". The clowns take back the control of the spaceship to fly over the city.

Suddenly, a bell tower takes off. The clowns decide to follow it. After a trip in space, the spaceship arrives to a mysterious planet. The clowns and the audience decide to explore this planet to see if they can find the inhabitants of Bordeaux.

Once arrived on the planet, one of the clowns puts on a spatial suit in order to leave the spaceship. Through the windshield several rocks can be seen. The equipped clown goes behind the screen, and a corresponding avatar appears in the virtual environment. The audience is asked to send the (virtual) clown to locations on the planet. When the clown arrives next to the rocks, specific actions take place, as for example the apparition of a monster. The clown comes back in the real environment and explains how he has living the situation. A member of the audience is also sent in the virtual environment.

After having explored the planet, the audience and the clowns take off to explore other planets. They try to find indications about the disparition of the Bordeaux inhabitants.

5   Technical Solutions

Three components have to be taken into account for the production of interactive scenarios using VR technologies. The first one concerns the scene modeling. The second one concerns the perception of the generated scenes. Finally, interfaces have to be proposed for the interaction with the visualized scenes. In the following we present the tools and techniques that we used for the development of our interactive scenario.

5.1   Modeling

We used two main techniques for the scene modeling. The small scenes and some key objects have been generated using classical 3D modelers. They can also be generated using photo-modeling applications. The 3D model of the city of Bordeaux has been generated using automatic and generic processes. It consists of about 10,000 buildings and some decor elements like trees or rivers. The generation process has initially been used for an application of 3D geomarketing [4]. We have developed a set of algorithms allowing the generation of 3D virtual cities from the cadastre of any real city.

We focused on the generation of optimized 3D models for real-time uses: simplification, scene graph organization, level of details, and so on. We use the VRML format for the description of the 3D models. The textures representing the appearances of the buildings are chosen in a database organized in terms of number of windows and number of levels. The only modification of this database allows modifying the entire aspect of the city. For example, it is possible to use real pictures for realistic atmospheres or drawings for more artistic atmospheres. Fig. 2 shows a view of the model generated from the cadastre of Bordeaux, with three different atmospheres.

5.2 Perception

The actual version of our experiment takes place in a SGI Reality Center for the perception of the scenes. It consists of a 10x3 meters curved screen on which images are displayed with three high-resolution video projectors. This equipment allows immersing several persons in a virtual environment. A surrounding sound system enables to produce high-quality sounds and musics. The application has been developed with OpenGL Performer and runs on an Onyx2. Fig. 3 shows Hemicyclia, our large-display VR environment.

5.3 Interaction

We use two innovative interfaces for the interaction with the virtual environment. The first one is a 6 degree of freedom input device called the CAT [3]. The CAT has been developed for an intuitive and efficient interaction with virtual environments displayed on large screens. It is a freestanding device looking like a circular table as shown in Fig. 4. Users can apply rotations in the environment by freely orientating the tabletop in space. They can perform translations by applying forces on it. When released, the tabletop does not move and consequently does not induce modifications to the environment. The CAT can be used without any equipment stage. Consequently, users are not constrained by the device. During our experiment, the clowns (and the audience) are able to travel in and over Bordeaux in complex and smooth 3D trajectories with easiness, and with few learning. Then, they can release the CAT without any difficulties to play with the audience.

The second interface consists in using laser pointers as an alternative to the mouse. Three cameras attached under the video projectors film the screen and allow recovering the position of a laser pointer spot on it. This position is interpreted as mouse coordinates. Hence, laser pointers can be used to replace the mouse. The advantage of the laser pointers is that several participants can easily share them. Moreover, users have a direct access to the objects by pointing them while freely moving in front of the screen. During our experiment, the audience points to locations in the planet in order to send the clowns to specific targets, as shown in Fig. 5.

6 Discussion

Until now, the performance was given three times. Everytime, the members of the audience were very enthusiastic about what they were living. Several factors contributed to this good acceptation.

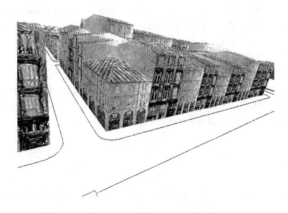

Fig. 2. The model of Bordeaux with different atmospheres.

Fig. 3. Hemicyclia: Our large-display VR environment.

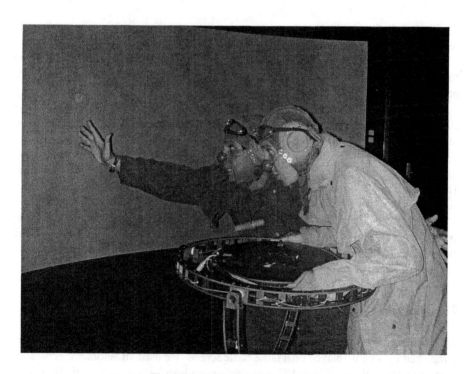

Fig. 4. The CAT used to fly in VEs.

Fig. 5. Using laser pointer to point to location.

First of all, the clowns lead the audience in a fantastic story, with humour and poetry, resulting in a really artistic show.

Secondly, the audience had access to new technologies that cannot be encountered, for the moment, somewhere else than in research labs. The audience was really impressed by the new technologies surrounding them.

The members of the audience traveled in an urban environment corresponding to a city they know (the city of Bordeaux). They were pleased to recognize their city, and to see it as they never did before.

As the modeling process is quite fully automatic, the urban environment corresponding to the city in which the performance take place can be generated in few time. The most time-consuming task consists in adding some reference landmarks (e.g. a particular church or a stadium).

Finally, the audience loved having the possibility to interact with the VE. The story evolved in real-time according to the audience actions. Consequently, the members of the audience were not only spectators anymore. They did not see a show but they participated at an experience.

7 Conclusion

We have put on a interactive demo experience in which the classical physical scenery is replaced by VEs displayed on a large-scale screen. We used an automatic generation process to create the displayed VE. Two innovating interfaces have been used to allow the participants to interact with the environment in an intuitive way.

This kind of experiment is beneficial for the different involved groups. The audience discovers new experiences. It gives the clowns a new investigation field. The modification of the environment in which they are living permanently gives them possibilities for improvisation.

For us, such an experiment allows to show that Virtual Reality is not reserved to complex scientific applications. It allows to contribute to the expansion of VR technologies. Moreover, it opens numerous research areas, as for example the development of intuitive interfaces for 3D interaction.

The actual performance takes place in our large-display VR environment, but is not limited to it. We would like to use lightweight equipments to allow itinerant performances like PCs, simple projectors, web cams, and modular screens.

References

1. Cruz-Neira, C., Sandin, D.J., DeFanti, T.A.: Surround-Screen Projection-Based Virtual Reality: The Design and Implementation of the CAVE. In ACM Computer Graphics, Vol. 27, Number 2 , July 1993.pp 135-142.
2. Exploration of Virtual Realities: University Theatre and Department of Theatre and Film at the University of Kansas, www.ku.edu/~ mreaney/shows.html
3. Hachet, M., Guitton, P., Reuter, P., Tyndiuk, F.: The CAT for efficient 2D and 3D interaction as an alternative to mouse adaptations. To appear in Proceedings of Virtual Reality Software and Tecnology (VRST 2003), november 2003.
4. Hachet, M., Guitton, P.: From Cadastres to Urban Environments for 3D Geomarketing. In Proceedings of IEEE/ISPRS joint Workshop on Remote Sensing and Data Fusion over Urban Areas, Roma, november 2001, pp 146-150.
5. Jessel, J.P., Jaspart, C., Flores J.J.: Computer Animation and Virtual Reality for Live Art Performance. Proceedings of Virtual Storytelling 2001 (LNCS 2197), Avignon, september 2001, pp. 205-207.
6. Théatre du chapeau: www.theatre-du-chapeau.com
7. Virtual Reality Application Center: http://www.vrac.iastate.edu/
8. Worcester Polytechnic Institue: www.wpi.edu/Academics/Depts/HUA/TT/vr.html

Storytelling for Recreating Our Selves: ZENetic Computer

Naoko Tosa[1,2,3], Koji Miyazaki[2], Hideki Murasato[3], and Seigo Matsuoka[4]

[1] Massachusetts Institute of Technology /JST/ATR
N52-390, 265 Massachusetts Ave. Cambridge, MA USA
naoko@mit.edu
[2] Japan Science Technology Corporation "Interaction & Intelligence"
2-2-2, Hikaridai, Seika-cho, Soraku-gun, Kyoto
619-0288, Japan
[3] ATR Adaptive Communications Research Laboratories
2-2-2, Hikaridai, Seika-cho, Soraku-gun, Kyoto
619-0288, Japan
[4] Editorial Engineering Laboratory,
7-6-14 Akasaka, Minato-ku, Tokyo
107-0052, Japan

Abstract. We present a interactive storytelling system that aims to help us "recreate" our conscious selves by calling on traditional Japanese concepts and media. "Recreating our selves" means the process of reconciling our conscious 'daily self' and our 'hidden self'. This requires deep stimulations which are difficult to achieve through conventional logic based interactions. Users create, enter and dynamically interact with a virtual world expressed as a 3D "Sansui" ink painting, encountering fragments of stories and ambiguous provocations. The user physically interacts with the system through various media including a Sumie (ink painting), a rake in a Zen rock garden, touching screen images, drawing or clapping hands. The interaction system includes a dynamical chaos engine which is used to couple activity of the user to the generation of high dimensional context and evolution of the storytelling.

1 Introduction

We have developed an interactive storytelling system that aims to help us "recreate" our conscious selves by calling on Buddhist principles, Asian philosophy, and traditional Japanese culture through the inspirational media of traditional ink paintings, kimono and haiku. "Recreating ourselves" means the process of making the consciousness of our 'daily self' meet that of our 'hidden self'. through stimulation of activity deep within us. It is difficult to achieve this through traditional logic-based interactions. Our system is a new approach which incorporates traditional media and methods in an interactive computer system. The interactive storytelling stimulates

O. Balet et al. (Eds.): ICVS 2003, LNCS 2897, pp. 220–226, 2003.
© Springer-Verlag Berlin Heidelberg 2003

deep imagination and allows users to develop connections between their hidden selves, full of imagination and creative energy, and their daily conscious selves, which directly interpret the ambient reality [1].

2 Philosophy of ZENetic Computer

The user creates a virtual world by manipulating 3D images of Asian *sansui* ink painting on a computer display with an intuitive and enjoyable interface tool. These images, which typically symbolize nature and philosophical precepts, provide a dramatic departure from our view of daily experience. This awakens us from our daily consciousness and gives free reign to subconscious imagination [2]. Based on the user's *sansui* design, the system infers his or her internal consciousness and generates a story that the user can 'enter' via the computer display. This story further shakes the user's consciousness. This is not a complete story, such as those in the movies or novels, but fragments of short stories. Experiencing these episodic stories makes users feel uneasy and arouses their subconscious desire to construct a whole story by linking the fragments. In each of these inchoate stories, the system stimulates interaction through Zen dialogue or haiku as a form of allegorical communication. The user is asked questions that do not have "correct" answers. He or she is forced to deal with these ambiguous provocations while subconsciously struggling to answer the questions.

This subconscious effort inspires the user to find ways of linking the stories into an original whole. The user responds to objects presented by the interactive system, whether a graphic image or a provocative statement, by manipulating input media, such as a virtual calligraphy brush or rake of a Zen rock garden, on-screen images, or simply clapping hands. Coupled with the subconscious effort exerted to link the fragmentary stories, these user interactions decrease the gap between daily self and hidden self. This process of bringing our selves together is called MA-Interaction; ma is a Japanese concept that stresses the ephemeral quality of experience. In the final phase, the user has a dialogue with a "bull," which is used as a metaphor of our hidden self in Zen Buddhism. Through this dialogue, users experience a virtual unification of their daily self and their unconscious self into a recreated conscious self.

3 Technical Realization

Key technologies used to realize the system include a digital 3D *sansui* ink-painting engine which allows the users themselves to compose an ink painting to enter, a neural network engine which classifies the user's 'hidden personality' revealed in the ink painting into Buddhist Goun categories, and a dynamical chaos engine which is injected with signals from Goun categories and other user actions to generate high dimensional data for the context and evolution of the storytelling. The following are the main components of the system structure.

3.1 Software Integration [3]

The flow of the system is as follows:

1) User makes 3D Sansui ink-painting picture by manipulating symbolic icons
2) User's hidden self is classified into Goun categories.
3) User enters the Sansui picture and a journey begins. Haiku is used to generate story fragments that are presented in Sansui.
4) User experiences various stages of MA-Interaction
(User may experience Steps 3 and 4 several times).
5) Finally, the Ten Bulls Story Interaction takes place.

3.2 Hardware Structure

Figure 1 shows the overall hardware structure of the Zenetic Computer System.

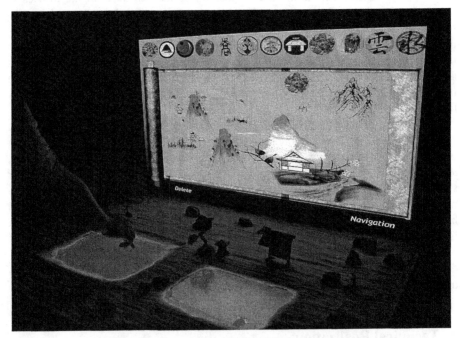

Fig. 1. User makes ink painting by ZENetic Computer

3.3 3D Sansui Ink-Painting Engine

A key part of the system is the user interaction with a digital 3D ink-painting engine. Depending on how users compose their initial ink-painting, the system classifies their intrinsic personality using a neural network. The personality corresponds to a point in a Goun space. Goun is a categorization from Buddhism based on the view that five basic spirits and materials make up the world. The five categories of personality based on goun can be summarized as follows.

a) 色 *Shiki* is how nature and materials actually exist.
b) 受 *Jyu* is the intuitive impression.
c) 想 *So* is the perceived image.
d) 行 *Gyo* is the process of mind that activates your behavior.
e) 識 *Shiki* is the deep mental process that lies behind all of the above processes

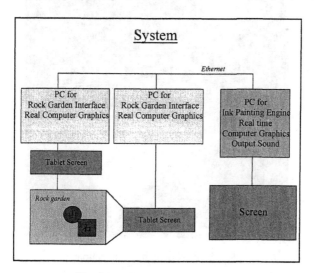

Fig. 2. ZENeticComputer System

User data is also obtained at later times from various interactions between the user and the system, and used to determine a pseudo Goun personality. Depending on how the user is affected by the evolving story, the pseudo Goun personality may differ from the intrinsic (=hidden) personality. Conversely, the difference between the pseudo personality and the intrinsic personality will affect the evolving story via an engine, called a chaos engine.

3.4 Storytelling Generated by Chaos Engine

A dynamical chaos engine is used to couple activity of the user, via the difference between the pseudo personality and the intrinsic personality, to the generation of high dimensional context and evolution of the storytelling. The chaos engine consists of three dynamic components, which we call agents. We name the three agents, User, Target and Master. The agents each have internal chaotic dynamics, and also move around in Goun space. The three agents are coupled so that there is an interplay between their motions in the Goun space and the synchronization [4] of their internal dynamics. The transient dynamics of the chaos engine are sampled and used to create the sounds and images experienced by the user, and also to control the evolution of the story.

Fig. 3. ZEN dialogue Interaction

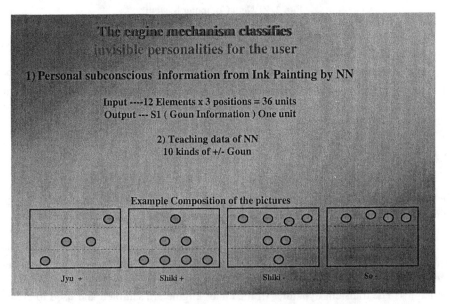

Fig. 4. Examples of neural-net classification of the composition of pictures created by a user into Buddhist Goun categories corresponding to "hidden self"

Fig. 5. Compass for navigation in your ink painting world

In the current implementation of the chaos engine for the ZENetic computer, the position of the User agent corresponds to the user's pseudo personality, and the position of the Target agent corresponds to the momentary view of the user's pseudo personality obtained from the latest user interaction. The User agent starts at the position of the intrinsic personality and tends to move toward the position of the Target agent. The User agent is coupled to the Target via the Master in such away that if there is no interference from the Master, the User tends to synchronize to the Target and move toward the Target position, so that the User and Target become identical. On the other hand, if there is interference from the Master, it is more difficult for the User to synchronize with the Target, and so less likely that the User will reach the Target. The strength of the Master's interference depends inversely on the distance between the pseudo personality and the hidden personality - the smaller the distance, the stronger the influence of the Master, and hence the more difficult it is for the User to synchronize and merge with the Target.

4   Conclusions and Future Work

Real-time interaction with individual consciousness and subconscious is a long-term challenge for computer systems. Interactive storytelling is a frontier which allows us to explore this challenge. Science says that human consciousness may have a chaotic nature. By incorporating chaotic mechanisms, our system aims to provide a rich and dynamic interaction which entangles the conscious and subconscious. Responses to questionnaires from users who have experienced the ZENetic Computer show that they tend to feel relaxed and stimulated in a way that they had never felt before. Both

English and Japanese versions have been developed. This system will be exhibited at the MIT Museum, KODAIJI - ZEN Temple (Kyoto, Japan) and around the world. [5]

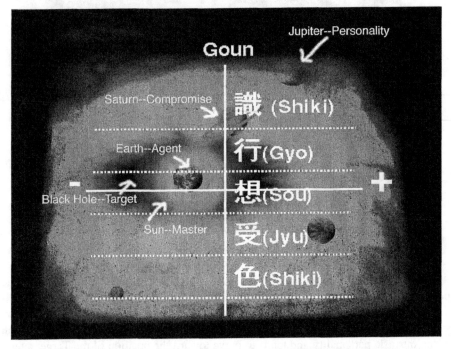

Fig. 6. Visualization of your own Chaos engine in ZENetic Computer

Acknowledgements

This research was supported in part by the Telecommunications Advancement Organization of Japan. Thanks to Dr. Peter Davis for helping to design and tune the chaos engine.

References

1. S. Matsuoka,"The Science of the beauties of nature," Shunjusha (1994) (In Japanese)
2. S. Matsuoka, "Sansui Thought" Gogatsu shobo (2003) (In Japanese)
3. N. Tosa, Chapter19: Expression of emotion unconsciousness with art and technology, "AFFECTIVE MINDS," ELSEVIER, pp. 183-201 (2000)
4. Y. Liu, P. Davis, "Dual synchronization of chaos", Physical Review E, 61 pp. R2176-R2179 (2000)
5. http://web.mit.edu/~naoko/

A Distributed Virtual Storytelling System for Firefighters Training

Eric Perdigau, Patrice Torguet, Cédric Sanza, and Jean-Pierre Jessel

IRIT – Computer Graphics and Virtual Reality Group
118, rte de Narbonne, F-31062 Toulouse Cedex
{perdigau,torguet,sanza,jessel}@irit.fr

Abstract. The aim of the proposed paper is to present a virtual reality scenario managing application which has been distributed according to the DoD (Department of Defense) High Level Architecture (HLA) standard. The system works over several implementations of the Run-Time Infrastructure (RTI, HLA software part), on networked PCs. The main scenario is a networked Firefighters Training Simulation where each computer can control one or several avatars either through human piloting or through Artificial Intelligence (AI) based behaviors using Learning Classifier Systems.

1 Introduction

The main goal of our system is to manage various types of distributed Virtual Reality applications for social, cultural and emotional immersions, in order to use learning scenario in various fields. The firefighters scenario (Fig.1.) aims to train firefighters for leadership in crisis situations. Various categories of people may be involved : different ranks of firefighters, wounded people, victims, neutral persons, and also the SAMU (emergency medical service), the prefect, etc... All those kinds of virtual people can either be autonomous characters or human controlled characters.

Other work has already been done in that precise field (crisis simulations) : for firefighters [8], for mine safety training [4], for emergency rescue teams against terrorist attacks [5], for security in a refinery [6], for buildings fire detection systems [2] or again for shipboard firefighting training [11].

All of this work clearly show that Virtual Environments are a convincing tool for crisis situations training and understanding. However our point of view tries to introduce an emotional and social dimension to improve interactions in such simulations. Indeed to be more immersive and interactive Virtual Worlds obey to some constraints inherent to the subject : physical constraints, communicational constraints and social constraints (emotional responses, personalities, wishes, ...). Credibility of a training simulation relies on the capability of the avatars to communicate, to react emotionally to events during the simulation and the possibility to collaborate with other humans via good network functionalities.

2 Distributed Features

The first issue we want to discuss is the network part of the application. The system is similar to a Virtual Environment for Training (VET), as the scenarios aim to immerse

O. Balet et al. (Eds.): ICVS 2003, LNCS 2897, pp. 227–230, 2003.
© Springer-Verlag Berlin Heidelberg 2003

several human beings in a virtual world. They can identify themselves, collaborate with each other and perform actions as they would do in reality. The crisis simulation consequently must run in real-time on several machines geographically distant from each other. Each of the participants can directly interact either with autonomous entities (buildings, objects, fires, autonomous persons, ...) or with human participants (others firefighters, victims, wounded persons, ...) through their avatars. Interactions must be done without discontinuity and the virtual world must be the same on every site in order to keep the necessary coherency of the simulation. All the network transfers must be fast and the modifications in the scene quite instantaneous everywhere. Thus we decided to adapt our storytelling system to the High Level Architecture (HLA) standard because it is specifically conceived for distributed simulations.

Fig. 1. A view of our application

The HLA [3] is a general purpose architecture for simulation reuse and interoperability. It was developed under the leadership of the Defense Modeling and Simulation Office (DMSO) to support reuse and interoperability across a large number of different types of simulations. It was adopted as the Facility for Distributed Simulation Systems 1.0 by the Object Management Group (OMG) in November 1998. Moreover it was approved as an open standard through the Institute of Electrical and Electronic Engineers (IEEE Standard 1516) in September 2000. HLA defines a distributed simulation as a set of applications running on several machines [7]. The applications are called Federates and the set of Federates is a Federation (Fig.2.). Federates communicate through the use of a well defined API which is implemented by a library and one or more server processes (called a RTI) [1][10].

3 Behavioral Features

The second issue of our project is to give life to autonomous entities. The main difficulty is to ensure coherent interaction between all the entities. Indeed, the human entities must then possess communicational, reasoning and emotional capacities. In that way we have chosen to use Learning Classifiers Systems (LCS) to generate their deliberate actions and decisions and the non intentional actions for avatars controlled by humans (like the orientation of the head while speaking, ...). LCS are well-known for their ability to automatically adapt to the environment, enabling continuous evolution and constant efficiency.

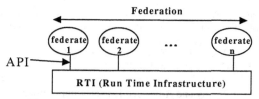

Fig. 2. a logical view of an HLA simulation

A classifier system is a reinforcement system based on a set of binary rules called classifiers (Fig.3.). The structure of a rule includes the condition part, the action part and the strength (evaluation). The interface between the LCS and the environment is composed of :

- the perception module (sensors),
- the action module (effectors),
- the reward system (fitness),
- the genetic algorithm.

At each time step, a classifier system gets information from its environment through the perception module. Then, it selects the best-adapted rule and triggers the action part of this rule. Finally, the reward system updates the strength of the rule thanks to a pre-defined fitness function that represents the goal to achieve. Periodically, the genetic algorithm is called to generate new rules from existing ones by using operators like mutation or crossing-over.

We use an extended classical LCS called αCS [9]. The features of αCS system are a multi-goal system and a communication interface that enables a dialogue based on the knowledge (rules) between several entities. The most interesting contribution of this work in our storytelling system is adaptation. Indeed, our virtual worlds become more and more interactive and non intentional actions are easier to produce. We also plan to use a Linux PC Cluster which will permit us to parallelize a huge amount of LCS corresponding to many characters in the scene.

4   Conclusion

Firefighters training needs all the components included in real life, like collaboration with humans or social and emotional factors. This environment gives a lot of opportunities either on learning or training sessions, and also on technology progress with the emotional states in virtual worlds. Furthermore, building on lessons learned during the design and implementation of such applications as well as on previous research work in the Networked VR field (we have built a distributed VR system called VIPER [12]), we are currently developing an architecture which will ease cluster and network distributed VR application creation.

References

1. Bréholée B., Siron P., CERTI: Evolutions of the ONERA RTI Prototype., 2002 Fall Simulation Interoperability Workshop, Orlando (2002).
2. Bukowsky R., Séquin C., Interactive Simulation of Fire in Virtual Building Environments, SIGGRAPH '97, Los Angeles, (1997)

3. Calvin J.O., Weatherly R., An introduction to the High Level Architecture (HLA) Runtime Infrastructure, 14th Workshop on the Standards for the Interoperability of Distributed Simulations, Orlando, Floride (1996).
4. Filigenzi M.T., Orr T.J., and Ruff T.M., Virtual reality for mine safety training, App Occup and Environ Hyg (2000) 15(6) 465-469
6. Haller M., Kurka G., omVR A Safety Training System for a Virtual Refinery, ISMCR'99, Workshop on Virtual Reality and Advanced Human-Robot Systems, Tokyo (1999)
7. Miller D.C., The DOD High Level Architecture and the Next Generation of DIS, 14th Workshop on the Standards for the Interoperability of Distributed Simulation, Orlando, Florida (1996)
8. Querrec R., Chevaillier P, Virtual Storytelling for Training : An Application to Fire Fighting in Industrial Environment, International Converence on Virtual Storytelling 2001, Avignon, LNCS 2197, Springer Verlag (2001) 201-204
9. Sanza C., Heguy O., Duthen Y., Evolution and Cooperation of Virtual Entities with Classifier Systems, Eurographics Workshop on Computer Animation and Simulation, Springer Computer Science, ISBN 3-211-83711-6, Manchester (2001)
10. Siron P., Design and Implementation of a HLA RTI Prototype at ONERA, 1998 Fall Simulation Interoperability Workshop, Orlando (1998)
11. Tate D.L., Sibert L., Virtual Environments for Shipboard Firefighting Training, IEEE Computer Graphics and Applications (1997)
12. Torguet P., Balet O., Jessel J.P., Gobbetti E., Duchon J., Bouvier E., CAVALCADE: a system for collaborative virtual prototyping, Journal of Design and Innovation Research, volume 2 number 1 special "virtual prototyping" (2000).

CITYCLUSTER
"From the Renaissance to the Megabyte Networking Age"
A Virtual Reality & High Speed Networking Project

Franz Fischnaller

Electronic Visualization Laboratory
School of Art and Design, University of Illinois at Chicago
106 Jefferson Hall, 929 W. Harrison Street, Chicago, IL 60607-7038
Ph: 312-996-3002, Fax: 312-413-7585
franz@evl.uic.edu
http://www.evl.uic.edu

Abstract. CITYCLUSTER is a virtual-reality networking matrix, a high-tech container with original technological features, navigation and interactivity, graphic and content style. In which multiple environments, ambiences, cities both real and imagined, can be hosted, coexist and be interrelated within themselves through a common, virtual territory, interconnected by high-speed network, enabling remote participants to interact and collaborate in shared environments. The framework, may be expanded and modify in accordance of the environments to be incorporated. A Virtual networking interface display was designed ad hoc, as interactivity tool for the user. Visitors, navigating and interacting with avatars becomes protagonist, free citizen. Buildings can be exchanged between the two cities to thus create an ideal environment (urban setting). From the Renaissance to the Megabyte Networking Age, is the first CITYCLUSTER-VR application. The implementation of CC has given rise to a range of technological challenges. New features and enhancements were added to the YGdrasil software.

1 Introduction

"From the Renaissance to the Megabyte Networking Age" is the first CC virtual-reality application. Which offers its visitors a thrilling interactive journey departing from the Renaissance until arriving and shifting to the Super Broadband Networking and electronic Age, breaking the barrier of time and space in real time. Florence metaphorically represents the "Renaissance Age", Chicago the "Gigabits Networking Age". Each virtual city is inhabited by a group of avatars: David, Venus and Machiavelli in Florence, and Mega, Giga and Picasso in Chicago. Primarily designed to run in the CAVETM and on the AGAVETM. It can run either locally or through remote networking in both SGI's and Linux platform. The networked experience can take place in real time between the CAVE™ and the AGAVE™. Both platforms interconnect and run over high-speed networks, enabling local and remote visitors to navigate, interact, and communicate with each other through the avatars as well as with three-dimensional models over distance in real time, in a common virtual space.

O. Balet et al. (Eds.): ICVS 2003, LNCS 2897, pp. 231–234, 2003.
© Springer-Verlag Berlin Heidelberg 2003

2   Virtual Environments

The virtual environments are characterized by multiple narrative spaces that comprise animated sculptures, interactive phenomena, high-tech performances, and characters of distinct and peculiar behavior. Emphasis was given to aesthetics and content quality, to the use of visual design in the virtual environment, to the dual concept of the perspective and to the intensity of the interaction thus bringing out the content to its fullest expression. The application is articulated by twelve scene: Florence, Machiavelli &Florence planes scene, Venus, David, the Academy, Picasso, Cathedral of Santa Maria del Fiore scene, The Baptistery, Grotto's Bell Tower, Lorenzo the Magnificent gallery, Chicago city, Hancock skyscraper, Sears skyscraper, Chicago 'planes', Chicago bridges. Is a large-scale environment. Each component of the environment covers a large virtual space, using hundreds of megabytes for models, texture-maps, and audio clips to link multiple scenes. The navigation and interaction are often surprising. The surprise factor in relation to body space and to the absence of temporal schemes is considered a pivotal experience between the remote visitors of the virtual-reality. This creative approach allows for multiple viewpoints and repeatedly generates an original multi-linear participatory interactive experience for the visitor. Legendary buildings can become cyber gateways teleporting the visitors from one city to the other. Renaissance or Megabyte digital interactive fragments are found strewn across the VR cities or floating randomly through the atmosphere... Masterpieces' detail morphs into three-dimensional creatures. The city itself can morph into a painting, transparent and penetrable, hosting a myriad of ethereal elements.

Fig. 1. In CC, the legendary room like the "Tribuna" becomes a cyber gateway

Fig. 2. Interacting with Meta Net Pave over the net with City Cluster virtual environments

2.1   Florence

The Renaissance virtual environment allows a wide range of actions, space transformations, and the entwining of time and space. Within the virtual city of Florence coexisted objects and interactive creatures of peculiar behavior: Diavolis Nerboroti, Nety screens, Gigabits digital fragments, the avatars Venus, David, and Machiavelli, as well as other selected elements and personages extracted from other works of art from the period. The buildings and squares that dominate the scenery are Palazzo Vecchio, Catedral of Santa Maria del Fiore, Brunelleschi's Dome, the Baptistery, Giotto's Bell Tower, Uffizi Gallery, Palazzo Medici Riccardi, Santo Spirito, Ponte

Vecchio, Chiesa di SS Annunziata, Academy, Piazza del Duomo, Piazza Signoria and others.

2.2 Chicago

The virtual city of Chicago appears under a unreal atmosphere, immersed within a cold, bio, gloomy and gelid environment. Contrasting against this landscape, some of the most outstanding buildings of the city such us Hancock Skyscraper, Sears Tower, Harold Washington Library, the Art Institute of Chicago emerge, volumetric and realistic forms filled with intensely luminous light. Depending on the visitor interaction the shoreline of Lake Michigan can become a dense accumulation of optic fibers of diverse colors and will generate musical sounds and other audio effects.

3 Avatars

The avatars embody the visual and graphic representation of specific concepts and symbols of diverse ages. Each virtual city is inhabited and guided by a group of avatars. David, Venus, and Machiavelli are 15th-century sphinxes, historical icons, narrative myths conceived, sculpted, and enriched by the collective imagination which today form part of the pantheon of figures related to the "rebirth" of art in Italy which was connected with the rediscovery of ancient philosophy, literature, artistic styles, and science as well as the evolution of empirical methods of study in these fields. Mega, Giga and Picasso are virtual embodiments of the Gigabits Networking Age, a time in which the invisible is no longer formless. These avatars embody the generation of electronic era, high-speed power, politics, networking, tele-presence, cloning, fear, and networking. Through the Avatars, City Cluster's net visitors see and experience the projection of themselves into a virtual body, or alter-presence, within the virtual environment which in turn transports them to live emotionally in another state and brings their body to interrelate, interact, and become immersed within this alter-physical reality.

4 Meta-net-Page

− Allows detecting information, images and details that are invisible or intangible zones for the naked eye.
− Indicates the user coordinates and provides more detailed information about the objects within its view.
− Acts as a sort of net mirror: the visitor can reflect their avatar in it by turning it around toward himself or herself while they are within the VR environment.
− Allow the user to fly up into the sky; to "teleport" immediately to the location shown on the view panel.
− Permit the user to zoom in or out by moving the panel closer or farther away from their own eye.
− Allows to take pictures (snapshots) and storage them. Which will serve as a placeholder for a specific location and heading.
− Allow the user to "grab" onto a building shown within the panel and move it to another location or even to another city.

Fig. 3. The virtual environments of Florence and Chicago are characterized by multiple narrative spaces with its Avatars: David, Venus and Macchiavelli

5   Exchanging Buildings from City to City over the Net

One of the most intense interactive experiences that the visitor can have is to exchange objects and buildings from one city to the other in real time over the Net. The Dome of Florence, for example, can be transported to Chicago or the Sears Tower to Florence and so forth... Buildings may be moved to recreate a new city or urban environment comprising elements and vital parts of Chicago and Florence.

6   Technology and Innovation

The project presented diverse creative technical challenges, which in turn revealed innovative aspects and salient feature relative to content management, the development of juxtaposed virtual environments, networking interactive techniques, avatar design, architecture, and virtual effects. Alex Hill, the lead technical advisor of the project, has advised the project manager and author of the project. YGdrasil, the software utilized for developing the project, has been upgraded and enhanced to address these issues.

XPn," an Authoring System for Immersive Art Exhibitions, presently known as the Ygdrasil system, created by Dave Pape (PhD, EVL UIC), was the software utilized for developing the MMB project by Franz Fischnaller. The XP system provides a framework for creating large scale, interactive virtual-reality applications. By dividing the development of applications into two distinct components - the coding of nodes that encapsulate specific behaviors, and the assembling of these nodes into a scene - XP allows teams comprising both artists and programmers to work on projects efficiently. It has been used to develop several successful artistic virtual worlds. Although originally developed for art applications, the general system should be useful in building a wide range of virtual worlds.

A Storytelling Concept for Digital Heritage Exchange in Virtual Environments

Stefan Conrad[1], Ernst Krujiff[1], Martin Suttrop[2],
Frank Hasenbrink[3], and Alex Lechner[3]

[1] Fraunhofer IMK, Sankt Augustin, Germany
[2] rmh, Cologne, Germany
[3] Vertigo Systems, Cologne, Germany

Abstract. This paper describes a software infrastructure and design methodology for the presentation of cultural and ecological heritage content in virtual environments, using a nonlinear storytelling approach. We set up a process guideline for the design of the story that leads to artifacts which can be seamlessly transformed and refined what we call an *executable story*. The result of the scenario design (story authoring) is an XML based description of the story including an enumeration of the resources like geometric models, sounds, and others. This XML based specification is immediately executable on a *StoryEngine* which has to be provided by the target virtual reality system.

1 Introduction

For the research project which is the base of this work, *DHX*[1] [1], a variation of different scenarios from cultural and ecological heritage are set up to exchange the content across country borders.

The scenarios are:

Beethovenhaus Bonn: Interactive exploration of Ludwig van Beethoven's biography in an immersive environment.

An Italian Drama Theatre of the 19th Century: Information about the theatre of the 19th century typically found in northern Italy, can be gathered interactively by visiting a fictional 3D-reconstruction in a VE, and querying a comprehensive database through an immersive interface.

Visual and Acoustic Tour of the Baptistery of Pisa: The user is able to have a remotely avatar-guided tour through a virtual model of the baptistery accompanying the "leaning tower" on the Piazza dei Miracoli in Pisa, Italy.

Samaria Gorge, Crete: A virtual visit of the Samaria gorge on Crete, Greece, a natural habitat of typical Mediterranean wildlife.

Yellow Dragon Temple: 3D-reconstruction and collective immersive experience of the ancient city of Gyeong-ju, the capitol of the Shilla dynasty in Korea.

The main requirements of these scenarios are the exchange of content between countries, shared experience from collaborative remote sites and transfer of content across different underlying VR[2] systems. Using collaborative VE technology and

---

[1] Funded by the EU (IST - 2001 - 33476).
[2] Virtual Reality.

O. Balet et al. (Eds.): ICVS 2003, LNCS 2897, pp. 235–238, 2003.
© Springer-Verlag Berlin Heidelberg 2003

avatars, a user in Germany will for example be able to make a tour through the Samaria gorge on Crete [2], remotely guided by an expert from the remote site in Greece. The nonlinear storytelling approach has been chosen to be able to provide a certain degree of freedom for the user while he is navigating through the content, along with a story like guidance which defines the minimal set of information which is presented to the user during a visit. The story will lead the user to predefined mandatory stations while he is able to choose his way through the content within given limits. Since our approach is plot oriented in opposition to character oriented approaches [3], we have chosen hierarchical finite state machines (HFSM) as the central model for the story and scenes. (see also [4] about narrative patterns in VR.)

2   Related Work

The *alVRed* project presents a set of tools for the creation of nonlinear storytelling content for VE[3]. It has a broader approach, and separates strictly between authoring and programming [5]. The step from authoring to programming is done with an export from the authoring tool and an import to the VR-system. Authoring is done completely offline. Timothy Griepp documents the use of XML[4] as a definition language for VE development in [6]. This approach proposes the use of XML in textual form, without dedicated tools.

3   Process and Architecture

The core work flows in our view on the story production process are authoring, modelling, story programming, VR-system programming and testing. We focus here on authoring and story programming. *Authoring* denotes the overall planning of the plot, the decomposition of the story in scenes and identification of required resources. It is comparable to the design phase from traditional software development. The author decomposes the scenes in hierarchical finite state machines and describes requisite objects, which will have a central role in the story.

The artifact of the authoring work flow is an XML description of the story, containing entities shown in the simplified model in figure 1. The story contains scenes which have a scenery and requisite objects assigned. The *scene* in our model is more a dramaturgical unit than a locality or geometric unit. The *scenery* describes a collection of passive background objects which form the scenes set, comparable to the background canvas in a theatre. Requisite objects can have properties and behaviour. Scenery and requisites reference resources like geometrical models and sounds. The whole story and the scenes are HFSM. The collaborative aspects of the scenarios are inherently supported by *AVANGO*s built in distribution support.

The *StoryEngine* is taking the description from the authoring and creates objects in the underlying VR system, which represent the entities of the story description. The storytelling support, based on HFSM according to the UML standard, became integral

---

[3] Virtual Environment.
[4] eXtensible Markup Language.

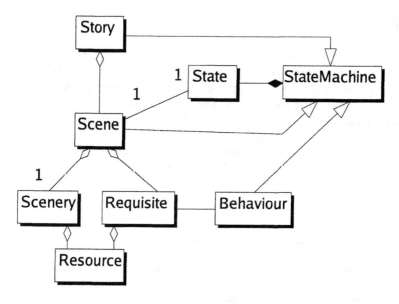

Fig. 1. Class diagram of the main classes of the *StoryEngine*

part of the primarily used VR[5] system, *AVANGO* [8], though the methodology is not leashed to a particular VR framework. State machine objects in *AVANGO* execute the state machine model of each scene. Requisite and scenery objects from the story description result in abstract wrappers of native scenegraph renderer objects, containing the geometry and other resources. Since the authored story description can be immediately transfered into a representation in the VR system, there is no need for a break between authoring and programming.

We are developing a visual tool for editing the state machine diagrams and for manipulating the scenegraph structure and node properties online (in the running VE). This tool is based on the *VR-Tuner* from the *alVRed* project. The author is immediately creating "living" objects in the VR system by using this tool. Following this approach, the authoring is seamlessly continued by the *story programming* with visual programming methods. Hand written scripts enrich the created objects and complete the visual story design.

Everything that has been created visually and is part of the XML story description is portable across VR systems that implement the *StoryEngine*. Scripts are still system specific (*AVANGO*), since most other VR systems do not support scripting. They are stored in the XML file but are not portable between systems. The XML description can be seen as the persistent state of the *StoryEngine*. The step from authoring to programming does not necessarily require the indirection via the XML file. Since objects and state machines are created immediatly in the *StoryEngine*, authoring and programming can go together in small project cycles. When system portability is not an issue, the XML file only serves for persistency between development sessions.

---

[5] Virtual Reality.

4 Conclusion

We proposed a methodology for the creation of storytelling content using visual programming capabilities that follow the development process guideline. The tight integration of authoring, and story programming supports the iterative development approach. Authoring, programming and testing can be combined in small development units. The scenarios mentioned above are currently in the phase of elaboration. The visual programming tools are being developed and enhanced under the concrete measure of the real project requirements. This immediate feedback from the *real world* provides a proper evaluation of the presented tools and methods.

References

1. Digital artistic and ecological heritage exchange. Website, 2003.
   http://www.eurasian-dhx.org.
2. Virtuelle reisen: Einmal kreta und zurueck in 15 minuten. *Focus*, jun 2002. german.
3. J. Bates. The nature of characters in interactive worlds and the oz project. Technical Report CMU-CS-92-200, Carnegie Mellon University, 1992.
4. Maria Roussos. The interplay between form, story and history: The use of narrative in cultural and educational virtual reality. In *Proceedings of the ICVS 2001*, Avignon, 2001.
5. G. Trogemann et al. Nichtlineare dramaturgie in vr-umgebungen. In *Tagungsband der 2. Internationalen Statustagung 'Virtuelle und Erweiterte Realität' des BMBF*, Leipzig, Germany, nov 2002. german.
6. Timothy Griepp and Carolina Cruz-Neira. Xjl–an xml schema for the rapid development of advanced synthetic environments. In *Proceedings of the IEEE Virtual Reality 2002 (VR2002) conference*, Orlando, mar 2002.
7. Ivar Jacobsen, Grady Booch, and James Rumbaugh. *The Unified Software Development Process*. Addison Wesley, 1998.
8. Henrik Tramberend. Avango: A distributed virtual reality framework. In *Proceedings of the IEEE VR 1999*, 1999.

Author Index

Lecture Notes in Computer Science

For information about Vols. 1–2812
please contact your bookseller or Springer-Verlag

Vol. 2850: M.Y. Vardi, A. Voronkov (Eds.), Logic for Programming, Artificial Intelligence, and Reasoning. Proceedings, 2003. XIII, 437 pages. 2003. (Subseries LNAI)

Vol. 2851: C. Boyd, W. Mao (Eds.), Information Security. Proceedings, 2003. XI, 443 pages. 2003.

Vol. 2852: F.S. de Boer, M.M. Bonsangue, S. Graf, W.-P. de Roever (Eds.), Formal Methods for Components and Objects. Proceedings, 2003. VIII, 509 pages. 2003.

Vol. 2853: M. Jeckle, L.-J. Zhang (Eds.), Web Services – ICWS-Europe 2003. Proceedings, 2003. VIII, 227 pages. 2003.

Vol. 2854: J. Hoffmann, Utilizing Problem Structure in Planning. XIII, 251 pages. 2003. (Subseries LNAI)

Vol. 2855: R. Alur, I. Lee (Eds.), Embedded Software. Proceedings, 2003. X, 373 pages. 2003.

Vol. 2856: M. Smirnov, E. Biersack, C. Blondia, O. Bonaventure, O. Casals, G. Karlsson, George Pavlou, B. Quoitin, J. Roberts, I. Stavrakakis, B. Stiller, P. Trimintzios, P. Van Mieghem (Eds.), Quality of Future Internet Services. IX, 293 pages. 2003.

Vol. 2857: M.A. Nascimento, E.S. de Moura, A.L. Oliveira (Eds.), String Processing and Information Retrieval. Proceedings, 2003. XI, 379 pages. 2003.

Vol. 2858: A. Veidenbaum, K. Joe, H. Amano, H. Aiso (Eds.), High Performance Computing. Proceedings, 2003. XV, 566 pages. 2003.

Vol. 2859: B. Apolloni, M. Marinaro, R. Tagliaferri (Eds.), Neural Nets. Proceedings, 2003. X, 376 pages. 2003.

Vol. 2860: D. Geist, E. Tronci (Eds.), Correct Hardware Design and Verification Methods. Proceedings, 2003. XII, 426 pages. 2003.

Vol. 2861: C. Bliek, C. Jermann, A. Neumaier (Eds.), Global Optimization and Constraint Satisfaction. Proceedings, 2002. XII, 239 pages. 2003.

Vol. 2862: D. Feitelson, L. Rudolph, U. Schwiegelshohn (Eds.), Job Scheduling Strategies for Parallel Processing. Proceedings, 2003. VII, 269 pages. 2003.

Vol. 2863: P. Stevens, J. Whittle, G. Booch (Eds.), «UML» 2003 – The Unified Modeling Language. Proceedings, 2003. XIV, 415 pages. 2003.

Vol. 2864: A.K. Dey, A. Schmidt, J.F. McCarthy (Eds.), UbiComp 2003: Ubiquitous Computing. Proceedings, 2003. XVII, 368 pages. 2003.

Vol. 2865: S. Pierre, M. Barbeau, E. Kranakis (Eds.), Ad-Hoc, Mobile, and Wireless Networks. Proceedings, 2003. X, 293 pages. 2003.

Vol. 2867: M. Brunner, A. Keller (Eds.), Self-Managing Distributed Systems. Proceedings, 2003. XIII, 274 pages. 2003.

Vol. 2868: P. Perner, R. Brause, H.-G. Holzhütter (Eds.), Medical Data Analysis. Proceedings, 2003. VIII, 127 pages. 2003.

Vol. 2869: A. Yazici, C. Şener (Eds.), Computer and Information Sciences – ISCIS 2003. Proceedings, 2003. XIX, 1110 pages. 2003.

Vol. 2870: D. Fensel, K. Sycara, J. Mylopoulos (Eds.), The Semantic Web - ISWC 2003. Proceedings, 2003. XV, 931 pages. 2003.

Vol. 2871: N. Zhong, Z.W. Raś, S. Tsumoto, E. Suzuki (Eds.), Foundations of Intelligent Systems. Proceedings, 2003. XV, 697 pages. 2003. (Subseries LNAI)

Vol. 2873: J. Lawry, J. Shanahan, A. Ralescu (Eds.), Modelling with Words. XIII, 229 pages. 2003. (Subseries LNAI)

Vol. 2875: E. Aarts, R. Collier, E. van Loenen, B. de Ruyter (Eds.), Ambient Intelligence. Proceedings, 2003. XI, 432 pages. 2003.

Vol. 2876: M. Schroeder, G. Wagner (Eds.), Rules and Rule Markup Languages for the Semantic Web. Proceedings, 2003. VII, 173 pages. 2003.

Vol. 2877: T. Böhme, G. Heyer, H. Unger (Eds.), Innovative Internet Community Systems. Proceedings, 2003. VIII, 263 pages. 2003.

Vol. 2878: R.E. Ellis, T.M. Peters (Eds.), Medical Image Computing and Computer-Assisted Intervention - MICCAI 2003. Part I. Proceedings, 2003. XXXIII, 819 pages. 2003.

Vol. 2879: R.E. Ellis, T.M. Peters (Eds.), Medical Image Computing and Computer-Assisted Intervention - MICCAI 2003. Part II. Proceedings, 2003. XXXIV, 1003 pages. 2003.

Vol. 2880: H.L. Bodlaender (Ed.), Graph-Theoretic Concepts in Computer Science. Proceedings, 2003. XI, 386 pages. 2003.

Vol. 2881: E. Horlait, T. Magedanz, R.H. Glitho (Eds.), Mobile Agents for Telecommunication Applications. Proceedings, 2003. IX, 297 pages. 2003.

Vol. 2883: J. Schaeffer, M. Müller, Y. Björnsson (Eds.), Computers and Games. Proceedings, 2002. XI, 431 pages. 2003.

Vol. 2884: E. Najm, U. Nestmann, P. Stevens (Eds.), Formal Methods for Open Object-Based Distributed Systems. Proceedings, 2003. X, 293 pages. 2003.

Vol. 2885: J.S. Dong, J. Woodcock (Eds.), Formal Methods and Software Engineering. Proceedings, 2003. XI, 683 pages. 2003.

Vol. 2886: I. Nyström, G. Sanniti di Baja, S. Svensson (Eds.), Discrete Geometry for Computer Imagery. Proceedings, 2003. XII, 556 pages. 2003.

Vol. 2887: T. Johansson (Ed.), Fast Software Encryption. Proceedings, 2003. IX, 397 pages. 2003.

Vol. 2888: R. Meersman, Zahir Tari, D.C. Schmidt et al. (Eds.), On The Move to Meaningful Internet Systems 2003: CoopIS, DOA, and ODBASE. Proceedings, 2003. XXI, 1546 pages. 2003.

Vol. 2889: Robert Meersman, Zahir Tari et al. (Eds.), On The Move to Meaningful Internet Systems 2003: OTM 2003 Workshops. Proceedings, 2003. XXI, 1096 pages. 2003.

Vol. 2891: J. Lee, M. Barley (Eds.), Intelligent Agents and Multi-Agent Systems. Proceedings, 2003. X, 215 pages. 2003. (Subseries LNAI)

Vol. 2893: J.-B. Stefani, I. Demeure, D. Hagimont (Eds.), Distributed Applications and Interoperable Systems. Proceedings, 2003. XIII, 311 pages. 2003.

Vol. 2895: A. Ohori (Ed.), Programming Languages and Systems. Proceedings, 2003. XIII, 427 pages. 2003.

Vol. 2897: O. Balet, G. Subsol, P. Torguet (Eds.), Virtual Storytelling. Proceedings, 2003. XI, 240 pages. 2003.

Vol. 2899: G. Ventre, R. Canonico (Eds.), Interactive Multimedia on Next Generation Networks. Proceedings, 2003. XIV, 420 pages. 2003.